Frommer's®

irreverent
guide to
San Francisco

2nd Edition

By
Liz Barrett

A BALLIET & FITZGERALD BOOK
MACMILLAN • USA

a disclaimer

Prices fluctuate in the course of time, and travel information changes under the impact of the varied and volatile factors that influence the travel industry. Neither the author nor the publisher can be held responsible for the experiences of readers while traveling. Readers are invited to write to the publisher with ideas, comments, and suggestions for future editions.

about the authors

Liz Barrett is a lifelong resident of the San Francisco Bay Area who not only attended the first Human Be-In, but actually remembers it. Her articles have appeared in many national publications and have been syndicated by the *New York Times*. She has also been a special guest on National Public Radio.

Balliett & Fitzgerald, Inc.

Editorial director: Will Balliett / Line editor: Holly Hughes / Executive editor: Tom Dyja / Managing editor: Rachel Aydt / Production editor: Maria Fernandez / Associate editor: Vijay Balakrishnan

MACMILLAN TRAVEL

A Simon & Schuster Macmillan Company
1633 Broadway
New York, NY 10019
Find us online at www.frommers.com

ISBN 0-02-862239-1
ISSN 1085-4835

Macmillan Travel Art director: Michele Laseau
Interior design contributed to by Tsang Seymour Design Studio

special sales

Manufactured in the United States of America

what's so irreverent?

It's up to you.

You can buy a traditional guidebook with its fluff, its promotional hype, its let's-find-something-nice-to-say-about-everything point of view. Or you can buy an Irreverent guide.

What the Irreverents give you is the lowdown, the inside story. They have nothing to sell but the truth, which includes a balance of good and bad. They praise, they trash, they weigh, and leave the final decisions up to you. No tourist board, no chamber of commerce will ever recommend them.

Our writers are insiders, who feel passionate about the cities they live in, and have strong opinions they want to share with you. They take a special pleasure leading you where other guides fear to tread.

How irreverent are they? One of our authors insisted on writing under a pseudonym. "I couldn't show my face in town again if I used my own name," she told me. "My friends would never speak to me." Such is the price of honesty. She, like you, should know she'll always have a friend at Frommer's.

Warm regards,

Michael Spring

Michael Spring
Publisher

contents

INTRODUCTION   **1**

NEIGHBORHOOD MAP   **6**

YOU PROBABLY DIDN'T KNOW   **7**

ACCOMMODATIONS   **12**
    Winning the Reservations Game (15)
    Is There a Right Address? (16)
    THE LOWDOWN   **18**
        Irresistible deals (18)
        Grande dames worth considering (19)
        Petite dames worth more than they charge (20)
        In search of painted ladies (20)
        When money is no object (21)
        When money's too tight to mention (22)
        Lavender lodgings (22)
        Turning Japanese (23)
        For writers in search of a muse (23)
        For movie-hounds (25)
        Taking care of business (25)
        Family values (26)
        If there's a pet in your entourage (26)
        Euro-style lodgings (27)
        Luscious love nests (27)
        Provident penthouses (28)
        I'm with the band (29)

That's why they call it modern art (30)

We gotta get outta this place (31)

THE INDEX   **32**

An A to Z list of places to stay, with vital statistics

MAPS   **44**

DINING AND CAFES   **48**

Only in San Francisco (50)

How to Dress (51)

When to Eat (52)

Getting the Right Table (52)

Chefs (52)

Cafe Society (54)

Navigating the Coffee Trail (54)

THE LOWDOWN   **56**

Grills in the mist (56)

For committed carnivores (57)

Seafood supremo (57)

If you're George Jetson on an expense account (57)

See-and-be-scenes (58)

Hold the hype (58)

Some like it hot (59)

Tastiest tapas (60)

Pass the dumplings, darling (60)

Best Chinese in Chinatown (61)

Ultra-chic Chinoise (61)

South of the border in the Mission (61)

Seoul food (62)

A passage to India (63)

Asian delights (63)

Japanese jewels (64)

The French connection (64)

Super supper clubs (66)

Vegging out (67)

North Beach classics (67)

Athens al fresco (68)

The rest of the world (68)

Goofy decor, fabulous food (69)

Kid pleasers (70)

Where to seal a deal (71)

Cheap eats (71)

Eating with insomniacs (71)

The morning after (72)

The cafe superhighway (72)

Wake-up call: cafes that open before 8am (73)

How about a little fresh air? (73)

Cafe con angst (74)

All-day hangouts (74)

Live music (75)

Jack Kerouac woke up here (75)

Hippie holdouts (75)

THE INDEX 76
An A to Z list of restaurants and cafes, with vital statistics
MAPS 90

DIVERSIONS 94
Getting Your Bearings (96)
THE LOWDOWN 98

Must-sees for first-time visitors from Peoria (98)

Only in San Francisco (100)

Special moments (101)

Morbid landmarks (102)

The roar of the fish stalls, the smell of the crowd (103)

Looking for a few good whales: Marine World (103)

Urban ferry tales (104)

Cruising Golden Gate Park (104)

Museum meccas outside Golden Gate Park (106)

Freebies at the major museums (107)

Museums for special interests (107)

Museums for really special interests (109)

Outlandish out-of-town archives (110)

The Bongo-Rama Beatnik tour (111)

Tune in, turn on, drop out (111)

The last-call saloon crawl (113)

Painted ladies (113)

Mural, mural on the wall (114)

Are we there yet? (Fun with the kids) (115)

Fabulous footsteps (115)

THE INDEX 117
An A to Z list of diversions, with vital statistics

GETTING OUTSIDE 126
THE LOWDOWN 128

Parks (128)

Stretching your legs (129)

Pedal pushing (131)

Working up a sweat (132)
Hitting the beach (133)
Bathing in the buff (135)
Poolside plunges (136)
Water sports (136)
Reeling them in (137)
Par for the course (137)
Lawn bowling (138)
Islands with a past (138)
Fantasy islands (139)
Day trips (140)
Soothing spas and marvelous massages (142)

SHOPPING   144

Target Zones (146)
Bargain-Hunting (148)
Trading with the Natives (148)
Hours of Business (149)
Sales Tax (149)

THE LOWDOWN   149

Shopping bags to show off (149)
Are you being served? (149)
One-stop shopping (150)
For foot fetishists (150)
If it's July, you're going to need a sweater (150)
For men who want to look like Cary Grant (150)
For men who'd rather look like Lou Reed
    than Cary Grant (151)
If you can't make it to Hong Kong, but you're
    into custom-made shirts (151)
If you simply can't live without a feather boa
    and a new tiara (151)
Recycled regalia (151)
Cheap thrills: nonprofit thrift shops (152)
In the outlets (152)
Politically correct splurges (152)
Crystals and other assorted New Age voodoo (153)
Baubles, bangles, and beads (153)
Goofatoriums (154)
Gumby for grown-ups (154)
If you've got an itch for leather (155)
Everything you ever wanted to know about sex (155)
Or sexy underwear (155)

Uncommon scents (156)
Sweets to go (156)
Italian treats to go (156)
The best deal on the best bubbly (157)
Kid stuff (157)
Words, words, words (157)
In search of 12-inch vinyl (158)
Music meccas (158)

THE INDEX   **159**

An A to Z list of shops, with vital statistics

NIGHTLIFE   **172**

Liquor and Smoking Laws (175)

THE LOWDOWN   **175**

It's only rock 'n' roll (175)
All-night techno parties (176)
All that acid jazz (177)
All that other jazz (178)
Blues joints (178)
Disco infernal (179)
Cool cocktail lounges (179)
Kiss me, I'm Irish (180)
Just your basic, friendly neighborhood bar (181)
Three babes and a bus (181)
Bustling brew pubs (182)
Swingy supper clubs (182)
Lookin' for love (183)
Drag clubs (183)
Where the boys are (184)
Where the girls are (185)
Poker palaces (185)

THE INDEX   **186**

An A to Z list of nightspots, with vital statistics

ENTERTAINMENT   **196**

Sources (199)
Getting Tickets (199)
THE LOWDOWN   **201**

The play's the thing (201)
On the fringes (202)
The main drag (203)
Mostly Mozart (203)
Men in tights (204)

Dancing with the avant-garde (205)

Grand opera (205)

Take me out to the ballgame (205)

THE INDEX   **207**

An A to Z list of venues, with vital statistics

HOTLINES & OTHER BASICS   **212**

Airports (213)

Airport transportation to the city (213)

All-night pharmacies (214)

Babysitters (214)

BART (214)

Buses (215)

Cable cars (215)

Car rentals (215)

Cash advances, check cashing, and ATM cards (215)

Chauffeurs (216)

Climate (216)

Concierges (216)

Convention center (217)

Dentists (217)

Doctors (217)

Driving around (217)

Emergencies (218)

Events hotline (218)

Ferries (218)

Festivals and special events (219)

Gay and lesbian resources (220)

Liquor laws (221)

MUNI Metro streetcars (221)

Newspapers (221)

Parking garages (221)

Phone facts (222)

Taxis (222)

Time (223)

Tipping (223)

Visitor information center (223)

Introduction

San Francisco, so Rudyard Kipling said, "is a mad city inhabited by perfectly insane people whose women are of remarkable beauty." What he didn't say was that half of those women are men.

It is no secret that San Francisco is the gay capital of the world, but that is emphatically not the city's only personality. Olive O'Suddin, the roller-skating nun-in-drag who leads the peripatetic Sisters of Perpetual Indulgence, is a treasured icon here, no doubt about it, but so is Herb Caen, the Pulitzer Prize-winning *Chronicle* gossip columnist who once dubbed the city "Baghdad by the Bay" and had major streets renamed after him before his death in 1996.

That counterpoise is precisely what makes San Francisco such a great city. You can go to the opera in blue jeans or have a hamburger in a tuxedo. Let a snooty doorman in white gloves carry your Louis Vuitton luggage into the Fairmont Hotel on S. Nob Hill or toss it into a rental car and check into the Phoenix, a funky Tenderloin motel where John F. Kennedy Jr. once got double-booked into a room with ex-Blondie star Debbie Harry. Dress in black from head to toe and squish belly-to-butt with the South of Market hordes at Slim's, a nightclub started by musician Boz Scaggs, or dust off your gold sequins and sip champagne at Bimbo's 365, a swank time-warp supper club where you almost expect to see Lucy and Ricky Ricardo at the next table, especially when Tito Puente is onstage.

Do anything you want, any way you want, and you'll fit right in. Visitors, in fact, tend to feel so simpatico with San Francisco that they can't resist comparing it to their own hometowns. New Yorkers justify their fondness for the city by saying it's not like the rest of the West, that it is the only city with any real culture west of the Mississippi (or west of the Hudson, for that matter). Europeans insist that San Francisco is much more like Europe than America. Even expatriates of cozy heartland locales have found parts of the city wonderfully familiar.

In truth, San Francisco is not New York at all, nor would it want to be. People don't come here to make the Big Time, they come to have a good time. When you sit down at a bar, fellow drinkers may well strike up a conversation with you, but you probably won't be asked what you do or where you went to school or who your daddy is. Frankly, nobody gives a damn. It's not that San Franciscans are indifferent or without ambition; it's just that they are more focused on a cordial lifestyle than on an impeccable pedigree. Besides, it wouldn't be polite to ask, and San Franciscans are nothing if not polite. (If you've ever attempted to negotiate the streets of New York in an automobile, you'll be relieved to know that Bay Area drivers do not cruise the city with their horns permanently engaged in the honk mode.)

There are also a few flaws in the whole San-Francisco-is-so-much-like-Europe idea. Being considered the "Paris of the West" is a compliment, one supposes, though it is highly doubtful that all those chain-smoking French existentialists would ever put up with San Francisco's tough no-smoking laws. Nor would the city's vigorous entrepreneurial mentality be likely to appeal to that crowd. It was suggested to one young French waiter, for example, that he was lucky to work for Alain Rondelli, the superb chef whose restaurant on Clement Street is one of the finest in the city. "Lucky?" he asked incredulously. "Lucky to have a job?"

"Ah, you are French," the customer replied.

The waiter smiled proudly. "To the bone," he said. Voilà.

North Beach is supposedly the most European-style neighborhood in the city. It's true that you can drop by Figone Hardware for a set of imported Italian bocce balls, but just down the block in Washington Square, dozens of Asian senior citizens gather on Sunday mornings for group tai chi. You can observe this hardly European thing from a window seat across the street at Mario's Bohemian Cigar Store, a cafe with the best focaccia sandwiches in town.

Half-Italian, half-Asian, North Beach is also the very womb from which thoroughly American beatniks originally sprang. It still houses Lawrence Ferlinghetti's City Lights Bookstore and Vesuvio's on opposite sides of Jack Kerouac Street as well as many other active Beat volcanoes. Farther down the Columbus Avenue umbilical cord, psychedelic shops staffed by the progeny of sixties hippies sell original Fillmore concert posters for a small fortune and blast Richie Havens' albums at decibel levels that left their predecessors among the hearing-impaired. Lyle Tuttle, whose tattoo client list included Janis Joplin, has his own mini-museum in celebration of painted flesh. It's a fitting bookend to a neighborhood bordered on the other extreme by strip joints and peep parlors. You make the call; is this Europe?

It's easy to see how exiles from college towns find the Haight and the Mission District so familiar and yet still exotic enough to entice them. Both neighborhoods are constantly reinventing themselves, and each new incarnation includes remnants of past lives, like apartments that have collected eccentric odds and ends left behind by a succession of short-term tenants. The corner of Haight and Ashbury now houses a GAP and a Ben & Jerry's ice cream store, but the sidewalk is still a loitering ground for restless, purple-haired teenagers in tie-dyed T-shirts and leather jackets. The smell of illegal smoking materials is so thick, you can take a single deep breath in passing and get happy for the rest of the day. Within one 3-block stretch is the Piedmont Boutique, a glamorous gewgaw shop that caters to drag queens and strippers; Cha Cha Cha, a trendy, crowded tapas bar; and Aub Zam Zam, home to a bartender who's famous for mixing what is commonly believed to be the best martini on the planet.

The Mission District is itself another planet, or so it seems. Part Latin Quarter and part New Bohemia, it mixes traditional Mexican and Central American culture with lesbians, beatniks, poets, musicians, artists, hipsters, and assorted pretenders of virtually every urban persuasion. Vivid murals dress the neighborhood (especially 24th Street) like a Diego Rivera fantasy, and virtually every corner taqueria is worth a tastestop. The sidewalks on Mission Street are trimmed in bright orange-and-blue tiles, and the center of the barrio is lined with palm trees. Yet a block away, cafes, bookstores, restaurants, bars, nightclubs, and a vibrator museum have turned Valencia Street into "the hippest hood in the city," according to Chip Conley, whose lively hotels have lodged everyone from Brenda Lee to Nirvana. Valencia Street is no gentrification project, though. It retains a low-rent, funky feeling and a solid respect for the Latin culture in which it is centered. While punk cha-cha bands play at the Latin American Club, mariachis stroll a few doors down to play a few tunes and pass the hat at La Rondalla, and live jazz may be on the menu at Radio Valencia. It's casual. It's friendly. It's inexpensive. It's like taking a vacation to two completely different and equally festive countries at the same time. There's no place like it anywhere else.

Nor is there any place like San Francisco itself—much to the relief of conservative talk-show hosts and other petulant patriots, who often liken the place to Sodom and Gomorrah. Face it, the city has always been a haven for those who are a tad on the weird side by Presbyterian standards. That's why people came out here in the first place—to escape from the oppressive conventions of an East Coast dominated by Old World principles, and that's essentially why they keep on coming. If San Francisco had a Statue of Liberty, she would beckon, "Send us your odd, your bizarre masses, your tired beatniks, ancient hippies, drag queens, poets, and artists, your temperamental opera singers and recalcitrant pastry chefs, your feminist firebugs and immortal quarterbacks, your transsexual tennis players yearning to be free."

Lest you get the idea that the entire city is an alternative universe populated strictly by the cast of *La Cage Aux Folles*, it should be clearly stated for the record that scads of utterly "normal" people reside in San Francisco's many diverse districts, from the breezy bayside Marina to the steep cliffs that bounce crashing waves back out to the Pacific Ocean. The Sunset District seems like a middle-class suburb, cut off from the city's clamor by Twin Peaks and Golden Gate Park. The Marina has a Safeway where singles congregate to squeeze more than the melons, but the neighborhood also houses little old ladies and upwardly mobile lawyers alongside millionaire ballplayers and stately yachtsmen. St. Francis Woods is a hidden, fairy-tale neighborhood with private drives and storybook houses. Pacific Heights—renamed Specific Whites by *Betty and Pansy's Severe Queer Review*—is a beautifully manicured enclave for San Francisco's richest and most powerful elite. (There is a pit bull inside one of those gigantic Victorian mansions, but the discreet sign merely warns: "Chien bizarre." Apparently they expect their burglars to speak French.) The modern apartment complexes in Diamond Heights could be in Pocatello, Idaho, and no one would know the difference, at least not from an architectural standpoint.

The irresistible beauty of San Francisco lies in its gentle refusal to fit into any mold, beginning with the very ground upon which it is built—steep hills and wide valleys dropping off suddenly at the edge of the continent. It's cold in the summer and warm in the winter, with sudden and notable exceptions, of course. It has been struck by earthquakes that would have destroyed other cities, but merely brought out the best in San Francisco. During the 1989 earthquake, a New York sports writer who happened to be here covering the World Series at Candlestick Park observed, "If this had happened at Yankee Stadium, we all would have been trampled to death in a stampede." Not here. Ordinary citizens jumped out of their cars and directed traffic on the streets. Plumbers, truck drivers, and major-league ballplayers climbed into the rubble with rescue workers to try to save people trapped in the collapsed freeway. There was virtually no violent crime on record for nearly three days—no looting, no rioting, not even any hoarding of supplies. When the World Series resumed three weeks later, 64,000 people—some wearing hard hats just in case—joined hands and sang out with homegrown rock icons Jefferson Starship: "We built this city on rock and roll."

This is it. This is why Tony Bennett left his heart here. This is why Betty and Pansy offer visitors the following advice: "Give yourself one year, and then if you don't like San Francisco, you can leave....San Francisco is a wonderful place to change your mind. Nobody holds you to yesterday's decision."

San Francisco Neighborhoods

you
probably
didn't know

Can I call it Frisco?... Most locals would sooner hear fingernails scratching across a chalkboard. "Frisco" sounds too much like "Vegas" or some other honky-tonk town. And it certainly doesn't suggest a place where you'd leave your heart. In any case, it's best to skip the indelicate nickname unless you're willing to accept dirty looks, slow service, and tables by the ladies' room.

Where are the best "vertigo views" of the city?... Standing at the top of some of San Francisco's steeper hills, you may feel a tad trembly and nauseous, like Jimmy Stewart in the Hitchcock film *Vertigo*. To heighten this sensation, take a glass-elevator ride, available for free in several of San Francisco's elegant hotels. The Westin Saint Francis (Union Square) has the fastest elevator in the city, ascending at 1,000 feet per minute. If you can keep your eyelids up and your stomach down, you'll catch panoramic views of downtown, Coit Tower, and the bay. Around the corner from the Saint Francis, the Pan-Pacific Hotel has a 17-story ride, but the cars face the inside of the building, looking onto an atrium that's one of the most elegant in the city. Five blocks away, at the Fairmont Hotel, take the skylift, which zips up at about 100 feet per minute to the Fairmont Crown, 24 floors up, for a leisurely view of Chinatown, Nob Hill, the Financial District, Coit Tower, and the South Bay Peninsula. Beware of small weddings in the elevators—they can seriously cramp your view. Down at the Embarcadero Center, the Hyatt Regency's glass lifts take you to a revolving restaurant/cocktail lounge that offers a great 360-degree view and ridiculously overpriced drinks that invariably include the requisite hardware—paper umbrellas, swizzle sticks, pineapple chunks, you name it. Mel Brooks panicked on the way up here in *High Anxiety*.

Where's the best place to hop on a cable car?... When you catch a ride on a cable car—yes, they do look like the ones in the Rice-A-Roni commercials and, yes, they do ring those bells—don't wait in line with all the tourists at the turnaround stops at the beginning and end of the lines. Walk a few blocks up the line (follow the tracks) and do as the locals do: Hop on when the car stops, hang on to a pole, and have your $2 ready to hand to the driver. He'll take coins or bills, and can even make change. Warning: Don't stand too close behind the gripman or his elbow might smash into your chest when he yanks the brake to stop the car. And whatever you do, don't call them "trolleys"—you'll be branded instantly as a tourist.

How does one dress for fog al fresco?... From June through August—summertime in the rest of the Western world—fog tends to engulf San Francisco from late afternoon until noon the next day. If you're a baseball fan, you'll soon discover one of the main reasons the Giants are building a new ballpark: Candlestick (now 3Com) Park is so chilly at night that it's equipped with one of the bay's 26 foghorns. Locals don't mind the mist, though. They dress in layers and immerse themselves in it. To make the most of a glorious foggy morning, sip a frothy cappuccino in a cozy neighborhood cafe until around noon, when the fog burns off and you can tie your sweater around your waist, roll up your shirtsleeves, and soak up the sun for a few hours. And no matter what the weather seems like during the day, always bring a coat or jacket along at night.

What is meant by "basic black and perils?"... If you're going to wear black, stay out of the ocean. Sure, thousands of local surfers have worn black wetsuits and survived, but others have found Pacific sharks to be most unreasonable—their vision isn't all that great and they have a fierce appetite for sea lions, a hazardous combination for unidentified black-coated mammals floating around at suppertime. Fortunately wetsuits come in a variety of bright colors. (While you're out catching a few waves, be on the lookout for rock star Chris Isaak. He loves to surf near his home at Ocean Beach.)

Where is the best place to park?... That's a question that baffles even the meter maids. A quick survey of the neighborhoods will reveal cars parked and double-parked on sidewalks, in front of fire hydrants, in towaway zones, on corners, in crosswalks and, in the Mission District, right down the middle of the street. The math is fairly simple: There are around 800,000 cars in the city on any given day, and less than 600,000 parking spaces. That adds up to 2.3 million parking tickets a year and unknown numbers of drivers still circling the city in a frenzy. There are a number of downtown, city-run garages that won't require you to mortgage your house in order to park for a few hours, but in most private garages you can pay up to $22.50 for a Friday night in popular areas like North Beach. Avoid the whole mess by using public transportation or cabs.

What's the best way to avoid getting mugged?... Muggers aren't a huge problem in San Francisco, but the city does have its share of pickpockets and other assorted scam artists who tend to prey on tourists. Standard rules of urban behavior apply: Don't keep your wallet in your rear pants pocket, and leave your purse at home or keep your hand on it all the time, especially when you're riding a bus (a favorite haunt of pickpockets). The favorite crime in San Francisco, actually, seems to be car vandalism, especially in the Mission District, where a car parked on the street for more than an hour has at least a 50/50 chance of getting its mirrors smashed. Solution: Take a cab.

What do you say to San Francisco cabbies?... The most-often-asked cabbie question in San Francisco is, "How often do you have to change your brakes?" Believe me, you don't want to know. One driver estimates that the hills are so treacherous he has to change his brakes once a week, while another casually replies, "Oh, a couple times a year, maybe." Either way, most drivers would rather avoid the topic, especially if you're headed down a grade that would rival K–2. Best advice: Forget the slope; look out the side windows instead.

What's the quickest way to get a date?... If you're a heterosexual type (fondly known as a "breeder" by the gay community), in town alone and wishing you weren't, you might want to check out the *Guardian*'s singles' events. A mixed bag of singles—shy desirables, curious newcomers, horny Hetero Sapiens, and, yes, some terminally unattractive loners—usually meet at a local watering hole, where some sort of appetizerish food-like substances are served; the *Guardian* throws in a free looking-for-love ad for attendant mixers and minglers. At least it's not sleazy, and who knows? Call the *Guardian*'s Romance Hot Line (tel 800/278–2226 or 800/278–2251) for information.

What's the best-kept secret about the symphony?... If you're a morning person who loves classical music, the San Francisco Symphony's open rehearsals have a seat with your name written on it. Before most major concerts, the symphony allows the public to attend open rehearsals at Davies Hall ($15 for unreserved seats, $25 for reserved.) Aside from the bargain-basement price, many afficionados prefer these rehearsals over the concerts because the music is equally exquisite and you get to see and hear the performers and conductors in a relaxed, intimate circumstance. Most open rehearsals take place on Wednesday mornings, 9am to noon. They sell out quickly for popular international performers, so call the Symphony box office (tel 415/864–6000) for a schedule while you are still planning your trip, and order tickets in advance if possible.

Who was the last emperor?... Around the time of the Gold Rush, San Francisco was home to California's first monarch—not a butterfly or a drag queen, but a self-coronated royal who called himself Emperor Norton. (He also claimed to be Protector of Mexico.) Still commemorated 150 years later by a town that cherishes its oddballs, the emperor was a real, live person who got invited to all the society affairs, whether or not the city fathers believed his claims to sovereignty. The old codger had a lot of influence on local customs and was apparently quite an impressive figurehead. A century later he gained further immortality, portrayed as a close friend who visited Ben Cartwright at the Ponderosa on the television show "Bonanza." Even Hoss tipped his hat to His Majesty. If that's not proof of authenticity, what is?

How long has San Francisco been a gay capital?... During the Gold Rush, "real" women were so scarce that desperate prospectors gladly paid them 3 ounces of gold for a single kiss. No one knows how many enterprising impostors whipped out the Max Factor and painted their lips red to pick up a few extra nuggets back then, but mascara and falsies have rarely seen a sales slump since. According to Trevor Hailey, the city's premier gay historian, the city became an established haven for the gay lifestyle with the Gold Rush; then the opening of the Panama Canal led countless gay sailors to this port, followed by an influx of gay artists and entertainers during the Bohemian era of the twenties and thirties. World War II brought thousands of Pacific-bound military men— yes, queers in the armed forces, whether General Eisenhower knew it or not—many of whom returned after the war to live where their forbidden lifestyle was accepted. By the time the Beat movement bongoed to the cultural forefront in the fifties, there was no question that North Beach was the place for gay "angry young men" to proclaim their sexuality to the world. Every major city has a gay subculture, but there's nothing "sub" about San Francisco's gay culture—it is definitely a predominant and celebrated part of life here.

What does the future hold?... A *Chronicle* poll once estimated that 37 percent of Bay Area residents believe in astrology; virtually every newspaper in the city features a horoscope. The most eccentric is definitely Rob Brezsny's "Real Astrology" in *SF Weekly*. He might tell you that you are "the pothole in the road to ruin" or suggest that you "stroll on over to the oldest tree you know and pour a bottle of mountain spring water over your head while confessing all your sins."

What should you do if you fall in love with the city and decide to stay?... You're going to need a job, and the Westin Saint Francis Hotel just happens to be on a long-term job search for a dedicated coin-washer. Until a few of years ago, every coin that was tendered at the hotel was put through a sort of tumbler that sterilized those copper pennies and buffalo nickels so that no customer was ever given a coin in change that wasn't fit for the white glove test. The current manager regrets that the money laundering service, as it were, was indefinitely postponed when the career coinman retired; the hotel's human resource department has yet to find a candidate with the proper experience. Interested?

accomm

1

odations

San Francisco's
famous palace
hotels—which are
as suffocatingly
grand as grande
dames get—are
finally getting a

run for their money. Sure, the non-hip rich may still lust after a night in the **Fairmont Hotel**'s $6,000-a-night penthouse suite: a three-bedroom, four-bath mini-mansion with a grand piano two-story circular library with 4,000 volumes, dining room that seats fifty, 24-karat gold fixtures, lapus lazuli fireplace, secret passages, and its own vault. If that price tag's too high, the Fairmont's standard rooms, at $189 and up, are a bargain compared to equivalent accommodations in New York, London, Paris, or Tokyo. But these days, stylish celebrities—who can afford any room in the city—are shying away from the huge luxury hotels in favor of more chic, intimate boutique hotels that cater to a younger, more with-it crowd.

The center of San Francisco's boutique hotel universe is Joie de Vivre, a group of eccentric hotels and restaurants invented by Chip Conley, a thirty-something entrepreneur who is a cross between Conrad Hilton and a modern-day Mad Hatter. Conley followed the example of boutique czar Bill Kimpton, buying fading older properties and transforming them into chic, contemporary cash cows. The Kimpton Group includes the **Hotel Triton**, an abstract expressionist's dream come true; the **Hotel Monaco**, a renovated 1910 Beaux Arts jewel; the four-star **Prescott Hotel**, where guests get preferred seating at Wolfgang Puck's famous Postrio restaurant; and a dozen others. Kimpton hotels tend to be a bit more traditonal (and occasionally more expensive) than Joie de Vivre's lodgings, but both focus on creature comforts and meticulously designed interiors. Conley's lodgings range from the **Phoenix**, a psychedelic-tropical inner-city motel full of urban artistes to the understated but ultra-luxurious **Nob Hill Lambourne**, a spa for health-conscious business travelers. Neither Conley nor Kimpton has a corner on the celebrity market, though. When Luciano Pavarotti is in town, he stays at the elegant **Inn at the Opera**, a tiny, 25-foot-wide Victorian hotel where services include complimentary clothes-pressing upon arrival. Before his death in 1996, legendary poet Allen Ginsberg chose North Beach's **Hotel Bohème**, a hip, cozy, and surprisingly quiet haven on Columbus Avenue, just footsteps away from Lawrence Ferlinghetti's City Lights Bookstore.

If you're not particularly impressed with the notion of sleeping in the same digs as the rich and famous—or the in-debt and infamous—try one of the city's scores of neighborhood inns. Europeans love the **San Remo Hotel**, a three-story Italianate Victorian hidden away on a quiet residential block of

North Beach; rooms start at $50 and the funky little rooftop cottage/penthouse with its own sundeck and panoramic view is one of the best deals in San Francisco at $100 a night.

If your budget is tighter than Dwight Yoakam's jeans, you'll be happy to know that for less than $30 a night, you can stay in a private room at the fully staffed **Central YMCA**, where you'll get free coffee and muffins in the morning along with the use of the health club and pool. Or go super-cheap ($13 a night) and dorm up at the **San Francisco International Hostel** in Fort Mason, at the edge of the posh bayfront Marina District with close-up views of the Golden Gate Bridge.

Finally, in the "Too Weird To Leave Out" category, there is an RV park out by the Cal Train station near the China Basin, where the Giants are building their new ballpark. If the sight of a hundred Winnebagos lined up in neat little rows rings your bell, by all means check it out (they have their own website at www.sfrvpark.com). There's bound to be a canasta game going on there somewhere.

Winning the Reservations Game

First of all, forget the major hotels if you're planning to visit in October. Some of them are almost fully booked 20 years in advance during the best-of-all-possible months in San Francisco. Don't let that discourage you, though—the most interesting places to stay, and the best deals, are rarely on the standard list of hotels that appears on travel agents' computer screens, so they don't get booked up so fast. San Francisco's tourist season is year-round, and hotel prices tend to remain fairly fixed throughout the year (a few increase between April and October). You're not likely to find an off-season bargain rate around town, but many hotels, especially in tourist areas, offer special rates for multiple-night stays, including meals or discounts on tours and attractions. The deals range from downright pathetic—a free bottle of cheap, plastic-corked champagne and a Gray Line tour through Fisherman's Wharf—to the sumptuous, whimsical "romance packages" offered by the Joie de Vivre hotels, including the Phoenix, the Commodore, the Nob Hill Lambourne, the Abigail, and the Archbishop's Mansion. Not all packages are advertised, so always ask the hotel or reservation agent if any are available. If you want to stick to the tourist-and-conventioneer circuit, last-minute vacancies and special discounts may be available through reservation services, most of which are computerized so they know exactly which rooms are available. Many of these services offer 50% to 75% discounts. The San Francisco Convention and Visitors Bureau offers booking services to the general public through **Leisure Reservation Services** (888/782–9673). Or try **California Reservations** (tel 800/576–0003), **San Francisco Reservations** (tel 800/677–1550), **Central Reservations** (tel 800/548–3311), or **Hotel Reservations Network** (tel 800/964–6835). **Bed and Breakfast International** (tel 800/872–4500) can set you up in more than a hundred private homes, guest houses, and inns in San Francisco, starting at $70 a night (two-night minimum). Their specialty is matching travelers' tastes and budgets to their ideal place to stay, including a few private sublets of entire homes or apartments. Owner and director Sharene Klein has moved to the Los Angeles area, but her San Francisco staff can still tell you every detail about the properties, often down to the kinds of flowers that bloom in the garden. Tell them what kind of vacation you hope to have, and they'll put you in a place that's likely to make it happen. **American Property Exchange** (tel 800/747–7784) rents luxury apartments, condos, houses, and flats at $85 to $275 a night; **Best of Nob Hill–United Commercial Brokers** (tel 800/634–2567, 408/279–3747 outside California) handles five Queen Anne Victorian apartments with antique furniture, fireplaces, and laundry service at weekly or monthly rates of $125 to $200 per night (minimum two-night stay); and **Executive Suites** (tel 888/878-4837, 415/495-5151) has 100 luxury condominiums, including maid service, fitness centers, saunas, pools, and laundry for $65 to $145 a night, depending on length of stay (special government and corporate rates are also available). Many other short-term options are outlined in a free lodging guide available through the San Francisco Convention and Visitors Bureau (tel 415/974–6900).

Is There a Right Address?

Most of San Francisco's major hotels are located near the **Financial District**, **Union Square**, and **Fisherman's Wharf**. The prime spots for world-class luxury hotels are Union Square and **Nob Hill**. Many small boutique hotels and inns are mixed among the giant towers and palaces, so the touristy neighborhoods shouldn't scare you off completely—the location is extremely convenient for walking and for access to public transportation. But—and it's a big "but"—you can easily be sucked into paying much more money than is necessary for a room with about as much personality as a Holiday Inn in Elko, Nevada. The thing is, you can't tell from the outside of the building or from the lobby what the rooms will be like. Take the Westin Saint Francis, for instance. It's an absolute architectural gem, one of the loveliest hotel exteriors in the Western world, but the rooms in the tower are, well, ordinary. Sure, they're spacious and full of expensive furniture, but they still look like they were punched out of the Universal School of Semi-Fancy Hotel Room Design. The whole thing is just too pastel. The rooms are spectacular, but you can see those from the elevator, and that's free.

Neither **Chinatown** nor **Japantown** is loaded with hotels, but each is worth considering. Japantown isn't as interesting as it sounds—mostly a bunch of import shops and food stands in a bland mall—but it does have the most authentic Japanese hotel in the city, the Miyako, with Zen gardens, futon beds, and in-room Shiatsu massage. Chinatown is crammed with everything: Crammed with people, crammed with fish, crammed with aromas, exotic vegetables, cheap souvenirs, great little food joints—but it's not crammed with good places to spend the night. You can, however, find a bed in Chinatown for $30 to $40 if you don't mind sharing a bath. You can't beat the location—near downtown, Union Square, North Beach, and (perish the thought) Fisherman's Wharf.

The **Tenderloin**—usually called by other names to divert attention from its reputation as a seedy, whore-and-drug-infested pit—is a block-by-block situation. One minute you can be strolling past a series of charming little shops and neighborhood taverns, and the next you're being accosted by panhandlers in front of a dilapidated homeless shelter or a shop that sells pornography. On the outer edges of the neighborhood are some of the trendiest and most fun lodgings and restaurants in town, but as a rule, the hotels there are either faded old beauties or transient houses best left to guests who rent them by the hour for "professional" purposes.

Van Ness Avenue is a long stretch of wide road that cuts through the city from the Mission District to the Marina. Inch for inch, it probably has more chain hotels and motels in its immediate vicinity than any other street in the city. It also has some beautifully restored old standards, like the **Hotel Richelieu**, that are close to entertainment and theater but mercifully removed from the constant stream of pickpockets and hustlers who usually hover around theater districts. (The Great American Music Hall puts most of its performing artists up at the Richelieu.) The **Civic Center** area houses the ballet, the opera, the symphony, the main library, and City Hall, along with a number of wonderful boutique hotels such as the Inn at the Opera and the **Abigail Hotel**, and exquisite restaurants that are virtually empty after 8:30pm (San Franciscans tend to eat before performances). Right smack in the middle of it all is a plaza that has been a constant battle site for San Francisco's intractable homeless problem. Some people find that repugnant; others chalk it up as an integral part of urban life. Public transportation is a breeze in this centrally located neighborhood, and parking is very reasonable at the Civic Center garage. (Don't go to any of the private garages near the Opera House or you may have to call home for extra cash.) **Lombard Street**, in Cow Hollow, is Motel Row, dotted with low-profile, inexpensive places to stay. The area stretches from the Marina to the Presidio and there are plenty of scenic vistas and worthwhile seafood houses that are local favorites. Be warned, though: Some motels are a bit marginal and the neighborhood is far from the thick of the city's most interesting activities. The more residential neighborhoods—the Mission District, the Haight, the Castro, Noe Valley, the Sunset, Pacific Heights—have very few hotels, but many boast wonderful inns and bed-and-breakfast houses. The **Mission District** is a lot of fun, but has few places to stay; the **Castro**, the **Haight**, and **Pacific Heights** have several beautiful Victorian bed-and-breakfast options; **Noe Valley** is charming but primarily residential. Some of the inns in the outer reaches of the **Sunset District** offer the city's most gorgeous views of the Pacific Ocean.

The Lowdown

Irresistible Deals... Europeans and seasoned travelers love the **San Remo Hotel**, an Italianate Victorian jewel hidden away in a residential area of North Beach. The owners haven't raised their rates for so long that single rooms start at $50 (not a misprint), but the San Remo would be a delight at twice that price. Rooms are small but very cozy, with antique beds and armoires, old-fashioned ceiling fans, and lace-curtained windows that open wide to let in the cool bay breeze and the sounds of San Francisco's lively Italian neighborhood. The atmosphere is friendly, casual, and totally international; bathrooms are shared, and even the water faucets are European—cold on the left, hot on the right. The **Phoenix** is the exact opposite of the San Remo. It is New World all the way, as American as Velveeta and Andy Warhol. Of all the city's trendy lodgings, the Phoenix is still the favorite place for deviant minds to meet. Rock stars and other eccentric celebrities flock to this inner-city motel next door to **Backflip**, a cocktail lounge and restaurant that is a scene in its own right (see Dining).

Grande dames worth considering... The **Fairmont Hotel** is synonymous with elegant San Francisco. It sits on top of Nob Hill as though it alone were holding court over the city (never mind that the Mark Hopkins is virtually across the street). The lobby is fancy, fancy, fancy and the velvet furniture is red, red, red, matching the bellhops' uniforms. The overall effect is about a half-degree shy of gaudy, but its history keeps it within the grande dame category.

The **Mark Hopkins International** is a traditional favorite of San Franciscans who appreciate elegance but don't have much of a stomach for gewgaw. It shares the top of the hill with the Fairmont but is notably less glitzy. It's a few dollars more expensive than its Nob Hill neighbor, too, but by the time you're paying that much, who's counting? The rooms themselves are plush but not extraordinary, unless you want to pop for a large suite with a Jacuzzi and a view. The best part about the hotel is probably the famous Top of the Mark cocktail lounge, still one of the most romantic spots in the city and worth a visit even if you have no intention of staying at the hotel. It has been the traditional spot to kiss a lover good-bye since World War II. (Rumor has it that gay sailors started the tradition, or at least spread it around.) The charm of the **Westin Saint Francis** in Union Square decreased considerably when the huge tower was added on, but it still has a few merits. The front entrance, used for the television series "Hotel," remains magnificent, and stepping into the lobby will probably always make you feel like a million bucks (or at least like you might need a million bucks to stay there very long). Afternoon high tea in the Compass Rose is a civilized antidote to the shopping frenzy just outside the door. If you're intent on staying at the Saint Francis, get a room in the older part of the hotel—the tower rooms are big and boring, except for their views, and they cost more.

Petite dames worth more than they charge... For the elegance of a grand luxe hotel at as little as half the price, try the **Donatello Hotel** in Union Square or the **Hotel Monaco** at the edge of the Theater District. The lavish, French-inspired Donatello is worth a visit just to see the massive stained-glass dome above the valet parking area in front of the hotel. Inside, the rooms are all oversized, with tall ceilings and huge windows; many of the successful young corporate types who frequent the Donatello happily shell out an extra $100 for rooms that open onto private, landscaped terraces. The guests at the Monaco are less buttoned-down than at the Donatello, but they definitely have a few dollars to throw around. Inside this majestic Beaux Arts landmark, the interior design is more sensual than stately—perfect for the theater crowd. A huge staircase sweeps from the lobby to the living room, and the grand chimney piece in the "prefunction" room rises to a mural of floating hot-air balloons that recall the Wizard of Oz. The bellmen in full wooden-soldier regalia outside the four-star **Prescott Hotel** in Union Square are your first clue that this is a scaled-down version of the Fairmont. Your second clue is that the room rates are about the same, give or take a few dollars. But at the Prescott, you get more personalized service, and the penthouse suite only costs $1,200 a night (a fifth of the cost of the Fairmont's penthouse).

In search of painted ladies... San Francisco has no shortage of painted ladies, be they the brazen drag queen variety or the architectural type (Victorian mansions with elaborate paint jobs). Both are found all over town, but the most famous Victorian painted ladies— the ones featured in tourism posters—are on Alamo Square, virtually across the street from the **Archbishop's Mansion**, built in 1904 and now a bed-and-breakfast inn. The huge rooms and ornate decor almost make you dizzy, but "Texans love it," says the owner. "It makes them feel like they're in their own castle for a few nights." Most of the rooms have massive canopy beds, working fireplaces, and deep, old-fashioned bathtubs, and all guests are served breakfast in bed.

The **Red Victorian Bed and Breakfast Inn** in Haight-Ashbury, known affectionately as the Red Vic, is much more eccentric and much less expensive than the Archbishop's Mansion. It's right on Haight Street, and fits in perfectly, if that gives you a clue. Group meditation is offered every morning in the back of the lobby, and owner Sami Sunchild has left her artistic thumbprint all over the inn with poem-paintings that make you want to run right out and stick a flower in your hair. Each room has its own theme, from a Persian-esque suite that looks like a good home for a hookah-smoking caterpillar to a quasi-psychedelic "LOVE" wall that certainly does not appear to be conducive to sleep. Most rooms have shared baths; be ready for aquariums and other surprises when you go to wash your face. The Red Vic is fun, it's clean, and it's definitely only in San Francisco.

In the same neighborhood but not at all in the same vein is the **Victorian Inn on the Park**, at Lyon and Fell streets, just across the Panhandle from the house where Janis Joplin once lived. The inn, a registered historic landmark, is a restored Queen Anne Victorian that caters to a more subdued clientele than the Red Vic, though it, too, had its heyday as a hippie crash pad. It's an outstanding example of Victorian architecture, and the antique furnishings are comfortable and elegant, despite signs of wear.

When money is no object... The **Clift Hotel** (formerly the Four Seasons Clift) is just about flawless—a sophisticated, elegant retreat for aristocrats and other travelers with plenty of credit. The large, high-ceilinged rooms have been meticulously restored to their prime 1915 state, with all the modern luxuries added for dessert. The topper is the wonderful Redwood Room, a lusciously romantic art-deco piano bar. The **Stouffer Renaissance Stanford Court Hotel**, called simply Stanford Court by residents and taxi drivers, is a historic landmark up on Nob Hill that once housed the founder of Stanford University. Many San Franciscans consider this the ultimate landmark hotel, but some people find it a bit difficult to feel at home in a lobby with a stained-glass dome—church pews and a confessional wouldn't seem out of place. The antiques-filled rooms are more welcoming, but if they seem too stuffy, you can always head for the bathroom, where you can flick on the television, pick up the telephone, and lather yourself into a froth with French-milled soap.

When money's too tight to mention... There are lots of safe and comfortable, sometimes even scenic, cheap lodgings in San Francisco, starting as low as $10 a day per person. The best bets for quality and location are the YMCA, hostels, budget Chinatown hotels, and Lombard Street motels. The **Central YMCA** offers private rooms with shared baths from $29 a night, including free coffee and muffins in the morning and use of the health-club facilities and pool. There are also rooms with private baths and a dormitory (for AYH and IYH members only). The hotel is staffed 24 hours a day and there are no curfews; men and women are welcome.

Chinatown's bargains include the **Grant Plaza**, a clean, comfortable hotel that many locals recommend to budget-minded visitors. All rooms have a private bath, and start at $52; a Super Saver package includes breakfast and free parking. Another Chinatown cheap sleep is the **Hotel Astoria**, where rooms with shared bath start at $39 (some rooms also have private bath). Hostels include the **AYH Hostel at Union Square**, a relatively new facility for AYH members only, starting at $16 per night; the **Green Tortoise Guest House**, a North Beach spot that offers a choice of a hostel with dorm facilities ($15 to $18) or private rooms with shared bath (starting at $35 to $39); the **Inter-Club/Globe Hostel**, South of Market, with dorm and private rooms, a cafe, bar, and sundeck, starting at $14 a night; and the **San Francisco International Hostel** (AYH) at Fort Mason, a dormitory with a view of the Golden Gate Bridge starting at $16.

Lavender lodgings... Gay tourists are to San Francisco what Disney World pilgrims are to Orlando, Florida: Big business. So surrender, Dorothy. If the idea of seeing men holding hands is a problem for you, you're in the wrong town, especially during Gay Pride festivities in June. Basically, all San Francisco hotels are gay-friendly; many mainstream hotels offer special Gay Pride discounts (ask when you call for reservations), and some lodgings cater almost entirely to a gay clientele. Many others that are not gay per se are staffed by a predominantly gay workforce, which can turn an otherwise ordinary little spot into a really fun place for gay travelers to stay. For the inside word, one of the best and funniest sources is *Betty & Pansy's Severe Queer Review*, available from A Different Light Bookstore (tel 800/343–4002). Recommended gay-oriented lodgings include all the Joi de Vivre hotels; the inexpensive **Leland Hotel**, occupying a Victorian at Polk and Bush streets; the European-style **Pension San Francisco** (Market and Gough streets); the Western-themed **Black Stallion Inn** (Castro street between 19th and 20th streets); and two other converted Victorians—the **24 Henry Guesthouse** in the Castro District and the Italianate **Inn San Francisco** on South Van Ness Avenue. Lesbian options include tiny **Bock's Bed and Breakfast**, on Willard Street near Golden Gate Park and the **House O'Chicks**, in a Castro Victorian on 15th Street near Noe Street.

Turning Japanese... The **Miyako Hotel** is authentic Japanese, even when that means bowing to Americans by including Western-style beds and bathrooms in many rooms. It's so much like an elegant Tokyo hotel, in fact, that most Japanese tourists opt for other, more "American" hotels for their vacations in San Francisco. Here's what's best about the Miyako: The rates (much lower than Hotel Nikko in Union Square), the in-room Shiatsu massages, the deep Japanese soak tubs, the *tokonama* (alcoves for displaying Japanese art), the down comforters on the futon beds, the Zen gardens inside the traditional rooms, and the sunlight filtered through *Shoji* (rice paper) screens on every window. Don't confuse this hotel with the Best Western Miyako Inn nearby. One of the most Japanese things about **Hotel Nikko** (Union Square) is the astronomical fee it charges for a Japanese suite—$1,100 per night. If that doesn't make you feel like you're in Tokyo, nothing will. These suites are not that much better than the Miyako's, but they do feature a better view of the city and an in-room well for performing the traditional tea ceremony.

For writers in search of a muse... New York has the Algonquin, San Francisco has Union Square's **Hotel Rex**. Hang around the lobby or browse in the antiquarian bookstore and you're likely to rub shoulders with celebrated writers and artists gathered for roundtables, book signings, readings, or just socializing. Playwright Wallace Shawn is among the many regular guests here. The walls of the lobby and guest rooms are a gallery of local artists' work, which owner Chip Conley bought to infuse cash into the art community after the 1989 quake. Be sure to look at the lamps: Each one was individually thrown by a local potter and each shade is hand-painted. Even the most ardent literary historians haven't been able to establish with certainty the exact number or locations of all the places Allen Ginsberg is rumored to have slept in his beatnik heyday; in his last years, however, he is known to have stayed at **Hotel Bohème**, a tasty little North Beach hotel just a short walk from Lawrence Ferlinghetti's City Lights Bookstore. A small black awning on Columbus Avenue is the only clue to the hotel's whereabouts (next to Stella Bakery and Cafe); you have to push the doorbell to get buzzed in to the narrow staircase that leads up to the foyer and reception desk. Do it, even if you don't stay there, just to see the foyer's dozens of museum-quality photographs of North Beach in the forties and fifties, including many shots of legendary poets and musicians holding forth in local joints. It'll take a lot more money to spend a night at the **Sheraton Palace Hotel**, originally known as just the Palace, where only writers who had already become rich and famous could afford to stay. Oscar Wilde stayed here when he was 27 years old and apparently drank the entire town under the table; Rudyard Kipling arrived a few years later, but was rejected by both the *Chronicle* and Ambrose Bierce's *San Francisco Illustrated Wasp*. The Sheraton Palace is still lavish and elegant; modern conveniences have been installed, but the furnishings are restored antiques that will make you wonder if any of Oscar Wilde's molecules could still be floating around in the upholstery somewhere. Meanwhile, as long as you're spending some money, consider the **Huntington Hotel** on Nob Hill, where Eugene O'Neill and his wife moved from the Fairmont after they left Tao House in Danville, some 30 miles away in the country. Today the hotel is still a discreet lodging for the "old money" crowd that wants to be left alone, as far as possible from anything resembling flash or celebrity. The **York Hotel** is neither a fancy landmark nor a charming North Beach haven, but it was home for a while to Ron Kovic, who wrote *Born on the Fourth of July* and *Around the World in Eight Days*. While staying at the York, Kovic wrote eight novels in 38 days, according to Don Herron's *The Literary World of San Francisco* (City Lights Books). (It's also considered to be gay-friendly.)

For movie-hounds.... San Francisco is a favorite site of filmmakers, and hotels make perfect backdrops. The **Fairmont Hotel** played center stage in the movie *Bullitt*, Steve McQueen's classic suspense thriller that has one of the all-time best movie chase scenes. The **York Hotel** is a must-see for Alfred Hitchcock fans: The stairway scene in *Vertigo* was shot here. Many San Francisco hotels have been featured in movies, but only one was designed as a shrine to them. In the heart of the theater district, **Hotel Bijou** looks like a sumptuous movie palace from the 1930s, with Hollywood portraits on the walls and each guest room based on the theme of a movie that was shot in the Bay Area. (Those 65 movies are all available for check-out from the hotel's video library). Best of all, there is an ornate mini-theater that plays daily shows of San Francisco movies.

Taking care of business... To the business traveler, happiness is a warm fax machine; ecstasy is one right there in your room. Guests at **The Ritz-Carlton San Francisco** will find just that, along with a voice-mail system in every room, a fully operational business center, complimentary transportation, and every other amenity a generous expense account can buy. The **Nob Hill Lambourne** is a model hotel for health-conscious business execs. Not only does the Lambourne feature a full-service spa on the premises, every room has its own exercise equipment as well as personal computer, fax set-up, and compact stereo unit, all of which special treatment costs the same or less than a nondescript room at some of the major hotels in the area. A bit farther from the Financial District, in Japantown, the **Miyako Hotel** caters to a clientele of lots of Japanese business travelers, with fax machines and voice mail in the rooms, as well as translation services. Business travelers seeking offbeat accommodations could try the **Inn at the Opera** or the **Hotel Bohème**, both of which are equipped with in-room voice mail and fax/modem hook-ups, yet offer a European-style ambience quite different from the standard business-travel hotel.

Family values... Oh, to be a kid again. They get all the good stuff and don't ever even think of offering to pay. Even some high-end hotels make a point of catering to youngsters, possibly on the theory that rich children grow up to be rich adults. At **The Clift Hotel**, children are supplied, free of charge, with everything from toys and Nintendo to milk and cookies and smaller versions of the luxurious bathrobes Mom and Dad are wearing. Parents can be provided with a babysitter and, if by chance they left the baby bag at home, every item imaginable (bottles, diapers, clothes, etc.) needed for an infant. The **Westin Saint Francis'** Kids Club is another program geared toward pleasing guests 12 and under: Members receive a sports bottle or sippy cup with complimentary refills at the hotel's restaurant, along with free food from a special kids menu, while parents request such necessities as strollers, cribs, bottle-warmers, and stepstools. The Westin Saint Francis' glass-enclosed elevators add an amusement-park thrill to the whole experience. Or, for kids with a wacky sense of humor, here's a more unorthodox choice: The **Mansions Hotel**, a converted Victorian inn that has magic shows every night, as well as a document museum with papers signed by the likes of George Washington, Abraham Lincoln, and of course, Harry Houdini.

If there's a pet in your entourage... A number of San Francisco hotels make special provisions for pooches, ranging from simply tolerating their presence to greeting them in the lobby with a doggie biscuit. For the lowdown on off-leash parks and beaches, as well as restaurants and cafes that will allow you to bring Rover in with you, get *The Dog Lover's Companion* by Lyle York and Marcia Goodavage (Foghorn Press, tel 707/773–4260). Lodgings that accept pets include some lower-priced motel properties such as the **Best Western Civic Center Motor Inn**, the **Laurel Motor Inn** in Pacific Heights, and the **Rodeway Inn** on Lombard Street's motel row; big mass-market chain properties such as the immense **San Francisco Marriott** and even, surprisingly, a couple of top-end luxury hotels—the **Westin Saint Francis**, the

Campton Place Hotel (no dogs over 25 pounds—leave the Rottweiler home), and **The Clift Hotel**, whose Very Important Pet program includes a greeting with a biscuit. Some small distinctive properties that are canine-friendly include the whimsical **Mansions Hotel**, **Pension San Francisco**, and **Inn San Francisco**, which takes pets on occasion. Always call in advance for pet policies and required deposits.

Euro-style lodgings.... San Francisco's abundance of European-inspired small hotels and guest houses are part of the ambience that has led people to call it "the Paris of the West." The **Andrews Hotel** (Union Square) is a prime example. The small, family-owned Victorian is rich in history, going back to its incarnation as the Sultan Turkish baths, a turn-of-the-century men's club. Owner Henry Andrews oversees every detail, from the fluffy down comforters and fresh flowers in each guest room to the gourmet continental breakfast set up on each floor every morning. Insider tip: Ask for a "sunny bay king" room—they have lovely bay windows and are larger than standard rooms but they cost only two or three dollars more. The small **Juliana Hotel**, near Nob Hill, is a cozy, secure-feeling three-star hotel that is particularly popular with women traveling alone. It is also a secret hideaway for celebrities—at least, it was a secret until it was featured on *Lifestyles of the Rich and Famous*. You never know who you might meet at the free wine reception each afternoon. The comfy **Abigail Hotel**, a modest hotel near the Opera House and Civic Center, draws a young international crowd that prefers down comforters to backpacks, and appreciates the superb on-site vegetarian restaurant (Millenium). The rooms are a bit small, which makes the atmosphere even more European, and the "antique" furniture is old but not precious. With just ten guest rooms, **Jackson Court** is not exactly a hotel, but staying in this historic mansion in Pacific Heights will make you feel like European royalty. (In fact, many of the residents of this exclusive neighborhood are probably richer than royals.)

Luscious love nests... *Town and Country* said a night at the **Archbishop's Mansion** is "like a night in a well-written romance novel," which is ideal if you like romance novels. It's probably the only hotel in the city where you'll find a huge bathroom with a working fireplace and a claw-footed bathtub right in the middle of the room, smelling of perfume and just waiting for a candlelit soak for two. (Do you hear that mood music yet?) The next morning you can keep the spark alive as long as nature allows—the mansion staff will serve you both breakfast in bed. If that whole Danielle Steel thing bores you, perhaps the passion of the opera will get your motor running. Couples have been known to hold intimate wedding dinners in front of the fire at the Ovation restaurant at **Inn at the Opera**, then walk across the street to pump up the volume with a fervent aria at the Opera House. The Inn at the Opera is the most sumptuous small hotel in the city, and we do mean small—the entire building is only 25 feet wide, which kind of makes you wonder how Luciano Pavarotti keeps from feeling cramped when he stays there. Still, the sense is one of airy coziness, partially because all of the windows open for real fresh air. If you've got that truly, madly, deeply kind of thing going on, and you're willing to prove it with some serious money, take your amour across the bay to the lush, 22-acre **Claremont Resort Hotel, Spa & Tennis Club** and book a telescope suite, where San Francisco's lights will twinkle just for you all night long. It's one of the best views of San Francisco you'll ever find. The picture window is as big as a movie screen and is fitted with a wide, wraparound window seat custom-made for those spontaneous harmonic convergences. And if you pause to look out the window during the day, you'll see acres and acres of beautifully landscaped grounds (irrigated by the resort's own wells). Play tennis, swim, get massages, eat in the superb restaurants, have cocktails in the bar, do it all, but by all means get back to your room in time for a private bottle of California bubbly (the wine list is unbeatable) and the view.

Provident penthouses.... You don't have to spend $6,000 a night at the Fairmont to stay in an enchanting penthouse. For $100 a night, you can have your own little cottage and sundeck at the **San Remo Hotel** in North Beach. True, it is perched on a tarpaper roof and is more like a goofy houseboat than a luxury apartment, but the location and the view are great. Unfortunately, this little gem is no longer a secret, so you may need to book a few months in advance. On the other hand, not many people know about the two gorgeous terrace penthouses at the **Maxwell Hotel** near Union Square. If you ever want to impress your associates or entertain your friends, this is the place to splurge ($495). There is no cheesy gold-plated anything, no marble floors, no frou-frou at all—the decor is modern but luxurious, sort of high-end Pottery Barn. The view is to die for. Room service is from Gracie's, the hotel's stylish American brasserie. Going up the scale, the **Prescott Hotel**, also in Union Square, has a more opulent penthouse: Two fireplaces (including one in the bedroom), a baby grand piano, a state-of-the-art stereo system, and a dining room that seats eight for a private dinner catered by Wolfgang Puck's Postrio restaurant. If you charged your seven guests $175 a piece, you could cover the $1,200-a-night fee. Just a thought.

I'm with the band... You don't have to be on assignment for the *National Enquirer* to be curious about rock stars, but you do have to know where they stay at night if you want to sneak a peek. We'll tell you some of the best spots, but you have to promise to follow the two cardinal rules of stargazing: (1) don't stare; and (2) don't ask. The **Phoenix** is the supreme hot spot for rock stars and other nonconformist celebrities. Originally a kind of futuristic, sleek motel in the fifties, then a hooker hall in the seventies and eighties, it was bought in 1987 by Chip Conley, who managed to snag his first celebrity guest, Brenda Lee, when she stopped one day to ask for directions to another hotel. After that came Arlo Guthrie and a few others, and the celebrity guest register mushroomed. Sinead O'Connor, John F. Kennedy Jr., Deborah Harry, Wim Wenders, the Sex Pistols, Nirvana, the Red Hot Chili Peppers, M.C. Hammer, k.d. lang, R.E.M., John Waters, Dr. John, Etta James, River Phoenix, Keanu Reeves, Chubby Checker, David Bowie, Bonnie Raitt, Bo Diddley, and the Cowboy Junkies are just a few of the stars who have lounged by the infamous mural-bottomed swimming pool in the Tenderloin. Offbeat stargazing doesn't get any better, and the rooms start at under $90, so reserve well in advance. The **Hotel Richelieu** puts up a lot of the bands that play at the nearby Great American Music Hall, but the pickings are generally a little slimmer and far tamer than the Phoenix. The celebrity guest register is a bit iffy; your best bet is to find out who's playing at the Great American during your vacation. It might be Etta James and it might be the Bulgarian State Women's Chorus, you never know. The Richelieu has been hosting music stars since it was built in 1908 when the Great American was still just a bordello, and it proudly displays in the lobby the costume of one of its first celebrity guests, Jenny Lind. The staff is young and hip and friendly, and can direct you to all the happening clubs in town. Celebrity guests at the **Inn at the Opera** are more along the lines of opera stars, artists, and dancers—Mikhail Baryshnikov, Twyla Tharp, David Hockney, Placido Domingo, Oscar de la Renta, Robert Rauschenberg, Philip Glass, Herbie Hancock, the Tokyo String Quartet, and the principal dancers of the American Ballet Theatre—but there are a few surprises to round out the list, such as home-run king Hank Aaron, and Gaylord Perry, who holds the major-league record for spitballs. This superb hotel is very popular, so reserve well in advance.

That's why they call it modern art... Two hotels worth visiting purely for the *lobbies d'moderne* are the **Hotel Triton** and the **Commodore**. The Triton lobby looks like what would have happened if Kandinsky had gone into business as a hotelier. The furniture and the people who sit upon it are all part of the glorious confetti that make you want to walk right up to the front desk and say, "I don't care how much it costs, I want to join the party." The stylish desk clerks add to the sense of chic, but they often have that deadpan look of a bouncer at a trendy nightclub. The Commodore is an entirely different flight of fancy: It used to be an ordinary, clean, reasonably priced hotel, until Chip Conley (see The Phoenix, above) got hold of it—where have we heard this before?—and turned it into a modernistic, Alice-in-Wonderland Love Boat. The decor is Picasso-meets-Popeye, a sort of surrealistic cruise-ship motif. There are wavy aqua lines painted around imaginary portholes on the front doors, through which Keanu Reeves, Jon Bon Jovi, and dozens of other celebs have entered the lobby. While staying at the Commodore to film *Little City*, Bon Jovi loved hanging out in the attached Red Room cocktail lounge, the hottest bar in town when it opened in 1996; he even volunteered to bartend one night.

We gotta get outta this place... Fog getting to you? Think you'll scream if you see one more panhandler on Market Street? Here's the cure: Get a car and drive across the Golden Gate Bridge, then another 12 miles to Mill Valley, one of those cozy little towns that forces you to use the word "quaint" to describe it. (It was, however, the setting for the 1970s satire *Serial*, starring Martin Mull, Sally Kellerman, and a flotilla of hot tubs—luckily, most of the Marin County stereotypes that inspired this book and the 1980 movie have gone to spawn elsewhere.) Get yourself a balcony room at the **Mill Valley Inn**, a European-style *pensione* where your free breakfast is served at a popular local espresso cafe. Go ahead, mingle with the locals—half of them are screenwriters and you know how they love to talk. After that, you'll be ready to calm down a bit at **Tea Garden Springs** (see Getting Outside) with a massage and an herbal elixir. If that still doesn't do it, get back in the car, head farther up the coast to Point Reyes National Seashore and check into **Manka's Inverness Lodge**, a hunting lodge built in 1917 and later transformed into a romantic inn; the extraordinary restaurant here serves game grilled in the fireplace and local line-caught fish. Try to get one of the private cabins, and whatever you do, don't miss dinner in the restaurant. If you have time, it's worth the extra two hours to drive up to Mendocino's **Heritage House**, where the movie *Same Time Next Year* was filmed. When you settle into your own private cottage on the 37 acres overlooking the Pacific Ocean, you'll know why this was picked as the site where Alan Alda and his movie mistress Ellen Burstyn returned year after year. The grounds are reminiscent of the Irish countryside, soft and green and wrapped with mist in the morning. The Heritage House's nationally acclaimed chef is Lance Velasquez, who left San Francisco after making Moose's restaurant a huge success. The wine list is one of the best in the state and the bar offers special tastings of the world's finest unblended scotches; and after all of that, there's always a stroll around the grounds and a Jacuzzi in your room.

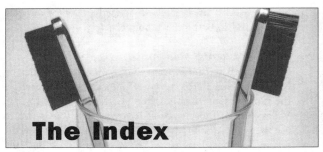

The Index

$$$$$	over $200
$$$$	$150–$200
$$$	$80–$150
$$	$50–$80
$	under $50

Abigail Hotel. This hotel is absolutely perfect for travelers who like charm, great food, international company, and an inexpensive bill when they check out (rooms start at $79).... *Tel 415/861–9728, 800/243–6510, fax 415/861–5848. 246 McAllister St., San Francisco, CA 94102, Civic Center BART/MUNI Metro station. 61 rooms. $$$* **(see p. 27)**

Archbishop's Mansion. This bed-and-breakfast inn has been hailed as the most spectacular place to stay in the city, and as the most elegant in-city hotel in the United States. Maybe yes, maybe no. Try a night in the Carmen Suite, and make up your own mind.... *Tel 415/563–7872, 800/543–5820, fax 415/885–3193. 1000 Fulton St., San Francisco, CA 94117, 5 MUNI bus. 10 rooms, 5 suites. $$$–$$$$$* **(see pp. 20, 27)**

Andrews Hotel. This cozy family-run inn near Union Square preserves many Victorian details. The atmosphere is continental; so is the daily free breakfast.... *Tel 415/563–6877, 800/926–3739, fax 415/938–6919. 624 Post St., San Francisco CA 94109, Union Square, Powell-Mason cable car. 48 rooms. $$$* **(see p. 27)**

AYH Hostel at Union Square. This hostel for AYH members only is in the heart of Union Square and features several rooms with private baths for families, as well as the normal dormitory facilities, starting at $16 per person. It is wheelchair accessible. Reservations are required.... *Tel 415/788–5604, fax 415/788–3023. 312 Mason St., San Fran-*

cisco, CA 94102, Powell-Mason cable car, 7B or 38 MUNI bus. 218 beds, 30 with private bath. $ **(see p. 22)**

Best Western Civic Center Motor Inn. This budget chain motel is nondescript, but clean and convenient. It has a sunny outdoor pool, offers free parking, and allows pets.... Tel 415/621–2826, 800/444–5829. 364 Ninth St., San Francisco, CA 94103, Civic Center BART/MUNI Metro station. 57 rooms. $$–$$$ **(see p. 26)**

Black Stallion Inn. The Severe Queer Review calls this the city's only "leather-levi-western bed and breakfast." It's right in the Castro District, and has a fireplace and a sundeck in the public rooms. Breakfast is included.... Tel 415/863–0131. 635 Castro St., San Francisco, CA 94114, Castro St. MUNI Metro station. 8 rooms. $$$ **(see p. 23)**

Bock's Bed and Breakfast. This tiny, non-smoking bed-and-breakfast near Golden Gate Park has sundecks, laundry facilities, and fax service. Continental breakfast is included. There is a two-night minimum stay.... Tel 415/664–6842, fax 415/664–1109. 1448 Willard St., San Francisco, CA 94117, 5 MUNI bus. 3 rooms. $–$$ **(see p. 23)**

Campton Place Hotel. This small luxury hotel is noted for its elegance (bathrooms have marble floors, brass fixtures, and cushy bathrobes) and comfortable intimacy. Personal service is a hallmark here. Tel 415/781–5555, 800/235–4300, fax 415/955–5536. 340 Stockton St., San Francisco, CA 94108; Powell-Hyde and Powell-Mason cable car; 2, 3, 4, 30, or 45 MUNI bus. 117 rooms, 10 suites. $$$$–$$$$$ **(see p. 27)**

Central YMCA. This reliable old standard in cheap lodgings is an especially good deal when you consider that the rooms are private (some with private bath) and include use of the health club and pool as well as free coffee and muffins in the morning. At $26 for a single ($36 for a double), that's a steal. (Rooms with private bath start at $37.50) Dormitory accommodations are also available to AYH and IYH members for $15, including all the same amenities. Both men and women are welcome.... Tel 415/885–0460. 220 Golden Gate Ave., San Francisco, CA 94109, Civic Center BART/MUNI Metro stop, 15 MUNI bus. 106 rooms, plus 6-bed dormitory. $ **(see pp. 15, 22)**

Claremont Resort Hotel, Spa & Tennis Club. This lush, romantic retreat, just four BART stops away from downtown San Francisco, was voted the best urban spa in the U.S. The 22 acres of landscaped grounds are just the backdrop for the landmark Victorian hotel (1915), the Bay Area's premier private tennis club (open to guests), and a $6 million holistic health and beauty spa.... *Tel 510/843–3000, 800/551–7266, fax 510/549-8582. Ashby and Domingo Aves., Oakland, CA 94623-0363, Rockridge BART station (plus a cab). 239 rooms. $$$$–$$$$$*

(see p. 28)

The Clift Hotel. A haven for aristocrats and romantics on a splurge, the Clift is the luxury hotel that other hotels want to be when they grow up. The divine rooms have high ceilings, marble bathrooms, fine art, and meticulously restored woodwork and moldings, true to old San Francisco (circa 1915); the service is impeccable.... *Tel 415/775–4700, 800/65-CLIFT, fax 415/441–4621. 495 Geary St., San Francisco, CA 94102; Powell-Hyde and Powell-Mason cable car, 2, 3, 4, 30, 38, or 45 bus. 326 rooms, including suites. $$$$$* **(see pp. 21, 26, 27)**

Commodore. You have to go by this one just to check out the lobby. It's a goofball version of a cruise ship, with a lobby full of furniture that looks like it came out of a cartoon. Every morning you get a tip sheet telling you what the hip happenings are in the city that day.... *Tel 415/932–6800, 800/338–6848, fax 415/923–6804. 825 Sutter St., San Francisco, CA 94109, California St. cable car. 113 rooms. $$–$$$* **(see p. 30)**

Donatello Hotel. The standard rooms may be the largest in the city, with 10-foot ceilings and huge windows; terrace suites open to lushly landscaped private decks. The clientele is international, and a bit conservative.... *Tel 415/441–7100, 800/227–3184, fax 415/885–8842. 501 Post St., San Francisco, CA 94109, Union Square, Powell-Mason cable car. 94 rooms, including suites. $$$$* **(see p. 20)**

Fairmont Hotel. This is probably the most famous hotel in San Francisco, at the very tip-top of Nob Hill, yet it's not incredibly expensive, provided you stay out of the suites. Rooms in the main building are more affordable than those in the tower, but don't miss the ride in the tower elevator. The staff is friendly and helpful, but not annoyingly deferential.... *Tel 415/772–5000, 800/527–4727, fax 415/772–5013. 950 Mason St., San Francisco, CA 94108, California St. cable car. 600 rooms, 62 suites, $$$$–$$$$$* **(see pp. 14, 19, 25)**

Grant Plaza. This bargain hotel in Chinatown is clean and comfortable. The rooms tend to have dreary mauve carpeting and floral bedspreads, but the windows are large and let in plenty of light.... *Tel 415/434–3883, 800/472–6899, fax 415/434–3886. 465 Grant Ave., San Francisco, CA 94108. 15, 30, 45 MUNI bus. 72 rooms. $* **(see p. 22)**

Green Tortoise Guest House. This non-smoking facility was originally made popular by super-cheap hippie bus trips from San Francisco to the Northwest and other destinations. It attracts lots of young people looking for a low-cost place to crash and some kindred souls. It also has a sauna, laundry, and organized tours.... *Tel 415/834–1000, 800/867–8647, fax 415/956–4900. 15, 30 MUNI bus. 100 beds, 10 rooms with shared bath. $* **(see p. 22)**

Heritage House. This 37-acre Mendocino retreat features a world class restaurant. The inn itself is an 1877 farmhouse; private cottages come with fireplaces, sundecks, and whirlpool baths. The only drawback is that you might never want to leave.... *Tel 707/937–5885, 800/235–5885, fax 707/937–0318. 5200 N. US Hwy 1, Little River, CA 95456. 65 rooms/cottages. $$$* **(see p. 31)**

Hotel Astoria. This super-cheap Chinatown hotel has plain, but not shabby, rooms, some with shared bath, some with private bath. Airport pickup and some business services are provided.... *Tel 415/434–8889, 800/666–6696, fax 415/434–8919. 510 Bush St., San Francisco, CA 94108; 30, 45 MUNI bus. 90 rooms, 40 with private bath. $*

(see p. 22)

Hotel Bijou. A shrine to the silver screen, this small hotel in the heart of the theater district looks like an old-time movie palace and features movie-themed guest rooms. There's even an on-site screening room with plush antique movie-theater seats. We give it two thumbs up.... *Tel 415/771-1200, 800/771-1022, fax 415/346-3196. 111 Mason St., San Francisco, CA 94102, Union Square, Powell-Mason cable car. $$$* **(see p. 25)**

Hotel Bohème. This Parisian-style beatnik villa is both comfortable and chic at the same time. It's right on Columbus Avenue, in the heart of North Beach, but the rooms are surprisingly quiet, elegant, and well-equipped.... *Tel 415/433–9111, fax 415/362–6292. 444 Columbus Ave., San Francisco, CA 94133; 15, 30, 45 MUNI bus. 15 rooms. $$$* **(see pp. 14, 24, 25)**

Hotel Monaco. This impeccably refurbished 1910 Beaux Arts landmark has won scads of design awards for its eccentric yet gracious interior design. A four-star hotel with all the amenities, the Monaco attracts discriminating non-mainstream types.... *Tel 415/292–0100, 800/214–4220, fax 415/292-0111. 501 Geary St., San Francisco, CA 94102, Union Square, Powell-Mason cable car, 38 MUNI bus. 167 rooms, 34 suites. $$$$* **(see pp. 14, 20)**

Hotel Nikko. This Japanese hotel is perilously close to the Hilton and it has rubbed off. Most of the rooms are very Western, though the traditional Japanese suites are lovely. Swimming pool, fitness center.... *Tel 415/394–1111, 800/645–5687, fax 415/394–1106. 222 Mason St., San Francisco, CA 94102; Powell St. BART/MUNI Metro station; Powell-Mason or Powell-Hyde cable car; 38 MUNI bus. 500 rooms, 22 suites. $$$$–$$$$$* **(see p. 23)**

Hotel Rex. This arts and literary salon/hotel draws artists and writers for roundtables, book-signings, and conversation.... *Tel 415/433–4434, 800/433–4434, fax 415/433–3695. 562 Sutter St., San Francisco, CA 84102, Union Square, Powell-Mason or Powell-Hyde cable car. $$$* **(see p. 23)**

Hotel Richelieu. This turn-of-the-century hotel is just a few blocks from the Great American Music Hall. The rooms are large but unremarkable—standard hotel-issue furnishings, complete with fitted bedspreads—but they do have coffeemakers, mini-bars, and private safes. Watch which direction you wander out the door—a few blocks down, Geary Street starts looking pretty grim.... *Tel 415/673–4711, 800/295–7424, fax 415/673–9362. 1050 Van Ness Ave., San Francisco, CA 94109, 38 MUNI bus. 150 rooms. $$$*
(see pp. 17, 29)

Hotel Triton. Plush, upholstered chairs that look like they came from Barbara Eden's bottle in "I Dream of Jeannie" sit next to the modern, angular front desk. Two huge columns that look like upside-down Doric pillars make the royal-blue carpet—splattered with gold stars—look like a right-side-up sky. The guests look as arty as the decor. Great location right across from the gate to Chinatown.... *Tel 415/394–0500, 800/433–6611, fax 415/394–0555. 342 Grant Ave., San Francisco, CA 94108; 30, 45 MUNI bus. 140 rooms. $$$–$$$$* **(see pp. 14, 30)**

House O'Chicks. Admit it, the name alone makes you want to check it out. This Victorian house is a lesbian lodging in the Castro District. Guests can feel free to use the kitchen, office, computer, and fax machine.... *Tel 415/861–9849. 2162 15th St. (near Noe St.), San Francisco, CA 94114, Church St. MUNI Metro station. $$* **(see p. 23)**

Huntington Hotel. Rooms are exquisitely—and individually—appointed, with museum-quality works of art and a blend of antique and custom-designed furniture. This Nob Hill landmark is definitely ruling class, so mind your manners.... *Tel 415/474–5400, 800/227–4683 in California, fax 415/474–6227. 1075 California St., San Francisco, CA 94108, California St. cable car, 1 MUNI bus. 140 rooms, 40 suites. $$$$–$$$$$* **(see p. 24)**

Inn at the Opera. This tiny European-style establishment is the most distinguished small luxury hotel in the city and one of the most romantic. A 25-foot wide Victorian jewel, nestled virtually in the backyard of the Opera house, it looks like a pen-and-ink illustration of a small rooming house in turn-of-the-century London or Paris.... *Tel 415/863–8400, 800/325–2708, fax 415/861–0821. 333 Fulton St., San Francisco, CA 94102, Civic Center BART/MUNI Metro station, 5, 21, 47, or 49 MUNI bus. 30 rooms, 18 suites. $$$–$$$$* **(see pp. 14, 25, 28, 30)**

Inn San Francisco. Once a private mansion, this gracious bed-and-breakfast offers a garden hot tub, rooftop sundeck, fireplaces in the guest rooms, and complimentary buffet breakfast.... *Tel 415/641–0188, 800/359–0913, fax 415/641–1701. 943 South Van Ness Ave., San Francisco, CA 94110, 5 MUNI bus. 21 rooms. $$–$$$$* **(see pp. 23, 27)**

Inter-Club/Globe Hostel. If you want to stay South of Market and bask on a sundeck, try this hostel. It has a dorm and private rooms, plus a pool table, cafe, and bar. Rates start at $14; reservations are highly recommended.... *Tel 415/ 431–0540, fax 415/431–3286. 10 Hallam Place (off Folsom St., between seventh and eighth Sts.). San Francisco, CA 94103, Civic Center BART/MUNI Metro station, 42 MUNI bus. 33 rooms. $* **(see p. 22)**

Jackson Court. Reserve at least six weeks in advance for this 10-room brownstone mansion in elite Pacific Heights. Somewhat ornate in parts, it's also warm and homey, with exceptionally comfortable beds (and exquisite bed linens). Tea and cookies are served by the fireplace every afternoon.... *Tel 415/929–7670, 800/738–7477, fax, 415/ 929–1405. 2198 Jackson St., San Francisco, CA 94115, Pacific Heights, 12 MUNI bus. $$$* **(see p. 27)**

Juliana Hotel. A haven for celebrities and for solo women travelers, who love the cozy, safe feel of both the inn and the neighborhood. For business types, there is limousine service to the Financial District every morning.... *Tel 415/392– 2540, 800/328–3880, fax 415/391–8447. 590 Bush St., San Francisco, CA 94108, Powell St. BART station, all cable car lines, 30 or 45 MUNI bus. $$$$* **(see p. 27)**

Laurel Motor Inn. This Pacific Heights motel has a great location plus kitchens and a complimentary continental breakfast; rates start at $73. Parking is free and pets are welcome.... *Tel 415/567–8467, 800/552–8735, fax 415/ 928–1866. 444 Presidio Ave., San Francisco, CA 94115, 3 MUNI bus. 49 rooms. $$–$$$* **(see p. 26)**

Leland Hotel. This Victorian Polk Street hotel is a great value, considering that you get rooms with bay windows, private baths, televisions, and in-room phones. For around $60, that's almost luxurious.... *Tel 415/441–5141, 800/258– 4458. 1315 Polk St., San Francisco, CA 94109, California St. cable car, 42 MUNI bus. 108 rooms. $$* **(see p. 23)**

Manka's Inverness Lodge & Restaurant. Locals rave about this small oceanside inn, with its remarkable restaurant, less than an hour from the city. The cheerful, rustic private cabins are delightful.... *Tel 415/669–1034. P.O. Box 1110, Inverness, CA 94937. On Point Reyes National Seashore. 14 units, 4 apartments with kitchens $$–$$$$* **(see p. 31)**

Mansions Hotel. This peculiar little hideaway features rooms named after famous or infamous San Franciscans; it's a combination of whimsy and Victorian elegance. Some of the rooms feature priceless antiques. Breakfast is complimentary.... *Tel 415/929–9444, fax 415/567–9391. 2220 Sacramento St., San Francisco, CA 94115; 1, 3, or 83 MUNI bus. 21 rooms.* $$$ **(see pp. 26, 27)**

Mark Hopkins International. Sometimes overshadowed by its Nob Hill neighbor, the Fairmont, this classic 19-story luxury hotel should not be overlooked. Every room has a marvelous view. The Mark Hopkins's low-key elegance makes it popular with locals.... *Tel 415/392–3434, 800/327–0200, fax 415/421–3302. 1 Nob Hill, San Francisco, CA 94108, California St. cable car. 390 rooms, 27 suites.* $$$$–$$$$$ **(see p. 19)**

Maxwell Hotel. You can't miss the real-life sculpture of a shopper outside the entrance to this restored 1908 art-deco masterpiece, a tribute to the high-end shopping nearby in Union Square. (Special package deals are offered for shopaholics.) The spacious guest rooms are done in deep, rich colors with plush fabrics and hand-painted lampshades.... *Tel 415/986–2000, 888/734–6299, fax 415/397–2447. 386 Geary St., San Francisco, CA 94102, Union Square, Powell-Mason cable car, 38 MUNI bus.* $$$ **(see p. 29)**

Mill Valley Inn. The perfect escape, this three-story European-style *pensione* looks like a cross between an Italian villa and a California Colonial lodge, at the foot of Mount Tamalpais, alongside a redwood grove. Reserve a month in advance.... *Tel 415/389–6608, 800/595–2100, fax 415/389–5051. 165 Throckmorton Ave., Mill Valley, CA 94941. 25 rooms, 2 cottages, 1 penthouse apartment.* $$$ **(see p. 31)**

Miyako Hotel. One of the most tranquil, gracious hotels in the city. Opt for the luxurious traditional Japanese rooms with their wonderful deep-soak tubs (shower first, then soak) and Zen gardens. American-style breakfast is included.... *Tel 415/922–3200, 800/533–4567, fax 415/921–0417. 1625 Post St. (near Geary Blvd. and Laguna St.), San Francisco, CA 94115, 38 MUNI bus. 218 rooms, 11 suites.* $$$–$$$$ **(see pp. 23, 25)**

Nob Hill Lambourne. This very sleek hotel looks like another ritzy, oh-so-spare hotel for the rich and private, but it's actually a reasonably priced lodging that attracts busy, health-conscious business travelers. Full-service spa on site.... *Tel 415/433–2287, fax 415/433–0975. 725 Pine St., San Francisco, CA 94108, Powell St. BART station. 20 rooms, 6 suites. $$$$–$$$$$* **(see pp. 14, 25)**

Pension San Francisco. A wide green awning welcomes you to this red-brick Victorian perched at the crossroads of the Mission District, the Hayes Valley, and Upper Market Street. The feel of the pension is almost French Quarter, with wrought-iron fire escapes on the front and ornate white wood railings surrounding the rooftop.... *Tel 415/864–1271, 800/886–1271, fax 415/861–8116. 1668 Market St., San Francisco, CA 94102, Van Ness Ave. MUNI Metro station or 7 MUNI bus. 36 rooms. $* **(see pp. 23, 27)**

Phoenix. One of the most wacked-out and popular lodgings in the city, this Tenderloin/Civic Center motel is best known for its famous guests. The decor is sort of psychedelic kitsch a la Rancho Tropicale, with lots of rattan faux leopard skin, and art d'moderne.... *Tel 415/776–1380, 800/248–9466, fax 415/885–3109. 601 Eddy St., San Francisco, CA 94109; 19, 31, or 38 MUNI bus. 44 rooms, 3 suites. $$–$$$* **(see pp. 14, 19, 29)**

Prescott Hotel. The flagship of the Kimpton Group, this luxurious boutique hotel features massive cherry-wood furniture in the Edwardian-style guestrooms. Guests get preferred seating at Wolfgang Puck's chic Postrio restaurant.... *Tel 415/563-0303, fax 415/563-6831. 545 Post St., San Francisco, CA 94102, Union Square, Powell St. BART station, Powell-Mason or Powell-Hyde cable car, 2, 3, 4, or 38 MUNI bus. $$$$* **(see pp. 14, 20, 29)**

Red Victorian Bed and Breakfast Inn. There should be a sign in front of this lovely and eccentric Haight-Ashbury inn that reads: Welcome Back to 1967. Each room has its own theme, documented in a photo book at the front desk, so you can take your pick.... *Tel 415/864–1978. 1665 Haight St., San Francisco, CA 94117; 7, 66, 71, or 73 MUNI bus. 18 rooms (4 with private bath), 1 suite. $$–$$$*

(see p. 21)

The Ritz-Carlton San Francisco. Handsome rooms, Italian-marble bathrooms, plush terry bathrobes, and twice-daily maid service (once to turn down your bed) are just some of the comforts here. Fully equipped fitness center—with indoor pool, whirlpool, and sauna.... *Tel 415/296–7465. 600 Stockton St., San Francisco, CA 94108, Stockton St. BART station. 336 rooms, 42 suites. $$$$$* **(see p. 25)**

Rodeway Inn. A bit more expensive than the other budget motels along Lombard Street, the Rodeway offers a restaurant, lounge, free parking, kitchens, and wheelchair accessibility. Pets are welcome.... *Tel 415/673–0691, 800/228–2000. 1450 Lombard St., San Francisco, CA 94123, 28 MUNI bus. 73 rooms. $$$* **(see p. 26)**

San Francisco International Hostel (AYH). Fort Mason is the hub of the beautifully scenic Golden Gate National Recreation Area, and right in the thick of it, this dormitory hostel is wheelchair accessible, provides free parking, and starts at $16 per person.... *Tel 415/771–7277, fax 415/771–1468. Building 240, Fort Mason, San Francisco, CA 94123; Powell-Hyde cable car; 30 or 42 MUNI bus. 150 beds. $* **(see pp. 15, 22)**

San Francisco Marriott. One thing is certain—you can't miss this gigantic building, looming like a huge jukebox over the Financial District. Locals either love it or hate it. Decor is typical Chain Hotel Moderne; there are three restaurants, three lounges, a pool, health club, spa, gift shops, airline ticket desks, and some unbelievable views of both the bay and the Golden Gate.... *Tel 415/896–1600, 800/228–9290, fax 415/777–2799. 55 Fourth St., San Francisco, CA 94103, Powell St. BART/MUNI Metro station, Powell St. cable-car turnaround. 1,500 rooms. $$$–$$$$* **(see p. 26)**

San Remo Hotel. This delightful, clean, European-style hotel starts at $50 and tops out at $100 for the rooftop penthouse cottage (reserve at least a month in advance). The other rooms are furnished with antiques and have comfortable beds, windows that open to let in salty sea air, and ceiling fans to whoosh it around. The shared bathrooms on each floor are sparklingly clean and well kept. It's also walking distance from Fisherman's Wharf.... *Tel 415/776–8688, 800/352–7366, fax 415/776–2811. 2237 Mason St., San*

Francisco, CA 94133, Powell-Mason cable car, 15 or 30 MUNI bus. 62 rooms, all shared bath. $–$$

(see pp. 14, 18, 28)

Sheraton Palace Hotel. Once the Palace Hotel, this San Francisco landmark has now been restored to its turn-of-the-century distinction. The antique-furnished rooms have all the modern conveniences, and the health club boasts a lap pool.... Tel 415/512–1111, 800/325–3535, fax 415/543–0671. 2 New Montgomery St., San Francisco, CA 94105; Montgomery St. BART/MUNI Metro station, 7, 15, 30, or 45 MUNI bus. 550 rooms, 32 suites. $$$$$

(see p. 24)

Stouffer Renaissance Stanford Court Hotel. The Stanford Court is one of the most impressive hotels in the city, with a stained-glass dome in the lobby, antique furnishings in the rooms, and possibly the ghost of railroad baron Leland Stanford, lurking in the hallways.... Tel 415/989–3500, 800/227–4736, fax 415/391–0513. 905 California St., San Francisco, CA 94108, Powell-Hyde and Powell-Mason cable cars, 1 MUNI bus. 393 rooms, 18 suites, 14 junior suites. $$$$$ **(see p. 21)**

24 Henry Guesthouse. This very intimate little Victorian guesthouse (non-smoking) in the Castro District offers such amenities as libraries, sitting parlors, and a complimentary buffet breakfast.... Tel 415/864–5686, 800/900–5686, fax 415/864–0406. 24 Henry St. (between Sanchez and Noe Sts.), San Francisco, CA 94114, J Church MUNI Metro. 5 rooms (4 with shared bath), 1 one-bedroom apartment. $–$$$ **(see p. 23)**

Victorian Inn on the Park. A beautifully restored historic landmark with 12 rooms, some of which have working fireplaces and terraces overlooking the Panhandle. Breakfast is included.... Tel 415/931–1830, 800/435–1967, fax 415/931–1830. 301 Lyon St., San Francisco, CA 94117, 7 MUNI bus. 12 rooms. $$$ **(see p. 21)**

Westin Saint Francis. Perhaps the most venerable grande dame, the Saint Francis is extremely well located if you don't mind staying amid the thousands of Union Square shoppers and tourists. Rooms in the original old building are

preferable to those in the bland modern tower, and are slightly less expensive than their Nob Hill counterparts.... *Tel 415/397–7000, 800/228–3000, fax 415/774–0124. 335 Powell St., San Francisco, CA 94102; Powell-Hyde and Powell-Mason cable cars, 2, 3, 4, 30, 45, and 76 MUNI buses. 1,200 rooms, including 83 suites. $$$$–$$$$$*
(see pp. 19, 26)

York Hotel. The hotel's formal script logo, emblazoned on deep-green awnings, belies the relaxed atmosphere that prevails at the York, a clean, peachy-colored Victorian that looks inviting from a block away.... *Tel 415/885–6800, 800/808–9675, fax 415/885–2115. 940 Sutter St., San Francisco, CA 94109, Powell-Mason or Powell-Hyde cable car, 38 MUNI bus. 96 rooms. $$$–$$$$* **(see pp. 24, 25)**

San Francisco Accommodations

Abigail Hotel **15**

Archbishop's Mansion **21**

Best Western Civic
Center Motor Inn **16**

Black Stallion Inn **25**

Bock's Bed and Breakfast **26**

Central YMCA **12**

Green Tortise Guest House **5**

Hotel Bohème **4**

Hotel Richelieu **10**

House O'Chicks **24**

Inn at the Opera **20**

Inn San Francisco **19**

Inter-Club/Globe Hostel **17**

Jackson Court **6**

Laurel Motor Inn **9**
Leland Hotel **11**
Mansions Hotel **7**
Miyako Hotel **8**
Pension San Francisco **18**
Phoenix **14**
Red Victorian Bed and
Breakfast Inn **22**

Rodeway Inn **3**
San Francisco International Hostel **1**
San Remo Hotel **2**
Sheraton Palace Hotel **13**
24 Henry Guesthouse **23**
Victorian Inn on the Park **27**

Union Square/Nob Hill Accommodations

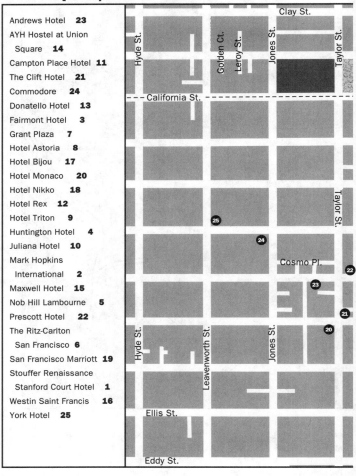

Andrews Hotel **23**

AYH Hostel at Union
Square **14**

Campton Place Hotel **11**

The Clift Hotel **21**

Commodore **24**

Donatello Hotel **13**

Fairmont Hotel **3**

Grant Plaza **7**

Hotel Astoria **8**

Hotel Bijou **17**

Hotel Monaco **20**

Hotel Nikko **18**

Hotel Rex **12**

Hotel Triton **9**

Huntington Hotel **4**

Juliana Hotel **10**

Mark Hopkins
International **2**

Maxwell Hotel **15**

Nob Hill Lambourne **5**

Prescott Hotel **22**

The Ritz-Carlton
San Francisco **6**

San Francisco Marriott **19**

Stouffer Renaissance
Stanford Court Hotel **1**

Westin Saint Francis **16**

York Hotel **25**

dining a

2

nd cafes

It's official: San
Francisco is the
best food town in
America. New
York had to accept
the backseat when
the City

by the Bay won all of the top James Beard awards (the Oscars of the restaurant world) in 1997. Best chef in the country. Best restaurant in the country. Best new restaurant in the country. Best "rising star" chef in the country. No other city had a chance. With some 3,500 restaurants representing every cuisine on earth (and a few from outer space), the city that spawned California cuisine has become North America's ground zero for ingenious chefs. They are drawn not only to the creative freedom that has always defined San Francisco, but also to the year-round abundance of fresh fruits, vegetables, herbs, fish, and seafood that are Northern California's unique bounty.

Oddly enough, it took local cooks until nearly the end of the twentieth century to figure out there was more to culinary life than steak and seafood, at which point they immediately went berserk with outlandish combinations of exotic ingredients and trickled raspberry vinegar on absolutely everything. Fortunately, most food fads—including that one—have the life span of a disposable razor, but there are some things you can always count on when you dine in San Francisco: A mélange of authentic ethnic eateries that is probably the most diverse in America; cafes, bistros, and formal dinner houses that serve extraordinary French food; a solid core of world-class restaurants inspired by California cuisine in all its transmutations; and, of course, the traditional grill fare that has been a staple since the Gold Rush. You could spend your entire vacation—and most of your money—eating at Masa's and other high-profile spots that have gotten more press than the O.J. Simpson trial, but the best way to enjoy San Francisco's lavish feast is to explore the nation's most exotic variety of ethnic food. Often the most interesting and delicious food is far less expensive than "see-and-be-seen" fare. There are far too many excellent restaurants to mention here, but the samples we offer will get you started on your own dining adventure.

Only in San Francisco

The sunny **Mission District** has long been famous for its Mexican restaurants and storefront taquerias, where locals take for granted lunchtime feasts of authentic barbecued pork *carnitas* and grilled steak (*carne asada*) for less than the price of a Big Mac. A steady stream of immigrants and refugees from Guatemala, El Salvador, Nicaragua, Chile, and Peru have brought dozens of new restaurants to the neighborhood, adding countless treats to the Latin American banquet table. Chinese food is also synonymous with San Francisco, but you can find that in almost every city. The true gems are the rarer **Asian/Pacific** cuisines such as Cambodia's complex mingling of coconut milk, lemongrass, lime, and classical French fish sauce; or Singapore's exotic seafood dishes that combine European, Indian, Chinese, and Malaysian influences.

Supper clubs are still the favored late-night haunts for gourmets, so swanky drinks like martinis are very chic, but San Francisco's own naturally fermented **Anchor Steam** beer and **Gordon Biersch** brews are high on the locals' list of favorite beverages (get it on tap, not bottled). Beer has been big in the city since the raucous Barbary Coast days, when the **San Francisco Brewing Company** pub (corner of Columbus and Pacific avenues) first opened its doors. After Prohibition, the 1907 establishment started legally producing its own beer (we love the Shanghai Pale Ale), which is available only at the pub or in extremely limited bottled batches at two neighborhood liquor stores (the **Jug Shop**, 1576 Pacific Ave., and **Coit Liquors**, 585 Columbus Ave.). Don't try to take it home as a souvenir—the beer is not pasteurized, so it must be refrigerated to last even two weeks. Finally, though Irish coffee is far from a local invention, a visit to the **Buena Vista Cafe** (2765 Haight Street, a National Historic Landmark, see Diversions) for a cup of it—especially on a foggy late afternoon—is a time-honored tradition among locals and tourists alike.

Take a chef home

No one can visit all of the city's best restaurants during one vacation, but you can take more than 100 of the top chefs home with you, including all of the 1997 James Beard Foundation award-winners. The Concierge Recommends is a collection of signature recipes selected as favorites by San Francisco concierges —everything from "Assassinated Chicken" or "Tower of Foie Gras" to "Warm Chocolate Cake with Chocolate and Butterscotch Sauces." Profiles of the chef, restaurant, and neighborhood are on the back of each recipe. This limited-edition cookbook is now available at some Bay Area department stores (Bloomingdale's and Nordstrom) and booksellers, or by mail order ($31.13 including tax and shipping) from Gala Publishing, 74 Tehama St., San Francisco, CA 94105, tel 415/541–7870, fax 415/541–7947.

DINING AND CAFES | INTRODUCTION

How to Dress

Jackets and ties are rarely mandatory at San Francisco restaurants, but common sense should dictate the obvious: If you're going to a fancy place, dress up a bit. You'll probably need some sort of jacket, anyway, simply because it's so cool at night, even in summer. At casual establishments, anything goes. As long as you don't look like you just climbed out of a dumpster, you'll probably be acceptable no matter what you're wearing.

When to Eat

Unlike their New York night-owl counterparts, San Franciscans tend to dine *before* they go to the opera or ballet, not afterward. That means you need to reserve weeks in advance if you want to have dinner before 8 in any popular restaurant near a major theater or concert hall. After 8:30, however, you can get a table on the spot at Stars, the Hayes Street Grill, or other popular "opera ghetto" restaurants (those clustered near the performing arts mecca centering on City Hall and the War Memorial Opera House). Very few restaurants serve dinner after 10, so get your grazing over with before you go out on the town or you may be stuck with burgers or all-night coffee-shop food (see Eating with Insomniacs). Most breakfast places serve all day, with specials often ending at 11:30, and lunch tends to be whatever you feel like eating between then and mid-afternoon, when many restaurants begin to gear up for dinner. Mexican food seems to work for breakfast, lunch, and dinner, so you'll never have to go hungry if you can find your way to the Mission District.

Getting the Right Table

Unless your major objective in going to a restaurant is to gawk at celebrities—or perhaps be mistaken for one—the right table isn't much of an issue in San Francisco. A few restaurants, such as the Ovation at the Inn at the Opera (see Accommodations), have one exceptional table (theirs is by a fireplace) worth booking in advance for a do-or-die romantic encounter, but the trendiest establishments tend to do the same thing as in every town: Pack in the hoi polloi wherever they fit. (The Index notes whether reservations are recommended.)

Chefs

The restaurant world is its own little soap opera. Every star chef was once some other star's sous chef, and the darling of one kitchen today is likely to be the hit of another restaurant tomorrow. **James Ormsby**, whose Italian-French soul food made the Financial District power-spot Aqua a huge hit in its inaugural nine weeks, left in 1996 to open his own Mission District supper club, Bruno's, and relinquished Aqua to

Michael Mina, who was named 1997's top "rising star" chef by the James Beard Association. Meanwhile **Pat Loston,** Aqua's adored dessert chef, moved on to North Beach's surrealistic Cypress Club. Before **Thomas Keller** took over French Laundry in Yountville and was named the best chef in the country by the James Beard Foundation, **Ron Siegel** won national honors there. Siegel now presides at Charles Nob Hill. **Timothy Au** trained in the "opera ghetto" with Stars' **Jeremiah Tower** before going to Washington Square Bar and Grill in North Beach; Tower also trained **Lynn Sheehan,** who worked in Union Square with **Julian Serrano** at Masa's before she moved on to Mecca, an Upper Market supper club. (Serrano took over Masa's after the death of founder **Masataha Kobayashi** several years ago.) **Scott Warner** left Restaurant Lulu (South of Market) for North Beach's busy Rose Pistola, voted best new restaurant in the country at the 1997 James Beard awards. **Anne** and **David Gringrass** opened Postrio (Union Square) with **Wolfgang Puck** before the debut of their own South of Market cafe, Hawthorne Lane. The list goes on and on—and some of the city's best chefs have commuted way farther than across town. **Alain Rondelli** came all the way from a three-star restaurant in Paris to open his Clement Street bistro at what used to be Le St. Tropez, owned by **Gerald Hirigoyen,** who now owns Fringale (South of Market) and Pastis (Financial District). **Fabrice Canelle** worked at Maxim's in Paris before crossing the Atlantic—and the United States—

Getting wired

Need something to do with those twiddling thumbs after you've downed enough espresso to raise the dead? Try tapping your fingers on a computer keyboard to get linked you to countless other cafe rats around the world. Since 1991, San Francisco cafes have offered coin-operated access to e-mail and community bulletin boards via SF Net, but no matter how many quarters spent, you still couldn't get onto the net. Now a number of cafes have computers at the tables, with free access to the internet and the world wide web. (See our section on the "The cafe superhighway.") To find Bay Area cafes that are hooked up to SF Net, check out www.sfnet. com. For links to cafes with their their own web-sites click on "internet cafes" at http://sfbay. yahoo.com or go to www.cyberiacafe.net/cybe ria/guide for a guide to net-connected cafes around the world.

DINING AND CAFES | INTRODUCTION

to take over Moose's. And **Sylvain Portay** jolted all of New York by abandoning Le Cirque in favor of San Francisco's stylish Ritz Carlton dining room on Nob Hill.

Cafe Society

When you hear people raving about the cafe scene in San Francisco, they're not referring to the posh bistros calling themselves cafes just to horn in on the French tradition of charging a small fortune for a dab of *je ne sais quoi*. They're talking about coffeehouses with names like **Jammin' Java Coffee House**, **Red Dora's Bearded Lady**, and **Mad Magda's Russian Tea Room**—neighborhood caffeine dens that are often much more popular than bars as places to meet, hear music, listen to poetry, read, write, talk about art and politics, or just sit and watch the general buzz. The best cafes are basically ongoing block parties.

In recent years, Seattle has often been mislabeled by the media as America's gourmet-coffee center—primarily due to the success of Starbucks coffee chain—but the problem with this whole Seattle blather is that coffee by itself is utterly insignificant. Seattle could sell enough coffee beans to fill up Mount St. Helens, yet it would still never be San Francisco. San Francisco's coffeehouses and cafes are the hearts and souls of their communities. When **Radio Valencia**—a small corner cafe instrumental in the revitalization of the city's "New Bohemia," the Mission District's Valencia Street—reopened after being smashed by a fire truck in a head-on collision, loyal customers lined up for almost a block, waiting as much as two hours to get back into their neighborhood hangout.

Such small cafes have been the center of the city's vital bohemian scene since the turn of the century, and have enticed some of the world's most interesting artists and writers to not only visit, but stay. Chain coffee stores owned by giant corporations miss the point—and the social experience—entirely.

Navigating the Coffee Trail

In many of San Francisco's neighborhoods, there are at least two cafes per block—parts of the Mission District and the Haight average twice that many. The key to your own adventures in cafe-land is to get a feel for a neighborhood, remember that most cafes are defined by who goes there, and discover your own favorite spots as you go.

North Beach has been a bohemian stronghold for more than a century, known best for the Beat movement that originated there in the fifties, when Jack Kerouac and Allen

Ginsberg were regulars at **Caffe Trieste** and **Enrico's Sidewalk Cafe**. Lawrence Ferlinghetti still hangs around—and displays his paintings—at Enrico's and **Caffe Puccini**.

There are more than 20 cafes in one six-block area alone—bordered by Union Street and Broadway on the north and south, and Grant and Powell streets on the east and west. The coffee and pastries are very Italian, as is the opera music commonly heard on the jukeboxes, and the customers range from neighborhood residents having their afternoon coffee break to visitors from all over the world.

The **Mission District** cafe scene is funky, neighborhood-oriented, and the command post of Beatnik Central. Very few tourist types make it out to Valencia Street's hip coffeehouses, but locals come from all over the city to take in the live music and spoken-word performances—and to congregate with young, anti-fashion fashion-setters. Most of the cafes (and bars) are concentrated in the area bordered by 16th and 24th streets on the north and south, and by Mission and Valencia streets on the east and west.

The Real Poop on Starbucks

When every Denny's in America serves cappuccino with the breakfast special, blame it on Seattle. Not so long ago, a decent shot of espresso was a rare pleasure in that neck of the woods (and we do mean woods). Then suddenly, Seattle was hailed nationwide as the undisputed coffee heaven of the New World. They had discovered espresso sort of like Columbus discovered America—with little or no acknowledgment of those who had already cultivated it for generations. The most obvious player, Starbucks, is a publicly held company with a huge chain of coffee bars that are about as avant-garde as Mrs. Field's. The company was started by a former San Franciscan who first imitated Berkeley's beloved family-owned Peet's coffee store, then bought Peet's, then sold Starbucks to venture capitalists (but kept Peet's), and now has to compete with Starbucks to try to stay alive. David created Goliath.

The **Haight** is still a hippie haven of sorts, but the post-punk species is far better suited than its flower-child predecessors to hours of angst-ridden malingering at local coffee joints. The neighborhood isn't all nose rings, purple hair, and Jerry Garcia murals, though. You'll find cafes for every taste, from tranquil little pastry shops to ultra-hip hangouts virtually vibrating from the blare of loud music and the jolt of caffeine. Walk along Haight Street from Central to Stanyan streets, and don't neglect to venture a block or two up or down the side streets.

Other cafes we mention are located in three areas where you'd expect to find the city's cafe culture well-represented: **Hayes Valley**, a small, sunny neighborhood perfect for strolling because it compromises only a few blocks along Hayes Street (between Franklin and Buchanan streets) with an occasional side-street detour; **South of Market**, an industrial neighborhood where artists, architects, multimedia gurus, filmmakers, and musicians live and work in warehouse lofts (below Market Street, between Second and Tenth streets); and the **Castro** district, San Francisco's infamous gay mecca (mostly south of Market to about 20th Street., between Castro and Sanchez streets).

Finally, there are the refuges—cafes that provide escapes from neighborhoods that are often overrun by tourists or other consumption-crazed breeds. The ones we mention are located in the **Financial District** (Grant Avenue at Sutter Street) and the gentrified section of **Fillmore Street** (near Steiner Street).

The Lowdown

Grills in the mist... Long before there was California cuisine or nouvelle anything, mesquite-grilled seafood was the most popular item at **Tadich Grill**, where mesquite has been the charcoal of choice since the 1920s. This turn-of-the-century Financial District landmark still entices the tourist trade and local traditionalists, but the surly waiters are no longer charming to diners who prefer to get their steaks before they're cold and their french fries before they are soggy. As you'll learn if you go on any of the Dashiell Hammett walking tours, **John's Grill** is the place where Sam Spade ate his chops (actually rack of lamb) while in pursuit of the Maltese Falcon. A replica of the black bird, donated by Warner Brothers, sits in a display case outside John's small Hammett museum. Founded in 1908, this downtown dinner house has wood-paneled walls, period furnishings, and perfectly grilled, tender steaks. South of Market's **Fly Trap Restaurant** has moved a few blocks away from its original 1898 address, where flypaper was tacked to the tables to keep the horses' pesky companions off the steaks, but it still bases its menu on traditional San Francisco grill fare. The decor is conventional but not stuffy—small cloth-covered tables with cafe chairs and a variety of maps and architectural drawings on the walls—and its comfort-food specialties follow suit. Fish and seafood are the mainstays of the **Hayes Street Grill** menu—which changes daily—and they may be sautéed or mesquite-grilled with a Mexican, American, French, Italian, or Asian accent, depending on which accompanying vegetables are freshest that day. Grilled Alaskan king salmon and pan-fried Hama-Hama oysters are typical favorites. Some purists bemoan the loss of the older, funkier decor—creaky floors and cafe chairs—to the carpeting and chic little banquettes of the new and improved Hayes Street Grill, but the food is just as good as ever.

For committed carnivores... The best pure-and-simple steak house in town is definitely **Harris'**, midway between Russian Hill and Pacific Heights on Van Ness Avenue, where luscious cuts of Midwestern corn-fed beef are dry-aged on the premises, killer martinis flow by the barrel, and the gigantic booths can swallow you whole. For more exotic flesh feasts, try the Texas antelope, Wyoming Buffalo, or locally raised ostrich. **Izzy's Steaks and Chops** is also a meat-eater's dream, but its true glory is its status as a lively Marina watering hole. The steaks, though tender and delicious, may not be quite as luxurious as those at Harris', but they cost a lot less.

Seafood supremo... Many tourists leave San Francisco without ever discovering that there's more to its seafood restaurants than the fish joints around Fisherman's Wharf. Don't you make the same mistake. Swim on down to **Aqua**, the elegant, understated Financial District seafood house. Its biggest splash was a highly publicized "quiet dinner" for lovebirds Marcia Clark and Christopher Darden a few days after the O.J. Simpson trial ended. Never mind that; Aqua is one of the finest restaurants in town, and chef Michael Mina was honored by the James Beard Foundation as the rising star chef of the year in 1997. The decor is sleek and simple, adorned only by lush, exotic-flower arrangements. Mina's extraordinary menu follows suit: It's clearly focused with carefully chosen, stunning details. His alderwood-smoked salmon with roasted potato, crème fraîche and caviar is exquisite, as is his signature tuna with foie gras.

If you're George Jetson on an expense account... The Mission District's ultra-hip, ultra-crowded **Flying**

Saucer is no longer the talk of the town, but people still line up and wait for a table to sample food that tastes out of this world. Squid, papaya, and vermicelli become basic elements of a sculptured entrée, with cilantro, lime, and mint as added texture and color, and Thai vinaigrette as auxiliary rocket fuel. The menu is based on French technique, but from there it sprouts wildly with California, Latin, and Asian flavors.

See-and-be-scenes... Where you go to be seen depends largely on whom you hope to see—and how long it takes the trendies to get bored with the place. For years, Jeremiah Tower's **Stars** (near Civic Center) has been the easiest place for commoners to rub shoulders with celebrities. If you're feeling "Absolutely Fabulous", snag a seat at the long bar and have a martini or a glass of champagne while you watch people watch each other. **Moose's** (North Beach) is a good place to go if you want to stare at fashion models and young Republicans—and you don't mind eating in a room that feels big enough to host a national convention. The best people-watching is on crowded weekend nights, when the long wait for a table leaves people milling around in the foyer near the bar. **Enrico's Sidewalk Cafe** in North Beach has always been a great place to people-watch, and nightly jazz makes it even more fun. You can have a full dinner or just stop in for a drink (try the lip-puckering Mojito, a rum, mint, and lime-juice concoction), but you'll always find someone to look at.

Hold the hype... No matter how endlessly food critics lavish praise on the super-restaurants, there are some sacred cows, like Berkeley's **Chez Panisse**, that aren't always worth the money and effort. To give credit where it's due, Chez Panisse has been the most important restaurant in the Bay Area's culinary development in the past two decades and chef/owner Alice Waters was honored as the 1997 Humanitarian of the Year by the James Beard Foundation. But sometimes students catch up with their teachers, and these days there are plenty of other restaurants with more innovative chefs and less expensive tabs. The fact that you have to reserve a month in advance for a weekend dinner may be a testament to the restaurant's reputation, but it's also a pain in the neck, especially when you don't know if you'll be in the mood for the set menu when the day finally arrives. The above-mentioned **Stars** is also untouchably popular with critics—and publicity agents—but it's often so loud you can't carry on a conversation without shouting and the commoners-hoping-to-hobnob-with-celebrities factor can make you feel like you're having a nightmare about Los Angeles.

Some like it hot... San Francisco's latest addition to the four-alarm category is **Firecracker,** a stylish new Chinese restaurant that's right at home with its fiery hot Latin neighbors in the Mission District. Chef Phil Lee denies the California-fusion label that is often applied to his low-oil, low-sugar cooking: His cuisine is actually true to traditional Beijing cookery, in which the scarcity of oil was compensated by lots of garlic and spice. Firecracker's environment is also contemporary, yet faithful, to Chinese history, with old photographs on the walls and Chinese opera music mixed in with modern jazz. For authentic Thai food that's unbelievably delicious, but not watered down for uninitiated Western tongues, the Upper Haight's **Thep Phanom** can't be beat. The Thai wait staff, whose traditional garb suits the gracious, antique-laden dining room, usually tries to warn you when a dish is hot. Believe them. They mean it. The super-hot delicacies include *larb ped* (duck salad with mint, hot chili peppers, red onion, and lemon); even the milder dishes, such as charbroiled catfish or deep-fried quail are served with a variety of hot dipping sauces. For cooler options, try any of the mild curries, especially those made with coconut milk. **Cha Cha Cha** is a Haight hot spot in more ways than one—it's an exhaustingly popular place, especially if you indulge in the house special Sangria in the funky bar area during your inevitable wait for a table. And the Cajun/Caribbean food (mostly tapas) is absolutely fiery. That's saying something in San Francisco, where Mexican food has numbed most locals to anything cooler than a jalapeño. If the huge plates of flawless spicy ribs, beef and chicken didn't already qualify **Flint's** of North Oakland as the undisputed barbecue-joint champion of the world, the fact that it serves until as late as 4am would definitely clinch the title. If you even *think* you like barbecue, hop on BART and ride over to North Oakland (Flint's is two blocks south of the Ashby stop)—there's nothing even close to this in San Francisco. It's all take-out, though, so if your craving comes at 3am, you may have to smuggle your greasy treasures back to your hotel room.

Tastiest tapas... Cities everywhere have gone a bit mad for those little Spanish tidbits that are more than an appetizer but less than a main dish. **Babaloo** and **Cha Cha Cha** serve variations on Cajun themes. Cha Cha Cha has a Caribbean-psychedelic-voodoo twist, while Babaloo is a full-fledged Ricky Ricardo tropical Cuban bash. Despite the touristy Marina District location, Babaloo is definitely an "in" place where locals eat, drink, and carry on. Dinner music is Latin American, hip-hop, Afro-Cuban, and reggae. Slurp the tropical fruit sangria and nosh on plantain chips with spicy black-bean dip at the bar, or grab a table and pig out on "bigger" food, like the classic *ropa vieja* (grilled flank steak with molé sauce), which comes with mushroom wild rice. The Mission District's boisterous **Esperpento**—decorated like somebody's surrealistic dream about a childhood piñata party—remains steadfastly and authentically Spanish. All of the tapas are worth tasting, so share them family-style; the most popular main dish here is probably the paella, a steaming mountain of shellfish, pork, chicken, and saffron-flavored rice served in the pan. But the ultimate tapas in town may be those at **Timo's in the Zanzibar,** an eccentric, semi-Bohemian place that shares its Mission District home with a neighborhood bar called the Zanzibar. The tapas are just like the ones you get in Spain—treats such as roasted new potatoes in aioli, and potato cakes and fish with cilantro-mint salsa—and the crowd is interesting, artistic, and decidedly local. The best part about going to **Carta** is that its Upper Market cuisine map changes every month. They always serve both "small plates" and regular entrees, but one month might feature Peruvian *jalea de pescado* (batter-fried fish and seafood with pickled onions), and the next might be Turkish *manti* (dumplings with yogurt, garlic, and tomato sauce). One of the most popular months is January, which always features a "best-of" menu from all over the globe. Sit at any of the tables by the window and you can watch the refurbished trolley cars from all over the world pass by on Market Street.

Pass the dumplings, darling... The other little morsels that make tastebuds quiver in ecstasy are served from dim sum carts—tender shrimp wrapped in paper-thin dumplings, tiny crab cakes, octopus with hot peppers, and dozens of other Chinese delicacies. For exceptionally delicate dumplings, **Yank Sing** has long been the favorite of locals on the weekends—Financial District types tend to crowd into its modern, somewhat upscale dining room during the week—but nearby **Harbor Village** is a more serene and majestic alternative at lunchtime (11am–2:30pm). You won't find any unidentified steamed objects on their carts; instead you'll find dozens of authentic delicacies served by a meticulous wait staff. Every porcelain dish and carved chopstick reflects the Imperial aesthetic Harbor Village claims to have brought from Hong Kong, and the dim sum tradition allows you to enjoy all its refinement without the high tab of its exquisite dinners.

Best Chinese in Chinatown... **R & G Lounge** serves probably the best food in Chinatown. The dining room used to be in the basement of a commercial building, but a brighter, upstairs room has opened to accommodate the burgeoning clientele drawn primarily by super-fresh seafood. If you think Maine has a corner on the lobster market, do yourself a favor and try a live one from R & G's tank. One huge plus is that the waiters will gladly translate the Chinese menu for Westerners, which expands the choices considerably.

Ultra-chic Chinoise... You usually don't think of donning a dinner jacket to chow down on Chinese food, but it's not a bad idea at **Tommy Toy's**, where elaborate meals are served by an army of tuxedoed waiters who will pick up your napkin before you realize you've dropped it on the floor. Unquestionably the most elegant Chinese restaurant in San Francisco, it's the top choice for both local and visiting celebrities, as the entryway gallery of Clint Eastwood memorabilia will attest. Whole, bright-red lobsters, trimmed and served tableside, are the house specialty.

South of the border in the Mission... The Mission District is crammed with Central and South American food that often outdoes native versions, thanks to the fabulous fresh ingredients that abound in San Francisco. Even the most ordinary taqueria beats a fast-food lunch by a mile. Start with our suggestions, then graze your own way through the neighborhood. **Los Jarritos** makes wonderful fresh tortillas and other home-cooked Mexican delights for a loyal following of locals, many of whom travel across the city—and sometimes the bridges—for its food and friendly ambience. Call in advance to find out when they'll be serving *posole* (a spicy chicken-and-pork stew) that takes all day to prepare and is rarely available outside of home kitchens. If you want to get in a good mood fast, go to **La Rondalla**. It serves standard Mexican fare such as enchiladas, *chiles rellenos* (stuffed chili peppers baked in egg batter), and other recognizable dishes, but there's nothing standard about the atmosphere, from the year-round Christmas ornaments to the strolling mariachis who serenade on weekends. **La Taqueria** is an immaculate neighborhood favorite famous for its shredded pork *carnitas*, which fill soft, fluffy tortillas to make the perfect taco.

Chef/owner Gus Shinzato of **Fina Estampa**, another comfortable storefront establishment, is Japanese-Peruvian, and his menu relies heavily on Peru's spicy cross-cultural coastal cuisine, made with fresh local catches. Specialties include *parihuela*, a tomato and chili soup laced with the freshest seafood he can find, including mussels, clams, shrimp, squid, and other Pacific delicacies. Modest **El Nuevo Frutilandia** is one of the few places in the city to get home-cooked Puerto Rican and Cuban food (the fresh fruit shakes are wonderful, as are the Puerto Rican dumplings made of crushed plantain and yuca, filled with shredded pork). The odds of running into a horde of tourists here are extremely slim. Right next door you can get one of the best dinner deals in town at **El Trebol**, a Formica-table kind of place that serves Salvadoran/Nicaraguan treats like *pupusas* (handmade corn patties stuffed with cheese or meat or both) for less than a dollar and full meals (including rice and beans) for less than $4.

Seoul food... At do-it-yourself Korean barbecue joints the food is as much fun to cook as it is to eat. You barbecue marinated beef and pork on grills built into the tables, wrap the meat in a lettuce leaf and add whatever condiments you like—kind of a Korean burrito. **Kyung Bok Palace** has made a name for itself among the many Korean eateries along Geary Boulevard (Richmond District) by offering at least 10 different varieties of kimchee (spicy, pickled cabbage) to go with dinner. It packs the house with a mix of local Koreans and non-Korean students and families. **Brothers Restaurant** is a bit smaller and less hectic, catering to a primarily Korean clientele—it's probably the most popular Geary Boulevard place with local Koreans, and the staff sometimes proves its own authenticity when you're making reservations in English. You can grill meats at your table's wood-fired hibachi or sample from the rest of the small menu. Brothers' kimchee is truly outstanding.

A passage to India... Many of the best Indian eateries in the Bay Area are outside San Francisco in the Indian and Pakistani communities of the East and South Bay, but the best in the city, **Gaylord of India**, is in an unlikely spot—the middle of touristy Ghirardelli Square. Unfortunately, you'll pay rather dearly for the gourmet quality (about $35 per person, à la carte) and its wonderful view of the bay. One way to economize is to order the *thali* plates ($22 to $29 per person), which allow you to sample a wide variety of either vegetarian or tandoori dishes; then you can splurge on a luscious dessert, such as *kulfi* (homemade pistachio ice cream). A much less costly alternative is a multicourse meatless feast at **Ganges Vegetarian Restaurant**, a cozy refuge in a Victorian house near the Haight. There are low tables with floor cushions in back and Western-style tables and chairs in front. Owner Malvi Doshi's vegetarian dinners include classic yogurt-cucumber salad, vegetables with assorted chutneys, stew or soup, curries, a variety of main dishes (vegetarian, of course) and, finally, dessert.

Asian delights... One of the first destinations on your San Francisco ethnic-food adventure tour should be **Angkor Borei**, the perfect place to sample Cambodia's intricate cuisine at the modest price tag locals have come to expect in the Mission District. The combination of spices in most any dish on the menu is intriguing—typically, sweet basil and tangy lemongrass are first to hit the tongue, then a short blast of hot chili pepper bursts through and, finally, soothing coconut milk brings the whole blend together. If the combination of tropical flavors and French culinary techniques make you want to try even more sophisticated Cambodian cuisine (at a considerably higher price), try **Angkor Wat**, an elegant Richmond District dinner house. To economize, take advantage of the weekday lunch special (call for current specifics).

Geary Boulevard's tropical, romantic **Straits Cafe** features extraordinary food from Singapore—an exotic hybrid of European, Indian, Chinese, and Malaysian tastes that mixes spicy-hot peanut sauces with cool cucumbers and coconut-milk curries. Chef Chris Yeo uses all these flavors and textures to create extraordinary dishes like *laksa* (tamarind-scented broth with fish, chili peppers, onions, and rice noodles), and *satays* (chunks of meat). For great Vietnamese food, check out the **Golden Turtle**, a modestly elegant restaurant near Russian Hill that looks and tastes much more expensive than it is. A choice of several French wines complements the delicately spiced entrees, ranging from steamed sea bass with fresh ginger to grilled beef with lemongrass. The **Saigon Sandwich Cafe** is a Civic Center take-out deli with incredible Vietnamese sandwiches—baguettes full of pork or chicken with spicy sauces, cilantro, and peppers, or the popular Vietnamese-style meatball sandwiches—both for around $2.

Japanese jewels... For a variety of Japanese country-style food—fluffy tempura, savory noodles, and dumplings—go to **Sanppo** in the heart of Japantown, a favorite of local Japanese, where you may be asked to share a table when the regular crowd elbows in. Sanppo's rustic, home-like decor is instantly cozy. The tempura is consistently excellent and the *gyoza nabe* (pot stickers in a savory broth with noodles and bean curd) is a wonderful meal in itself. **Cho-Cho**'s tempura bar makes it popular with the Financial District crowd for after-work martinis and snacks, but it's the *shabu-shabu*—an audience-participation delicacy that involves sitting at a large, low table and cooking pieces of seafood, fish, meat, and vegetables by dipping them into a steaming caldron of tasty broth—that makes it such a fun place to stay for dinner. For the freshest sushi in town, call in advance to **Hama-Ko**, a gracious little Cole Valley restaurant, and ask chef Ted Kashiyama to prepare his special deluxe meal of hot and cold dishes; the exact contents depend on what local fishermen have available that morning.

The French connection... **Masa's** used to be the name bandied about most often when people were bragging about the best restaurants in town—chef Julian Serrano is virtually worshipped by food critics and fledgling chefs

for his unflagging dedication to authentic, perfectly exe-
cuted French cuisine. But **Fleur de Lys** is San Francisco's
true gem among classic French restaurants. Chef/owner
Hubert Keller—who was the first guest chef in White
House history when he cooked for President Clinton—
was named best chef in California by the James Beard
Foundation (1997). It's tough to find anything critical to
say about this romantic, elegant Union Square restaurant,
where the regularly changing menu is full of sumptuous
dishes like boneless quail stuffed with swiss chard and
pine nuts, enhanced with foie gras and a rich Merlot
sauce. This is truly the very best of French dining—without the snotty waiters. Three bits of advice: Reserve well
in advance, try the "Symphony of Fleur de Lys Appetizers," and don't be surprised if a dinner for two costs as
much as your plane ticket. And if you really want to go
out of your way for great food, take a 90-minute trip from
the city to **French Laundry**, up in Yountville, a small
wine-country village. You'll have to reserve several
months in advance, but it's worth the drive, the wait, and
the money. Fleur de Lys' Hubert Keller was named best
chef in California, but French Laundry's Thomas Keller
snagged the title of best chef in the entire country that
same year, and has been the center of rave reviews all over
the nation ever since. A young, enthusiastic California
chef, Keller grows at least half of what he cooks in three
gardens on the premises of this tiny three-star restaurant
that has the feel of a private country home. He personally
oversees every bite that ends up on a diner's plate. You can
easily find far less expensive French food in more modest
bistros such as **Alain Rondelli** (Clement Street) and
Fringale (South of Market). Rondelli, who once cooked
for the president of France and ran a three-star kitchen of
his own in Paris, is so in love with food that he often
serves complimentary samples of unusual items to
patrons, and he regularly offers a $52 six-course tasting
menu to acquaint people with his approach. The fresh
scallops in plum-lime marmalade (seared to a crispy gold
on top and served with arugula), and the braised pork
shank in vinegar and juniper berry broth evoke audible
moans of pleasure. Fringale's menu reflects the chef's
Basque origins and his classic training; the place is reasonably priced, and so friendly and comfortable that you
never feel self-conscious, despite the studied indifference
of much of the too-hip-for-words clientele. The frisée

salad with warm bacon dressing and croutons is exquisite—soft but not soggy—and the pork tenderloin with
onion and apple marmalade is rich and velvety without
being overly sweet. If you want to feel as though you *are*
in Paris, stop in at a Financial District treasure, **Cafe
Claude**, where every fixture, chair, dish, and spoon was
imported from France. It's jammed with a lively, youngish
crowd who come to enjoy both the atmosphere and the
inexpensive but oh-so-French sandwiches along with a
glass or two of Rhine, Beaujolais, or Mâcon Blanc wine.

Super supper clubs... You don't have to line up and wait
an hour just to get in the door of a supper club anymore,
but the best ones are still extremely popular, and new
ones that hope to last longer than a Kleenex have to be
both good restaurants and good nightclubs at the same
time. **Bruno's** is one of the swankier spots, in spite of its
notably bohemian Mission District locale. An award-
winning "French-Italian soul food" menu from chef
James Ormsby and a consistent calendar of irresistible
contemporary and Latin dance music has kept Bruno's
on the A-list for young trendsetters. Look for slinky
cocktail dresses and dinner jackets alongside thrift-store
chic. Across town at Van Ness Avenue and Bush Street
(near Russian Hill), the "new" **Coconut Grove** is just
what you would imagine from its name: a Copacabana
redux that looks like it was transplanted from Miami
Beach. The "old" Coconut Grove had to shut down and
regroup after its target twenty-something cocktail crowd
refused to pay a $30 cover charge just to dance under
huge fake palm trees. Rejuvenated by chef Gert Rausch,
whose Gulf Stream cuisine is also a huge hit in her
restaurant in Austin, Texas, the new club has ditched its
high cover charge and is doing well again. Try the tiger-
prawn spring rolls with sweet and spicy dipping sauce.
The atmosphere at **Mecca** has been described as "rough-
edged opulence," a perfect fit for its Upper Market
address. The circular bar is the centerpiece of the restaurant, which features live music five nights a week and
serves dinner until midnight. Chef Lynn Sheehan's
Mediterranean menu would be reason enough to go
there, even if there was no entertainment. You can get
fancy, delicate entrees, but don't overlook the wood-oven
pizzas or the rich desserts. Union Square's **Biscuits and
Blues** isn't quite as funky as it sounds, though it defi-

nitely takes pride in presenting down-home food at its dressed-up best. Chef/owner Regina Charboneau serves up French-influenced contemporary Southern cuisine; don't miss her Mississippi catfish with jalapeño tartar sauce or the gospel music on Sundays. The Financial District is usually dead at night, but **Sol y Luna** keeps it humming with live Flamenco and Latin jazz, dancing, and a tempting menu of tapas and paellas from chef Gustavo Navarro. His Latin cuisine incorporates many Italian flavors, a reflection of the rich Italian influence in his native Argentina. Don't let the location between a couple of dull high-rises fool you—Sol y Luna is a lively, popular hangout.

Vegging out... The Mother of All Vegetarian Restaurants must be **Greens**, where there's a two-week waiting list to sample the fare that has spawned several cookbooks, international acclaim, and a devoted following that brings people hundreds of miles just for dinner. This is no hippie-veggie-health-food cafe; it is meatless *haute cuisine*, combining the best of French, Mediterranean, and California cookery. The menu changes regularly, but past favorites have included a puffy vegetable cake laced with ricotta and gruyère cheeses, topped with a tangy-sweet tomato and sherry sauce, and finished with a spoonful of crème fraîche. Add the gracious dining room with its knockout Marina view, and you'll see why this brainchild of San Francisco's Zen Center is considered one of the best vegetarian restaurants in the world.

Still, we'd rather go to **Millennium** in the Civic Center's hip Abigail Hotel, where the menu is smaller but more whimsical—with items like "Dr. Dunphy's Chinese Herbal Aphrodisiac Love Potion," which you're not likely to find at dignified Greens. Though the white linen is sufficiently upscale, the staff is mercifully less serene. Every ingredient is organic and purely vegan, so don't expect any butter with your fresh-baked herb bread. **Ganges Vegetarian Restaurant** is a great spot for people who love traditional Indian food but would prefer not to lay their eyes on any cooked flesh.

North Beach classics... Columbus Avenue's main strip (between Broadway and Washington Square) is loaded with calzone joints and trattorias, but the latest soon-to-be-classic in San Francisco's "little Italy" is **Rose Pistola,**

named the best new restaurant in the country by the James Beard Foundation (1997). The sleek decor might have been out of place in the midst of North Beach's unpretentious little cafes, but owner Reed Hearon (who previously turned a South of Market warehouse into the loud and trendy Restaurant Lulu) has managed to keep the place warm and inviting with a friendly bar and sidewalk tables for people-watching. Chef Scott Warner's menu runs from snacks to full meals, so you can stop for a minute or stay for as long as you want. Try his *cioppino*, a classic fish soup that was originally brought by Italian immigrants to San Francisco, where local Dungeness crab became the central ingredient. Farther up Columbus Avenue at Greenwich Street, you'll find rich, authentic Tuscan food that locals rave about at **Buca Giovanni**. Chef Giovanni Leoni works with produce he grows himself, and garlic lovers should be in heaven here—the smell of the stinking rose greets you well before you descend into the downstairs dining room (*buca* means "hole" in Italian) that gave the place its name. Plan on two to three hours for dinner—Leoni's hearty, mega-caloric cuisine (like veal ravioli slathered in *panzerotti salsa di noci*, a rich white sauce with walnuts) requires plenty of time to savor and digest.

Athens al fresco... What could be better than featherlight filo dough, made from scratch and layered into sweet, delicate baklava that melts in your mouth? Try all that plus a sunny afternoon in the outdoor garden upstairs at **Stoyanof**, a cheery Sunset District cafe. Georgi Stoyanof, now in his seventies, and his son Angel also wrap their delicate filo around Greek cheeses, spinach, and lamb; dinner is a bit more formal, featuring classic Macedonian seafood dishes and exotic appetizers. Or get a break from the fog zone at **Asimakopoulos Cafe**, a neighborhood cafe at the top of Potrero Hill. The country-style Greek fare, which devoted regulars insist is the best in town, has outlasted all of the city's transient food fads for almost two decades. Specialties of this airy, festive cafe include *muhumara*, a traditional Greek and Turkish appetizer made with walnuts, olive oil, and red peppers, and *kota voskou*, layers of chicken, feta cheese, celery, and mushrooms in filo. Unexpected treat: Sunday waffle brunch.

The rest of the world... You'd be missing out on three of San Francisco's most fun—and unusual—dining experiences if you bypassed Suppenküche, Yaya Cuisine, or Helmand. Fans of German food may find **Suppenküche** one of the only places in town to satisfy their appetite. A small, spirited Hayes Valley beer hall and cafe, it serves delicious German food and drink to a good-humored, youngish crowd. The staples, served at plain wood tables, are variations of sauerkraut and sausage—flanked by baskets full of fresh-baked breads or mounds of buttery Bavarian-style mashed potatoes—supplemented by the more refined choices on the daily special chalkboard. At **Yaya Cuisine**, Chef Yehya Salih, who learned at the stove of superchef Jeremiah Tower, has transformed the cuisine of his native Iraq into a mouth-watering Mediterranean/California hybrid. Salih's enthusiasm is evident in every aspect of this Sunset District restaurant: His giant mural of Babylon that covers an entire wall, his habit of leaving the kitchen to chat with customers, and an ambitious menu. Tables are set with Iraqi-style flatbread to be dipped in thyme-sesame olive oil and savored while you mull over your order: Try the steamed oysters or vegetarian dolmas (his are whole vegetables stuffed with bulgur and chili peppers), both dressed in yogurt-mint sauce, or such main dishes as a hearty lamb stew or the California-style roasted baby chicken. The Helmand River flows out of Iran through Afghanistan; the formal dinner house **Helmand** rests on the shores of Broadway, which flows from North Beach to Pacific Heights. The Afghani food here is exquisite, with flavors from Central Asia, India, and the Middle East, and owner Mahmood Karzai has done Westerners the favor of removing much of the fat from the traditional recipes. We recommend *aushak,* a delicate, triangular-shaped wheat dumpling filled with leek and served in a yogurt-mint or beef sauce reminiscent of the Far East, and *chowpan seekh,* a grilled rack of lamb on Iranian-style flatbread; don't be afraid to try lots of new things, like *kaddo borawni,* an appetizer of baked pumpkin with garlic-yogurt sauce.

Goofy decor, fabulous food... What used to be Miss Pearl's Jam House, the cartoon version of "Abbott and Costello Go To Gilligan's Island", has been reincarnated as **Backflip,** a poolside cocktail party at the Tenderloin's Phoenix Motel. Entering through the modernistic cocktail lounge, you may go temporarily blind from the iridescent blue (they may have gone just a teensy bit overboard on the pool-color theme). Either float into the circular bar or swim upstream to the dining room, where the young and beautiful staff is outfitted head to toe in, you guessed it, iridescent blue. Once you settle into your faux cabana—a table enclosed on the sides by curtains—a wandering 7-foot drag queen (very tall platform shoes) may stop by to talk a little harmless trash and make sure you're having a good time. And you will be. This place is fun and the food is fabulous. The menu is "cocktail food," a whimsical variation on tapas that ranges from gourmet nibbles like smoked pork bruschetta with fig jam and shaved asiago to "tater tots" (potato and spring onion croquettes). Have a chocolate "martini" for dessert (a rich mousse served in an oversized martini glass).

The **Cypress Club**, though reminiscent of a grand, baroque opium den, is the opposite of funky. The ultra-chic backdrop once made this North Beach dining room a temple of trendiness, with more patrons jockeying for a strategic spot at the "see-and-be-seen" bar than ordering food at the tables. The Trend Factor has waned a bit, but the menu remains impressive; it's as rich as the decor. Don't miss the venison.

Kid pleasers... Dining with the family can be tricky business, especially if your children vary in age, but you're always safe in any of the neighborhood eateries in the Mission District, where there is usually at least one six-year-old running between tables while apologetic parents try to pull in the reins. **El Nuevo Frutilandia** (24th Street) is an especially good choice, because the fruit shakes will appeal to all ages, even if the Puerto Rican food is a bit too spicy for the younger palate. **La Rondalla** (Valencia Street) is fun for lunch or early dinner because of the goofy decorations, and the traditional Mexican food familiar to most kids—and not too fiery. (Later in the evening, the bar livens up and the atmosphere is less suitable for younger children.) If the kids do like hot-and-spicy treats, take them to **Kyung Bok Palace** (Richmond District), where they can have a ball playing chef and cooking their own meat on the grills. You'll have to sign up on a waiting list at the door, but if you go early enough, the wait won't be long.

It's actually possible to please teenagers if you take them to the right places and pretend to be Hollywood agents instead of their parents. Try **Hamburger Mary's**, a funky South of Market spot that attracts a lot of hip X-Generation types and serves great burgers and other American standards with humor and aplomb.

Where to seal a deal... This, of course, depends upon the client. The Old-Boy network tends to be wary of fancy food and effusive waiters, which you'll never find at **Harris'** (Van Ness Avenue). It's not cheap, but it's the best steak house in the city, and a few of Harris' martinis can soften up even the toughest old buzzard. If your client is of the artistic persuasion, go to the **Cypress Club** (North Beach), where the ingenious, surrealistic decor is matched by the superb menu. Attorneys love the **Fly Trap Restaurant**, the traditional San Francisco grill (with a few culinary updates) across the street from the courthouse. If your clients are food lovers who don't want to be bothered with trendy trappings, take them to our favorite small French bistros—**Alain Rondelli** (Clement Street) and **Fringale** (South of Market).

Cheap eats... The Mission District is jammed with great food at very inexpensive prices, but the best buy of all is **El Trebol** (24th Street), where a full Salvadoran dinner including rice and beans comes in at around $4. Other haunts famous for good food for next to nothing are **La Taqueria** (Mission St. near 24th Street), a family-oriented Mexican cafe, and **El Nuevo Frutilandia** (now at 24 Folsom Street), where the fruit shakes are as popular as the Puerto Rican food. The best Vietnamese deli in the city is the **Saigon Sandwich Cafe** (near Civic Center), where $2 will buy a delectable pork or chicken sandwich with spicy sauce.

Eating with insomniacs... San Francisco is not known as an all-night town, but there are a couple of spots that stay open until the wee hours, if not all night, and are a cut above the 24-hour Market Street joints where the coffee is as greasy as the bacon and eggs. **Hamburger Mary's** is our first choice, though you may have to wait a bit on weekends, when the South of Market club crowd drops in to chow down and sober up. Floral wallpaper that looks like your Great Aunt Ida's drapes, family portraits of nobody in particular, and unmatched salt and pepper shakers have made Mary's a funky favorite for years. The classic burgers here are topped with whatever you like, from grilled mushrooms to chili and cheese. It's hip, full of thrift-store knickknacks, and it serves a wicked margarita—but it closes at 2. If you're still hungry after the bars shut down, head for **Sparky's Diner**, a 24-hour Church Street diner that serves a decent burger and a hearty breakfast to Castro and Upper Market locals. The lights are sometimes a bit too bright and the wait staff a bit too dim, but at least the breakfasts here avoid the white-bread toast and frozen hashbrown-type food substance that seem to be standard issue at all-night coffee shops.

The morning after... Two breakfast stops are mandatory when you visit San Francisco—Sear's, in Union Square, and the Seal Rock Inn, near the ocean. **Sear's Fine Foods** is best visited after 9 on weekday mornings, when the Financial District crowd has had time to get to work. Their coin-size Swedish pancakes are marvelous—thin and sweet like the best French crêpes—and you get almost a million of them (well, 18) stacked high on your plate. A family-owned coffee shop attached to a small inn, **Seal Rock Inn** is one of those breakfast places you can go to on a Saturday or Sunday morning and see who slept with whom the night before. The scenic location is unbeatable (two blocks from the Pacific Ocean, near the Cliff House), the eggs Benedict and omelettes are a local legend, and you can actually find a place to park on the street. There is also patio dining. If you don't have a night-before paramour, take your kids here and walk down afterward to the Musée Mechanique at the Cliff House.

The cafe superhighway... Just a couple of years ago, **SF Net** coin-operated computer terminals were sucking down quarters like parking meters on speed. For a quarter for five minutes, cafe rats could log on and chat with simpatico souls at other cafes around town, send and receive e-mail, and post messages on cyberspace bulletin boards. Coins are still clinking at more than two dozen locations in the Bay Area, including **Jammin' Java Coffee House**, **Horseshoe Coffee House**, **Muddy Waters Coffee House**, and **Brain Wash Cafe**, to name a few, but SF Net's limited services have taken a back seat to the city's new "cybercafes." South of Market's "Multimedia Gulch" includes such digital diners as **Coffeenet**, **Cyberworld**, and **Internet Alfredo**, where you can sip a *latte* while you hook up to the world wide web; SF Net doesn't have direct internet access. At CoffeeNet, you can surf the web for free with a $5 minimum purchase. Cyberworld caught the attention of the *Wall Street Journal* with its "Six Shooter" coffee special, but it's the fifteen computer terminals with all of the bells and whistles that attract local customers ($8 per hour). Internet Alfredo, the new kid on the block, has eight full-access terminals and is open 24 hours a day; you can do everything from desktop publishing to surfing the net and creating your own web page ($6 per hour). Cowabunga!

Wake-up call: cafes that open before 8am...

When you're up and at 'em at the crack of dawn—and you need a serious caffeine jolt—only a select number of cafes are open and ready to pamper you with a perfectly frothy cappuccino or cafe au lait, airy croissants, and the morning paper to boot. If you're staying in a downtown hotel, try the Financial District's **Cafe de la Presse**, a subdued French-owned refuge that is also an international newsstand. In North Beach, **Caffe Greco**, **Caffe Trieste**, and **Stella Pastry & Caffe** are early-morning favorites. There are even a few bohemian types who open their eyes before noon—**Cafe La Bohème** and **Muddy Waters Coffee House** serve daybreak espresso in the Mission District, while Haight Street early-birds go to **Jammin' Java Coffee House** or **Tassajara Cafe & Bakery**.

How about a little fresh air?...

San Francisco's narrow sidewalks don't leave much room for outdoor seating, and some neighborhoods strictly enforce ordinances against al fresco impediments to pedestrian traffic. A typical sidewalk seat is a bench—without tables—in front of the building. There are some notable exceptions, however, beginning with the granddaddy of the city's sidewalk cafes, **Enrico's Sidewalk Cafe** (North Beach). Huge awnings overhang the table-seating area that provides Broadway's best people-watching—you feel as though you have box seats at the opera. Then there's the elevated wooden deck outside the gay hangout **Cafe Flore** in the Castro. On a foggy day, it's like being in one of those pensive, French B-movies. On a sunny day, it's like being on the French Riviera. But no matter what the weather, it's almost impossible to get a deck seat unless you're there at opening time (8am) or have the patience to wait for someone to leave—and can sprint to the open table faster than anyone else. Our favorite backyard "gardens" are at **Mad Magda's Russian Tea Room** in the sunny Hayes Valley, where customers have been known to sunbathe topless, and **Red Dora's Bearded Lady** in the city's other sun belt, the Mission District.

Cafe con angst... Every once in a while, every self-respecting cafe-dweller must disregard the sheer bliss of everyday life and slump over a coffee-stained table to agonize over some irresolvable existential dilemma. The absurdist population is high at **Brain Wash Cafe**, surrounded as it is by not only the endless spinning of clothes in dryers, but by the barren industrial architecture of South of Market warehouses. Still haven't met your angst quota? Go back to the Haight and listen to the lyrics blasting from the sound system at the **Horseshoe Coffee House**. If the Horseshoe's whining, dysfunctional, alternative soundtrack doesn't send you running for the Prozac, nothing will.

All-day hangouts... One of the unwritten rules of cafe life is that customers get to linger as long as they wish, even if all they buy is one cup of coffee. But certain places are more conducive than others to the all-day, write-in-your-journal, plan-out-your-future type of pause. **Cafe La Bohème** (Mission District) is the ultimate spot to waste a day—dozens of unemployed poets, artists, and general layabouts have made a career of it. If you sit there long enough, you'll see—and probably meet—people of all different ages, ethnic backgrounds, professions, and talents. (You'll probably also be asked for spare change a dozen times.) The location of **South Park Cafe** makes it possible to hang out all day within arm's length of an espresso without having to stay inside the whole time. It's one of a Victorian necklace of stylish eateries that circle the oval lawn of South Park. The Mission District's **Radio Valencia** is at its all-day best on Sunday, when you can start the day with brunch and top off the evening with a wheat beer and live jazz. Some people like to watch the wait staff change shifts to see if listless service is an aberration or is simply endemic to twenty-something hipsters.

Live music... The Most Eclectic Assortment of Quirky Music Award goes to **Radio Valencia**, where, before the aforementioned fire-truck mishap interrupted the performance calendar, the regular house bands played swing, bluegrass, and "outside" jazz, with special performances by many top jazz musicians whose material was a bit too eccentric for other venues. We fully expect the resurrected cafe (which was due to reopen in November 1995) will continue the tradition. Meanwhile, **Enrico's Sidewalk Cafe**, a North Beach institution (see Nightlife), presents live jazz seven nights a week (no cover charge), ranging from Brazilian, bebop, and swing to Dixieland and jump & jive; North Beach's **Caffe Trieste** presents live opera music on Sunday afternoons; and the Mission District's **Cafe Istanbul** regularly offers live Middle Eastern music and belly dancing (call for details). Other cafes that occasionally present live music include **Brain Wash Cafe**, **Red Dora's Bearded Lady**, and **Mad Magda's Russian Tea Room**.

Jack Kerouac woke up here... Legendary writers have scribbled in notebooks and on napkins all over North Beach. Jack Kerouac and Allen Ginsberg were regulars at **Caffe Trieste**; Richard Brautigan hawked homemade copies of his poems and stories there. Francis Ford Coppola drafted a screenplay at one of the small tables at **Mario's Bohemian Cigar Store**, though a debate still rages over whether or not it was *The Godfather*. Lawrence Ferlinghetti is a regular at **Caffe Puccini**, where every seat is a window seat, and he still displays his art work at both Puccini and **Enrico's Sidewalk Cafe**.

Hippie holdouts... One of the few true hippie cafes left over from the sixties—it was a crash pad then—is **Sacred Grounds**, a Haight Ashbury classic that will make you want to tie-dye your entire wardrobe. The atmosphere is gentle, but not nostalgic. **Tassajara Cafe & Bakery** is hardly a hippie tradition—it's not old enough to remember the Summer of Love and it's usually well-stocked with medical students and other polo-shirted Cole Valley denizens—but because it serves organic food, its clientele includes a sizable contingent of die-hard hippies among its clean-living vegetarians. The Mission District's **Cafe La Bohème** welcomes virtually everybody, and always has its share of customers who look like extras from *Woodstock*.

The Index

$$$$	over $25
$$$	$15–$25
$$	$7–$14
$	under $7

Alain Rondelli. Warm, sensual decor—tawny-colored walls, cushy banquettes, and an intimate bar—enhances Rondelli's seductive, ever-changing menu and unforgettable six-course tasting menu ($52 per person).... *Tel 415/387–0408. 126 Clement St., 2 or 38 MUNI bus. Reservations essential. AE, DC not accepted.* $$$ **(see pp. 65, 71)**

Angkor Borei. This small, unpretentious, neighborhood restaurant serves fine Cambodian cuisine at Mission District prices. Try the delicate vegetable-filled spring rolls to warm up, then go for a spicy noodle dish.... *Tel 415/550–8417. 3471 Mission St., 14 or 49 MUNI bus. DC not accepted.* $ **(see p. 63)**

Angkor Wat. Possibly the best Cambodian restaurant in the western hemisphere. On Friday or Saturday night, you'll be treated not only to exquisite dishes that burst with tropical and French flavors, but also to performances by the Cambodian Royal Ballet.... *Tel 415/221–7887. 4217 Geary Blvd., 38 MUNI bus. Reservations recommended.* $$–$$$ **(see p. 63)**

Aqua. Celebrity lovebirds and hungry powerbrokers frequent this elegant seafood restaurant. Chef Michael Mina was named rising star chef of the year by the James Beard Foundation (1997).... *Tel 415/956–9662. 252 California St., Financial District, Embarcadero BART/MUNI Metro station, 42 MUNI bus. Reservations highly recommended.* $$$–$$$$ **(see p. 57)**

Asimakopoulos Cafe. The best Greek food in town, at a neighborhood cafe atop sunny Potrero Hill.... *Tel 415/552–8789. 288 Connecticut St. (at 18th St.), Potrero Hill; it's easiest to take a cab. $$* **(see p. 68)**

Babaloo. Lively, kooky Cuban/Caribbean tapas joint.... *Tel 415/346–5374. 2030 Lombard St., Marina District, 28 MUNI bus. $$* **(see p. 60)**

Backflip. Join rock stars, trendsetters, and people-watchers at this poolside restaurant/cocktail lounge adjacent to the Phoenix Motel.... *Tel 415/771–FLIP. 601 Eddy St. (at Larkin St.), Civic Center BART/MUNI Metro station, 5 or 38 MUNI bus. Reservations recommended for "cabana" tables. $$.* **(see p. 69)**

Biscuits and Blues. The dressed-up, down-home menu at this supper club includes treats like Southern-fried dill pickles and yam fries, along with jambalaya, chicken, catfish, and, of course, biscuits.... *Tel 415/292-BLUE. 401 Mason St., Union Square, Powell-Mason or Powell-Hyde cable car, Powell St. BART/MUNI Metro station, 38 MUNI bus. $$-$$$.* **(see p. 66)**

Brain Wash Cafe. Hang with the post-punkers or log onto SF Net while your whites, colors, and mixed loads are tumbling dry.... *Tel 415/861–3663. 1122 Folsom St. (near 7th St.), Civic Center BART station, 12 or 19 MUNI bus. $*
(see pp. 72, 74, 75)

Brothers Restaurant. This Korean barbecue spot has wood-fired hibachis at each table, dozens of food choices to grill, and a host of other dishes for those who choose not to barbecue.... *Tel 415/387–7991. 4128 Geary Blvd., 38 MUNI bus. Reservations recommended. AE, DC not accepted. $$* **(see p. 63)**

Bruno's. This swanky, retro supper club has a huge local following, not only because of its hip Mission District location, but because of chef James Ormsby's exceptional "French-Italian soul food." The bar is separate from the dining room.... *Tel 415/550–7455. 2389 Mission St., 24th St. BART station. $$$.* **(see p. 66)**

Buca Giovanni. Chef Giovanni Leoni's authentic Tuscan cuisine—created from produce he grows himself—is sinfully rich and hearty.... *Tel 415/776–7766. 800 Greenwich St., Powell-Mason cable car, 30 MUNI bus. Reservations recommended. $$* **(see p. 68)**

Cafe Claude. This great lunch spot tucked away in the Financial District is the most authentic Parisian-style cafe in the city; wonderful sandwiches and wines by the glass.... *Tel 415/392–3505. 7 Claude Lane (near Bush and Kearny Sts.), Montgomery St. BART/MUNI Metro station, 38 MUNI bus. $* **(see p. 66)**

Cafe de la Presse. Escape from the shopping frenzy of Union Square into this oh-so-French cafe. It's one of few places in the city where a "latte" is a "cafe au lait." Open 7am–11pm every day.... *Tel 415/398–2680. 342 Grant Ave. (near Sutter St.), 2, 3, 4, or 76 MUNI bus.* **(see p. 73)**

Cafe Flore. The food is good (a bit pricey) and the outside sundeck is one of the prime people-watching spots in the Castro District.... *Tel 415/621–8579. 2298 Market St. (at Noe St.), Castro St. MUNI Metro station, 8, 24, or 37 MUNI bus. $* **(see p. 73)**

Cafe Istanbul. Belly-dancing is no longer the main attraction, but the Middle Eastern atmosphere is reason enough to visit Cafe Istanbul. Sit cross-legged on the pillow platform and swig a pot of thick Turkish coffee or tea.... *Tel 415/863–8854. 525 Valencia St. (near 16th St.), 16th St. BART station, 26 MUNI bus. $$* **(see p. 75)**

Cafe La Bohème. Share big, wooden tables with artistic and often terminally unemployed cafe-dwellers at this all-day hangout. The crowd is multi-everything—multicultural, multiracial, and multigenerational.... *Tel 415/643–0481. 3318 24th St., 24th St. BART station. $*
(see pp. 73, 74, 75)

Caffe Greco. One of North Beach's most popular coffeehouses, partly because of its peerless espresso (imported Illy Caffe, touted as the world's finest).... *Tel 415/397–6261. 423 Columbus Ave., 15, 30, 41, or 45 MUNI bus. $*
(see p. 73)

Caffe Puccini. Named after the great opera composer, Giacomo Puccini, this cafe is deep Italian—as any good

North Beach spot should be—and manages to avoid becoming a trend trap despite its fair share of noted patrons and artistic types.... *Tel 415/989–7033. 411 Columbus Ave., 15, 30, 41, or 45 MUNI bus. $* **(see p. 75)**

Caffe Trieste. One of the last remaining beatnik haunts—Jack Kerouac and Allen Ginsberg were regulars—this legendary little cafe is a must for visiting coffeehounds. They also roast their own coffee—among the best in North Beach—but if you smell a faint scorch when you walk by, walk on.... *Tel 415/392–6739. 601 Vallejo St. (at Grant St.), 15 or 41 MUNI bus. $* **(see pp. 55, 73, 75)**

Carta. The "small plates" here come from a different country each month, but the fresh ingredients are always local.... *Tel 415/863–3516. 1772 Market St. (between Octavia and Gough Sts.), Van Ness MUNI Metro station or any Market Street MUNI bus. Reservations recomended. $$-$$$.* **(see p. 60)**

Cha Cha Cha. Every dish in this funky Caribbean tapas joint is a tongue-burner to some degree, which is as it should be in a Cuban/Cajun restaurant that looks like it was decorated by a voodoo queen on a sangria binge.... *Tel 415/386–5758. 1801 Haight St., 6, 7, 33, 66, or 71 MUNI bus. No reservations. $* **(see pp. 59, 60)**

Chez Panisse. Among restaurant reviewers, Berkeley's Chez Panisse is held sacred, but locals who have eaten there for years will tell you that it isn't consistent. Reserve at least a month in advance.... *Tel 510/548–5525. 1517 Shattuck Ave., Berkeley, North Berkeley BART station and a cab. Reservations essential. $$$* **(see p. 58)**

Cho-Cho. True to its classic Japanese theme and decor, Cho-Cho offers *shabu-shabu* and other traditional Japanese foods, including marvelous tempura, cooked to order at the tempura bar.... *Tel 415/397–3066. 1020 Kearny St., 15, 30, or 41 MUNI bus. DC not accepted. $$* **(see p. 64)**

Coconut Grove. Dance or dine on Gulf Coast cuisine beneath huge, shimmery fake palm trees. Cover charge for music $5–10.... *Tel 415/776–1616. 1415 Van Ness Ave., 2, 3, 4, 19, 42, 47, or 49 MUNI bus. Reservations recommended on weekends. $$$.* **(see p. 66)**

Coffeenet. Free internet access at your table is the main draw of this "Multimedia Gulch" cafe. Visit it on the web at www. Coffeenet.net.... *Tel 415/495–7447. 744 Harrison St. (between Third and Fourth Sts.), South of Market, 15, 30, or 45 MUNI bus. $–$$.* **(see p. 72)**

Cyberworld. Internet access is the calling card here, along with the super-strong "six-shooter" coffee drink. Catch it on the web at www.cyberworldsf.com.... *Tel 415/278–9669. 528 Folsom St., South of Market, 15, 30, 42, or 45 MUNI bus. $$.* **(see p. 72)**

Cypress Club. It looks like Salvador Dali's impression of the Mad Hatter's tea party, but after one glance at the menu, you can rest assured this is a serious place to eat, with some of the best game dishes in the city and a superb wine list.... *Tel 415/296–8555. 1500 Jackson St., 15 or 30 MUNI bus. Reservations recommended. $$$* **(see pp. 70, 71)**

El Nuevo Frutilandia. A casual, friendly neighborhood bistro, this brightly painted Mission District storefront is one of the few places in San Francisco that serve authentic Puerto Rican and Cuban home cooking.... *Tel 415/648–2958. 3077 24th St., 24th St. BART/MUNI Metro station. No credit cards. $* **(see pp. 62, 70, 71)**

El Trebol. This delightful little Salvadoran/Nicaraguan eatery on 24th Street in the Castro District is one of the best deals in the city.... *Tel 415/285–6298. 3324 24th St., 24th St. BART station. No credit cards. $* **(see pp. 62, 71)**

Enrico's Sidewalk Cafe. New owners resurrected what may be the city's favorite cafe and transformed it into a casual supper club that's both an excellent restaurant and an extremely popular spot for coffee, cocktails, and live jazz.... *Tel 415/982–6223. 504 Broadway, 15, 30, 41, 45, or 83 MUNI bus. Reservations recommended for dinner (essential on weekends). $$* **(see pp. 55, 58, 73, 75)**

Esperpento. Authentic, inexpensive Spanish paella and tapas in a jam-packed Mission District storefront. Sometimes lunch (11–3 daily) is less crowded than dinner.... *Tel 415/ 282–8867. 3205 22nd St., 24th St. BART station, 26 MUNI bus. Reservations recommended. No credit cards. $* **(see p. 60)**

Fina Estampa. Some of the most delectable Peruvian food you'll ever taste is served at this typical Mission District storefront— casual, comfortable, and completely unpretentious.... *Tel 415/824–4437. 2374 Mission St., 16th St. BART/MUNI Metro station, 14 or 49 MUNI bus. AE, DC not accepted. $*
(see p. 62)

Firecracker. In case the name didn't make it obvious, the exquisite Mandarin food here is hot and spicy. Hugely popular.... *Tel 415/642–3470. 1007 ½ Valencia St., Mission District, 24th St. BART station. $$–$$$.* **(see p. 59)**

Fleur de Lys. The ultimate for a major splurge. Critics and customers alike call it the best classic French restaurant in the city, if not the country.... *Tel 415/673–7779. 777 Sutter St. (at Taylor St.), Union Square, Powell-Mason or Powell-Hyde cable car. Reservations essential. $$$$.* **(see p. 65)**

Flint's. It's worth a trip to Oakland to this famed barbecue pit where the sauce comes in a few choices—hot, hotter, and hottest—and the ribs are piled so high you can barely carry them on the paper plates. It's strictly takeout, but you can sit outside during the day. Open as late as 4 am depending on how many people are watching and customer traffic.... *Tel 510/653–0593. 6609 Shattuck Ave. (at 66th St.), Ashby BART station. $* **(see p. 59)**

Fly Trap Restaurant. A long history of good humor and a menu based on traditional San Francisco grill food make this institution a refreshing choice amid the glut of tony, food-fad eateries South of Market. Sample the warm apple crisp.... *Tel 415/243–0580. 606 Folsom St., Montgomery St. BART/MUNI Metro station, 15 MUNI bus. Reservations recommended. $$* **(see pp. 56, 71)**

Flying Saucer. If Captain Kirk beamed the "Star Trek" crew to earth for dinner, the Flying Saucer would be a perfect site— as long as he didn't mind waiting for a table. Eccentric, exotically flavored creations double as culinary sculptures.... *Tel 415/641–9955. 1000 Guerrero St., 24th St. BART station, 26 MUNI bus. Reservations essential (2–3 weeks in advance, possibly same-day for weeknight off-hours). $$*
(see p. 57)

French Laundry. Thomas Keller, named 1997's best chef in the country by the James Beard Foundation, presides over this small gem out in the wine country.... *Tel 707/944–2380. 6640 Washington St., Yountville, CA. Reservations essential. $$$$.* **(see pp. 53, 65)**

Fringale. A cozy, curved blond-wood bar greets you the moment you open the door and makes you feel comfortable in this chic South of Market bistro. The food— French/Basque—is delightful.... *Tel 415/543–0573. 570 Fourth St.; 30, 45, or 76 MUNI bus. DC not accepted. $$* **(see pp. 65, 71)**

Ganges Vegetarian Restaurant. Malvi Doshi runs her small Indian restaurant near the Haight as though it were her own kitchen and each patron a long-lost friend. Don't miss her *kulfi*—homemade cardamom ice cream.... *Tel 415/661–7290. 775 Frederick St., 33 MUNI bus. AE, DC not accepted. $* **(see pp. 63, 67)**

Gaylord of India. The furnishings are elegant and the view of the bay exquisite, but the prices are somewhat high.... *Tel 415/771–8822. Ghirardelli Square, 900 North Point 9 (third floor); Powell-Hyde cable car, 19, 30, or 42 MUNI bus. Reservations recommended. $$$* **(see p. 63)**

Golden Turtle. Even the toughest food critics hail this modest but formal restaurant near Russian Hill for its elegant Vietnamese food and inexpensive prices.... *Tel 415/441– 4419. 2211 Van Ness Ave., 42, 47, 49, or 76 MUNI bus. DC not accepted. $* **(see p. 64)**

Greens. More than a decade ago—when California cuisine was still a baby—there was a six-month waiting list for reservations at this legendary vegetarian restaurant. Three cookbooks and a couple of chefs later, Greens can usually accommodate guests with just two weeks' notice.... *Tel 415/ 771–6222. Fort Mason, Bldg. A, Buchanan St. at Marina Blvd., 28 MUNI bus. AE not accepted. $$* **(see p. 67)**

Hama-Ko. Chef Ted Kashiyama's little Cole Valley restaurant offers a limited sushi-bar menu; for a full meal, you must order in advance. It's all the freshest in town.... *Tel 415/ 753–6808. 108 Carl St., 37 or 43 MUNI bus. Reservations*

essential except for sushi bar. AE, DC not accepted. $$
(see p. 64)

Hamburger Mary's. When you've got to have a burger, but it's past midnight (and you want a beer as well), this funky South of Market institution is the place to go.... *Tel 415/ 626–5767. 1582 Folsom St., Van Ness Ave. MUNI Metro station, 12 MUNI bus. Reservations accepted but not always practical. DC not accepted. $* **(see pp. 70, 71)**

Harbor Village. If the major appeal of Chinese food to you is its customary inexpensive price tag, don't bother with Harbor Village. The dinners are exquisite, but the real reason to go to Harbor Village is for the dim sum, served only at lunch (11–2:30, 10:30–2:30 Sun.).... *Tel 415/781–8833. 4 Embarcadero Center, Embarcadero BART/MUNI Metro station, 15, 45, or 76 MUNI bus. Reservations recommended. $$–$$$* **(see p. 61)**

Harris'. Anne Harris cooks and serves damn fine steaks. The best steak house in the city.... *Tel 415/673–1888. 2100 Van Ness Ave., 42, 47, 49, or 76 MUNI bus. Reservations recommended. $$$* **(see pp. 57, 71)**

Hayes Street Grill. Superb fish and seafood are the mainstays of the menu, sautéed or mesquite-grilled with a Mexican, American, French, Italian, or Asian accent. A loyal clientele dines here before opera, ballet, or symphony performances across the street.... *Tel 415/863–5545. 320 Hayes St., Civic Center BART/MUNI Metro station, 21 MUNI bus. Reservations essential for tables before 8:30pm. $$* **(see p. 57)**

Helmand. A formal dinner house on a stretch of Broadway between North Beach and Pacific Heights. Owner Mahmood Karzai's Afghani menu—easily the best in the city—incorporates tastes of Central Asia, India, and the Middle East.... *Tel 415/362–0641. 430 Broadway, 15, 30 or 45 MUNI bus. Reservations recommended. $* **(see p. 69)**

Horseshoe Coffee House. The nose-ring and tattoo capital of the city, hands down. If you like loud music (mostly alternative rock), huge *lattes*, cheap food, and bulletin boards that read like a stream-of-consciousness urban novel, check this place out.... *Tel 415/626–8852. 566 Haight St.*

(near Fillmore St.), 6, 7, 66, or 71 MUNI bus. $

(see pp. 72, 74)

Internet Alfredo. Internet insomniacs can surf the web 24 hours a day at this "Multimedia Gulch" coffeehouse.... *Tel 415/437–3140. 790–A Brannan St. (near Eighth St.), South of Market, 42 MUNI bus. $.* **(see p. 72)**

Izzy's Steaks and Chops. If you like a good, stiff drink with your T-bone, you'll like Izzy's. The steaks are thick, the drinks plentiful, the wait staff very friendly.... *Tel 415/563–0487. 3345 Steiner St., 10, 20, 30, 43, 60, 70, or 80 MUNI bus. Reservations recommended. $$*

(see p. 57)

Jammin' Java Coffee House. Just a few steps up from Haight Street, the decibel and frenzy level drop remarkably, and a sidewalk seat at Jammin' Java can rejuvenate your trend-weary soul—especially on a sunny afternoon. The clientele is a harmonious blend of young hipsters and older bohemians.... *Tel 415/668–5282. 701 Cole St. (at Waller St.), 6, 7, 33, 37, 43, 66, and 71 MUNI bus.*

(see pp. 54, 72, 73)

John's Grill. Now nearly 90 years old, this is a fun place to get a juicy steak or have a late-afternoon cocktail (the homemade vanilla ice cream is heavenly, too).... *Tel 415/986–0069. 63 Ellis St., Powell St. BART/MUNI Metro station. Reservations recommended. $$* **(see p. 56)**

Kyung Bok Palace. A smorgasbord of pickles, salads, and sauces accompanies the marinated beef and pork you cook to your own liking on live-coal grills built into the tables. Dinner starts at 5, and don't be fashionably late or your name may be at the end of a very long waiting list.... *Tel 415/221–0685. 6314 Geary Blvd., 38 MUNI bus. No reservations. AE not accepted. $$* **(see pp. 62, 70)**

La Rondalla. The traditional Mexican fare is tasty and substantial, a perfect prelude to a few gigantic margaritas at the crowded, lively bar.... *Tel 415/647–7474. 901 Valencia St., 16th or 24th St. BART station, 26 MUNI bus. No credit cards. $–$$* **(see pp. 62, 70)**

La Taqueria. A Mission District favorite, with its clean, comfortable cantina-style atmosphere—adobe walls, colorful murals, chunky wooden tables. Try the delicious shredded pork *carnitas.... Tel 415/285–7117. 2889 Mission St., 24th St. BART station, 14 or 49 MUNI bus. No credit cards. $* **(see pp. 62, 71)**

Los Jarritos. Anything you order at this friendly Mexican eatery will be authentic and tasty, but make sure you don't miss the homemade tortillas.... *Tel 415/648–8383. 901 South Van Ness Ave., 16th or 24th St. BART station, 33 MUNI bus. AE, DC not accepted. $* **(see p. 61)**

Mad Magda's Russian Tea Room. Not only can you drink your tea any way you like it at Mad Magda's, you can have your leaves read and find out what the future holds. If you're a devout coffee drinker, they'll read your tarot cards instead. (Readings during evening hours only.) The service is just a tiny bit too mellow.... *Tel 415/864–7654. 579 Hayes St. (near Octavia St.), Civic Center BART station or 21 MUNI bus. $* **(see pp. 54, 74, 75)**

Mario's Bohemian Cigar Store Cafe. This is our favorite North Beach cafe, not just because it has the best focaccia sandwiches in the city, but because despite the fact that it currently sells no cigars, it is still a closet-size corner cafe. (P.S. There are hardly any tourists.) A second location opened in Polk Gulch, but it's just not the same... *Tel 415/362–0536. 566 Columbus Ave. (at Union St.), 15, 30, 41, or 45 MUNI bus. $* **(see p. 75)**

Masa's. If you want a three-star meal so classically French it will rival the best of Paris—and you don't mind spending $300 or so for two people—by all means, sign up three weeks in advance for dinner at Masa's.... *Tel 415/989–7154. Adjacent to Hotel Vintage Court, 648 Bush St., any Powell St. cable car. Jacket required, tie optional but preferred; reservations essential. $$$$* **(see p. 64)**

Mecca. Cozy into a black-leather booth and be pampered by the attentive wait staff at this sensual supper club. The decor and the Mediterranean cuisine are both elegant yet congenial.... *Tel 415/621–7000. 2029 Market St. (between Dolores and 14th Sts.), Upper Market, any Market St. MUNI bus. Reservations recommended. $$$.* **(see p. 66)**

Millennium. This stylish vegan restaurant's inventive menu is the culinary equivalent of a world-beat concert.... *Tel 415/487–9800. 246 McAllister St., Civic Center BART/ MUNI Metro station, 5, 10, 20, 60, 70, or 80 MUNI bus. Reservations accepted. $–$$* **(see p. 67)**

Moose's. Proprietor Ed Moose's innovative menu—combining Southwestern, Italian, and Californian delicacies—is exceptional, but its the glam scene that fills the mammoth dining room.... *Tel 415/989–7800. 1652 Stockton St., 15, or 30 MUNI bus. Reservations essential. $$–$$$* **(see p. 58)**

Muddy Waters Coffee House. You won't have any trouble finding this Mission District cafe—its name is emblazoned in giant letters across the front window. Inside, the atmosphere is funky, bohemian, punked-out cybernerd—with an eclectic clientele to match.... *Tel 415/863–8006. 521 Valencia St. (near 16th St.), 16th St. BART station or 26 MUNI bus. $* **(see pp. 72, 73)**

R & G Lounge. The name sounds like a booze joint where a guy named Sam might be playing the piano, but it's actually a Chinatown restaurant offering some of the best seafood in the area.... *Tel 415/982–7877. 631 Kearny St., 15, 30, or 45 MUNI bus. $–$$* **(see p. 61)**

Radio Valencia. The small cafe that helped launch the hip revitalization of Valencia Street was redecorated rather abruptly in the summer of 1995 by a fire truck that smashed through the corner window. The 1996 resurrection had customers lined up around the block.... *Tel 415/826–1199. 1199 Valencia St. (at 23rd St.), 24th St. BART station or 26 MUNI bus. $* **(see pp. 54, 74)**

Red Dora's Bearded Lady. This is a popular lesbian hangout, but the crowd is definitely mixed at this delightful, eccentric, Mission District cafe near the projects. Weekend nights often feature live music or spoken-word performances, but call to confirm.... *Tel 415/626–2805. 485 14th St. (at Guerrero St.), 16th St. BART station. $* **(see pp. 54, 74, 75)**

Rose Pistola. This popular North Beach trattoria was voted best new restaurant in the country (1997) by the James Beard Foundation.... *Tel 415/399–0499. 532 Columbus Ave., North Beach, 15 or 30 MUNI bus. $$–$$$.* **(see p. 67)**

Sacred Grounds Cafe. Across the Panhandle from Haight Street, this sixties throwback—eclectic furnishings and works by local artists share the room with fine, Victorian-style wood paneling—is still a vital part of the Haight Ashbury scene. Live music and poetry readings continue to attract a dynamic crowd, especially students.... *Tel 415/ 387–3859. 2095 Hayes St. (at Cole St.), 21 MUNI bus. $*
(see p. 75)

Saigon Sandwich Cafe. Not a full-fledged restaurant, but it makes the best Vietnamese sandwiches in town—for around $2. Lunch only (7–4:30, 8–4 weekends).... *Tel 415/474–5698. 560 Larkin St., Civic Center BART/MUNI Metro station, 19, 31, or 38 MUNI bus. No credit cards. $*
(see pp. 64, 71)

Sanppo. Comfortable, inexpensive, and very good, it's right in the heart of Japantown.... *Tel 415/346–3486. Japan Center, 1702 Post St., 38 MUNI bus. AE, DC not accepted. $*
(see p. 64)

Seal Rock Inn. Neighborhood coffee shop just footsteps away from Sutro Park, which overlooks the Pacific Ocean.... *Tel 415/386–6418. 545 Point Lobos Ave., Ocean Beach, 38 MUNI bus. $–$$.*
(see p. 72)

Sear's Fine Foods. If you're anywhere near Union Square at breakfast time, it is mandatory to eat at Sear's diner, beloved for its teeny-tiny, rich, sweet Swedish pancakes.... *Tel 415/986–1160. 439 Powell St., Powell St. BART/MUNI Metro station, any Powell St. cable car, 76 MUNI bus. No credit cards. $*
(see p. 72)

Sol y Luna. Sandwiched between skyscrapers, this spirited Latin American supper club is one of the few late-night signs of life in the Financial District. Paellas and tapas are the specialty.... *Tel 415/296–8696. 475 Sacramento St. (between Battery and Sansome Sts.), Embarcadero BART/ MUNI Metro station. Reservations recommended. $$–$$$.*
(see p. 67)

South Park Cafe. This little South of Market spot has a delightful multiple-personality disorder. It starts as a casual cafe in the morning, then turns into a super-hip lunch bistro, then goes back to its casual cafe persona (at least in the front section) for the rest of the day. The restaurant serves exquisite food (French) at decent prices.... *Tel 415/495–7275. 108 South Park (near 2nd and Bryant Sts.), Montgomery St. BART station, 15, 30, or 45 MUNI bus. $$* **(see p. 74)**

Sparky's Diner. The wee-hours crowd at Sparky's can be a bit eccentric—and sometimes a tad inebriated, especially on weekends—but just mind your own business and pass the ketchup.... *Tel 415/621–6001. 242 Church St., Church St. MUNI Metro station. DC not accepted. $* **(see p. 72)**

Stars. Chef/owner Jeremiah Tower, the self-proclaimed inventor of California Cuisine, created Stars, commonly considered one of the top restaurants in the city. It's a little loud, though, and suffers from the customers' celebrity mania.... *Tel 415/861–7827. 150 Redwood Alley (near Van Ness Ave.), Civic Center BART station. Reservations highly recommended. $$$* **(see pp. 58, 59)**

Stella Pastry & Caffe. Owner Franco Santucci will be happy to expound on the virtues of his patented *Sacripantina*, Luciano Pavarotti's favorite San Francisco dessert and one of many delectable pastries baked on Stella's premises.... *Tel 415/986–2914. 446 Columbus Ave., 15, 30, 41, or 45 MUNI bus.* **(see p. 73)**

Stoyanof. A bright, cheery, neighborhood cafe in the Sunset District that serves the best Greek pastries in San Francisco.... *Tel 415/664–3664. 1240 Ninth Ave., N. Judah MUNI Metro streetcar, 71 MUNI bus. Credit cards for dinner only; DC not accepted. $* **(see p. 68)**

Straits Cafe. The coconut-milk chicken curry is as exotically delicious as the Singapore-style decor.... *Tel 415/668–1783. 3300 Geary Blvd., 38 MUNI bus. Reservations recommended. $$* **(see p. 64)**

Suppenküche. This small, inviting (often crowded and noisy) Hayes Valley beer hall/dining room steadily attracts a young crowd looking for good food, good beer, and good company all in the same place.... *Tel 415/252–9289. 601 Hayes St., Civic Center BART/MUNI Metro station, 21 MUNI bus. DC not accepted. $$* **(see p. 69)**

Tadich Grill. This landmark steak-and-seafood house has been run by the same family since the turn of the century. The french fries are a must.... *Tel 415/391–2373. 240 California St., Embarcadero St. BART/MUNI Metro station. No reservations accepted. AE, DC not accepted.* $$–$$$
(see p. 56)

Tassajara Cafe & Bakery. A bit up the hill from the Haight, in the quieter, less bohemian Cole Valley, Tassajara Cafe has the about the best cookies and pastries you can get.... *Tel 415/664–8947. 1000 Cole St. (at Parnassus St.), 6, 37, 43, or 66 MUNI bus, or N. Judah MUNI/Metro streetcar.* $
(see pp. 73, 75)

Thep Phanom. It's a good thing Thep Phanom is located in California, land of a zillion chili farmers, because they use tons of the red-hot peppers in their fiery Thai food. Keep plenty of water at your table—you'll need it.... *Tel 415/431–2526. 900 Waller St., 3, 6, 7, 22, 66, or 71 MUNI bus. DC not accepted.* $–$$ **(see p. 59)**

Timo's in the Zanzibar. There are two major draws to quirky, artistic Timo's: the tapas, which locals insist are the best in town, and the adjoining bar, the Zanzibar.... *Tel 415/647–0558. 842 Valencia St., 16th St. BART/MUNI Metro station, 26 MUNI bus. AE, DC not accepted.* $$ **(see p. 60)**

Tommy Toy's. This chi-chi Chinese dinner house is a favorite of visiting dignitaries and Hollywood stars.... *Tel 397–4888. 655 Montgomery St., Financial District, Montgomery St. BART/MUNI Metro station. Reservations highly recommended.* $$$–$$$$. **(see p. 61)**

Yank Sing. A guidebook staple that's worth the trip. The dim sum is always satisfying, especially the dumplings, which include many vegetarian options.... *Tel 415/362–1640. 427 Battery St., Embarcadero BART/MUNI Metro station.* $–$$ **(see p. 61)**

Yaya Cuisine. At this Sunset District restaurant, Chef Yahya Salih's native Iraq flavors the exuberant Mediterranean/California hybrid cuisine.... *Tel 415/566–6966. 1220 Ninth Ave., 66 or 71 MUNI bus. Reservations recommended. DC not accepted.* $$ **(see p. 69)**

San Francisco Dining

Alain Rondelli **4**
Angkor Borei **48**
Angkor Wat **3**
Asimakoupoulos Cafe **50**
Babaloo **16**
Backflip **20**
Brothers Restaurant **6**
Bruno's **44**
Buca Giovanni **11**
Carta **30**
Cha Cha Cha **33**
Coconut Grove **19**

El Nuevo Frutilandia **47**
El Trebol **46**
Esperpento **42**
Fina Estampa **39**
Firecracker **37**
Fly Trap Restaurant **27**
Flying Saucer **43**
Fringale **49**
Ganges Vegetarian Restaurant **34**
Gaylord of India **10**
Golden Turtle **18**
Greens **9**
Hama-Ko **35**

Hamburger Mary's **29**
Harris' **17**
Hayes Street Grill **25**
Helmand **14**
Izzy's Steaks and Chops **15**
Kyung Bok Palace **2**
La Rondalla **41**
La Taqueria **45**
Los Jarritos **40**
Mecca **32**
Millennium **26**
Moose's **12**

Rose Pistola **13**
Saigon Sandwich Cafe **21**
Seal Rock Inn **1**
Sanppo **23**
South Park Café **28**
Sparky's Diner **36**
Stars **22**
Stoyanof **8**
Straits Cafe **5**
Suppenküche **24**
Thep Phanom **31**
Timo's in the Zanzibar **38**
Yaya Cuisine **7**

Union Square & Financial District Dining

Aqua **15**

Biscuits and
Blues **3**

Cafe Claude **16**

Cho-Cho **7**

Cypress Club **8**

Enrico,s Sidewalk
 cafe **6**

Fleur de Lys **4**

Harbor Village **12**

John's Grill **5**

Masa's **1**

R & G Lounge **9**

Sear's Fine Foods **2**

Sol y Luna **13**

Tadich Grill **14**

Tommy Toys **10**

Yank Sing **11**

3

sions

First word of
advice: Stay away
from Fisherman's
Wharf. Ditto for
Pier 39 and the
cable-car turn-
arounds. That

is, unless your purpose in traveling all the way to San Francisco is to rub elbows with throngs of tourists, shivering in their shorts and souvenir tank tops despite repeated warnings about how cold it is in July. If you brought the kids, you may have to surrender, but get your wharf duty out of the way as quickly as possible (we give you a few survival tips later on in the chapter) so you can move on to the city's true delights.

There are a few things that are so utterly San Francisco that they absolutely must be experienced at some point during your visit—a cable-car ride to the Buena Vista Cafe for a cup of Irish coffee, a trip to Coit Tower, a walk across the Golden Gate Bridge, the view from the elevator at the top of the Fairmont Hotel—but the best way to get to know the city is to explore the neighborhoods where people actually live. Skip the taxicabs (unless it's after dark or you're in a questionable neighborhood): Take a bus or a streetcar instead, then poke around on foot. Wander around the Haight and count the shrines to Jerry Garcia. Take in the Spoken Word or an avant cha-cha band at a hip, side-street bar in the Mission District. Practice your tai chi with the Chinese senior citizens in Washington Square (North Beach). Gawk at the mansions in Pacific Heights. Visit the Castro for an undiluted dose of the predominant—and wonderfully irreverent—influence gay culture has on every aspect of life in San Francisco.

Lombard Street

The zigzags of "the crookedest street in the world" are negotiated by so many tourists that the bricks finally cracked and popped out of the pavement a few years ago. But the city never would have let one of the jewels of its tourist trade fall into disrepair for long. The famous block between Hyde and Leavenworth streets was closed to automobile traffic for around two years while work crews painstakingly repaired or replaced every errant brick. The street is again open to cars, but the best way to enjoy the view is still to walk down the staircases on either side.

No matter what neighborhood you visit, the best seat in the house is any table at a cozy cafe (see Dining and Cafes). Pull up a chair. Have a nice, frothy cappuccino. There is plenty of time for that trip to the museum—mañana.

Getting Your Bearings

Get a map. There's no other way to visualize San Francisco's irregular layout. The city is not one big grid like Manhattan;

it is totally akimbo with sub-grids that skirt its many hills and valleys in a roundabout way. You can rarely see what's over the next hill, so you may not realize that North Beach is the uphill next-door neighbor of Fisherman's Wharf (north) and Chinatown (south). That may not seem important to you yet, but when you think you're trapped at Pier 39, you'll be relieved to realize that the inviting cafes of North Beach are just a few blocks away.

When it comes to maps, you need two kinds—an overall view of the neighborhoods in relation to each other, and a comprehensive street map. A neighborhood map will show clearly, for example, that Haight Ashbury is right next to Golden Gate Park, which stretches from the middle of the city all the way to the Pacific Ocean (at Ocean Beach, near the Cliff House). You'll see that the Castro and the Mission District—right next to each other, and not too far east of Haight Ashbury—are both south of Market Street, but the neighborhood officially known as South of Market is quite a distance farther east, in the downtown area.

You'll also see that San Francisco—a city and county unto itself—is at the northern tip of a peninsula flanked by the San Francisco Bay on the east and the Pacific Ocean on the west. The

Pick a Card, Any Card
If you've already seen the in-flight movie nine times—before the airline censored it—and you're looking for a good way to amuse yourself on the plane ride to San Francisco, why not play cards? Forget Solitaire and Old Maid—you'll have much more fun with Lynn Gordon's special deck, 52 Adventures in San Francisco. There are no hearts, diamonds, clubs, or spades, but each card does bear a lively illustration on the front and directions for an enticing adventure on the back. Pick cards at random and find the best places to get ice cream—or to go bird-watching—or go through the whole deck and relish the thought of how much fun you're going to have when you finally land in the city. The decks are inexpensive ($5.95) and also double as souvenirs or substitutes for all those postcards you didn't send because you were having way too much fun to stop at the post office. Find them at your local bookstore or contact Chronicle Books, tel 800/722–6657.

Financial District sits on the eastern shore of the city, which curves northward as the Embarcadero passes North Beach and Fisherman's Wharf, eventually turning almost due west to the Golden Gate, where the Pacific Ocean meets the bay. If you stand just about anywhere in the city, you can see a tower that looks like a miniature space needle sitting atop Twin Peaks, the geographical center of the city.

The front section of the San Francisco Yellow Pages has several excellent maps, including transit maps, but if you want to get your bearings in advance, send $2 for a complete packet including useful booklets and a comprehensive visitor map to: San Francisco Convention and Visitors Bureau, P.O. Box 429097, San Francisco, CA 94102-9097 (allow three weeks for U.S. delivery; international mail sent via surface). You can also pick up a copy of the visitor map for free at the Visitor Center at Hallidie Plaza when you arrive. To get the official transit map by mail, send $2.50 to: MUNI MAP, 949 Presidio Ave., San Francisco, CA 94115 (allow two weeks for delivery). It includes all MUNI routes (cable cars, buses, and Metro street-cars), regional transit connections, frequency guide, travel hints, and points of interest. Ask them to include a copy of their excellent booklet, "Tours of Discovery," which features eight different routes you can ride on MUNI that will intro-duce you to San Francisco's most interesting views and neighborhoods—all for the price of a single fare (and a transfer). Transit maps, fares, schedules, and tours are down-loadable (free) at www.transitinfo.org.

The Lowdown

Must-sees for first-time visitors from Peoria...

There is one sure-fire perfect way to spend your first afternoon in San Francisco—take $2 out of your pocket, walk five or ten blocks up Powell from Market Street (away from the turnaround), and hop on the **Powell-Hyde cable car**. Don't even think about not doing it because it seems too "touristy"—locals have been known to invite out-of-town guests purely for an excuse to take this ride. The Powell-Hyde line is our favorite because it ends up just footsteps away from the Buena Vista Cafe (2765 Hyde St., tel 415/474–5044), a National Historic Landmark where a post-cable-car Irish coffee is an esteemed tradition, especially on a foggy afternoon. (The first Irish coffees ever served in America were mixed at the Buena Vista in 1952.) The ride itself twists through the city, climbing "halfway to the stars" atop Nob Hill, then plummeting back down on a breathtaking roller-coaster ride that levels out around the famous crooked section of Lombard Street ("The Crookedest Street in the World") before coasting down to the bay. No postcard can possibly capture what it feels like the first moment you glimpse that million-dollar view. (By the way, watch your teeth—many first-timers smile so broadly they collect stray bugs like radiator grills.)

Another mandatory awe-inspiring adventure is a bracing 15-minute walk across the **Golden Gate Bridge**. There is simply no other way to truly appreciate its immense scale and beauty. The best part is that the weather is absolutely predictable—it always feels cold and windy on the bridge (wear layers). To get an unbelievable view before you actually set foot on the bridge, take the 28 MUNI bus to Fort Point—a brick-and-granite strong-hold built in 1861—where you can climb up to the roof and behold the bridge above you before you set out on the pedestrian walkway. Once you are on the bridge, you'll feel it sway and vibrate as gusty ocean winds whip through its cables. Don't be alarmed. The bridge is not about to collapse. It held up under the ballast of more than a hundred thousand revelers who congregated there to celebrate its 50th anniversary (1987), and it didn't flinch during the 1989 earthquake.

Unless you take the lazy—and boring—way out (the 30, 39, or 45 MUNI bus), you'll probably need to fuel up for the steep hike to **Coit Tower**. We suggest starting out with a cup of super-strength coffee at Caffe Trieste (601 Vallejo St., tel 415/392–6739) because it's right on the corner of Grant Street, the most interesting route to the famous fire-hose-nozzle spire atop Telegraph Hill (where you turn right and head up the hill to the tower). Then head up Grant to Greenwich Street. Once you've actually begun the ascent, you may want to distract yourself from the daunting incline by imagining the tower's name-sake—Lillie Hitchcock Coit (1843–1929)—dressed as a fireman and racing around town with the volunteer brigade. Rumor has it that Ms. Coit found men's clothes appealing in other circumstances as well, particularly when she wanted to get into places where "ladies" weren't allowed. Though Ms. Coit's greatest achievement was to be made mascot of Engine Company 5—a reward for her help in fighting a fire—we love to think of Ms. Coit as San Francisco's most famous cross-dresser. No one really knows if Coit Tower was deliberately designed in the shape of a fire-hose nozzle. Up close, it doesn't matter. The Depression-era murals inside the lobby at the base of the tower are haunting images of Americans at labor, and the 360-degree view from the top of the tower (elevator ride $3) is unbeatable.

Only in San Francisco... San Francisco is full of sights and sounds that simply don't exist in other cities. Where else would a major-league baseball team blast a foghorn to celebrate home runs, or a county fair include a "fog calling" contest? The fog and the hills are San Francisco's natural treasures.

One of the best ways to enjoy the trademark topography is to hike down some of the stairways that have been built into the city's steep sidewalks and pathways. Allow at least an hour or two to walk the **Filbert Street Steps** (between Sansome Street and Telegraph Hill), a romantic favorite with locals because the path feels hidden from urban clamor as it winds past enchanting hundred-year-old cottages and lush gardens. The breathtaking view of the bay from the top of the hill has attracted artists, writers, and singers for years (Joan Baez and Armistead Maupin are among past residents). Start there, at Telegraph Hill Boulevard near Coit Tower, and work your way down. When you cross Montgomery Street to the lower steps, take a look at the art-deco apartment complex at 1930 Montgomery—you might recognize it from the movie *Dark Passage* (Humphrey Bogart and Lauren Bacall). You may want to take a sidetrack along Napier Lane, a lovely wooden walkway that leads to the public Grace Marchant Gardens, a particularly enchanting sight on Halloween, when more than 200 jack-o-lanterns light up the night for local trick-or-treaters.

Chinatown is one of the most celebrated neighborhoods in San Francisco, but it has never become merely a tourist trap—above all else it is a place where people *live*, the largest Chinese community outside of Asia. As soon as you cross under the ornate, dragon-crested gateway on Grant Avenue (at Bush Street), you're no longer in the Western world. Street signs are marked in Chinese characters, lamp posts are encircled by dragons, and store windows display strange medicinal herbs and animal parts you'd never find at a suburban drugstore. The best way to see this teeming neighborhood is early in the morning, when merchants deliver their wares in pushcarts and mothers rush down the street toting live chickens for that night's dinner. Wander up Grant Avenue or Stockton

Street to Sacramento and find Waverly Place, where you'll find **Tien Hon Temple** (125 Waverly Place, top floor) among the many brightly painted balconies. Back on Grant Avenue, a tiny bar with the single word **"Buddha"** on a sign over the door sits on the corner of Washington Street. Look inside. Old men with long braids and "thinking caps" sit at the bar. You're not only on a different continent, you're in a different century.

Every city has churches, but only San Francisco has the **Church of John Coltrane** (351 Divisadero St., tel 415/621–2054), an African Orthodox church that has been using Coltrane's music for the divine liturgy—and serving free food three days a week—for more than 22 years. Jazz lovers from all over the world flock to the small storefront church, where the house band, Ohnedaruth (the Sanskrit word for compassion and the spiritual name Alice Coltrane gave her husband when he died), plays their patron saint's music every Sunday. You never know who will be in attendance—or sitting in with the band. Bobby Hutcherson has stopped by more than once, as has Rashid Ali, Coltrane's last drummer. Once you get inside, you'll be in Coltrane heaven—the walls are adorned with more than a dozen contemporary versions of traditional Russian-style icons, including, of course, ones of Coltrane. The music seems to come from everywhere—the band sits near the altar, the choir takes up the entire first row of seats, and there are saxophones and other instruments spread throughout the congregation. It really is a divine spectacle. Come early to get a good seat; services usually start around noon and last for at least an hour-and-a-half.

Special moments... If a ride on the Powell-Hyde cable car or the view from Coit Tower hasn't already made you fall hopelessly in love with San Francisco, perhaps what you need is a view of the sun virtually melting into an orange-red-fuchsia pool as it sets on the blue Pacific. The ultimate spot is a window table at the pub in the **Cliff House** restaurant (1090 Point Lobos Ave., tel 415/386–3330), facing directly out to sea. The funky-nautical motif pub is a bit tacky, but it fades into the distant background the moment the sun begins its dazzling nightly show. Even the most jaded urbanites ooh and ahh at the display, so be sure to go at least an hour before sundown if you expect to get a good seat—or go outside and find a spot along the cliff.

If you have access to a car, don't leave the Bay Area without watching a sunset from the top of **Grizzly Peak** in the Berkeley Hills. Cars start lining up about a half-hour before sundown to watch the transformation from daylight to shimmering night lights—a magnificent sight in any weather, clear or foggy. The vista covers the entire bay, from San Mateo to the south, the city and the Golden Gate Bridge straight ahead, and Marin County to the north.

On Sundays, soak up the true "spirit" of the city with hundreds of other foot-tapping, hand-clapping, shoulder-swaying sinners at **Glide Memorial Church**'s morning celebrations. An hour or so with Reverend Cecil Williams and his exuberant gospel choir will surely shake your soul and let the glory out, no matter what your religious beliefs may be—everybody leaves this Tenderloin church wearing a major smile. Glide brings out the best in everyone—Bobby McFerrin drops by often, Maya Angelou visits when she's in town; even President Clinton has joined the crowd (fortunately he left his saxophone at home).

Morbid landmarks... For those who enjoy excursions to the dark side, here are a few points of interest that will never make it into San Francisco's public relations hall of fame.

The People's Temple, where crusader Jim Jones gathered disciples before leading them to their eventual death at a tragic mass suicide in Guyana, still stands at 1859 Geary Street. (It is now a Korean Presbyterian Church.)

It's hard to believe that **Charles Manson** recruited some of his deadliest "family" members—including Susan Atkins and Squeaky Fromme—during the peak of Haight Ashbury's peace-and-love scene, but he lived at 636 Cole Street for a few months in 1967 before heading to Southern California to organize his horrifying killing spree. (Manson now lives about 80 miles north of San Francisco at Folsom Prison, isolated from other inmates for his own protection.)

San Quentin State Prison, fondly known to its residents simply as "Q," has hosted some of California's most notorious criminals, including the aforementioned Mr. Manson, Sirhan Sirhan, and William Harris (one of Patty Hearst's kidnappers). They don't give tours of death row or anything like that, but you can take a ferry to Larkspur and hoof it to the prison, where there is a small museum (gas-chamber mementos and such) and a gift shop that sells items made by prisoners (no license plates).

Every hotel has gruesome moments it would rather not recall, but the **Westin Saint Francis** has a couple of whoppers—**President Ford's assassination attempt** (September 23, 1975) and **Fatty Arbuckle's lost weekend** (Labor Day weekend, 1921). President Ford was leaving the hotel through the Post Street entrance when Sara Jane Moore whipped out a gun and fired at him from across the street, but an ex-Marine standing next to her grabbed her arm, redirecting the bullet. (It was the second assassination attempt in one two-week trip to California.) Fatty Arbuckle was celebrating a multimillion-dollar movie contract inside the hotel at what has often been described as a drunken orgy when a young female guest was found unconscious in Room 1219. She died a few days later and Arbuckle was tried three times for her murder before finally being acquitted.

The roar of the fish stalls, the smell of the crowd... It has been decades since **Fisherman's Wharf** was actually a bustling fresh-fish market, and equally as long since **Pier 39** and the Port of San Francisco were a thriving part of the city's mercantile economy. Yet these two tourist traps are the first stop for most sightseers. (Pier 39, converted just over 15 years ago to an outdoor mall of shops and restaurants, is third on the list of the world's top 10 attractions, with more than 10.5 million guests each year.) There are precious few reasons to go near either place, but if you must (your kids will probably insist), here are some ways to make the best of it: Buy a fresh, whole crab at **Nick's** seafood stall (make sure it's still alive and wiggling), get them to cook and crack it for you on the spot, then pick up a sourdough baguette from **Boudin Sourdough Bakery**, and savor one of the best crab sandwiches around. Visit the sea lions—hundreds of them hang around Pier 39's K Dock, where docents from the Marine Mammal Center (remember it from *Star Trek IV*?) give out free books and teach visitors all about the barking pinnipeds (11–5). Then escape to **Pier 23 Cafe**, an almost-unnoticeable shack that attracts a local crowd with jazz, reggae, and calypso, as well as a beautiful view.

Looking for a few good whales: Marine World... One of the best ways to take the family to Pier 39 without actually lingering there is a ferry excursion on the Blue & Gold Fleet to **Marine World/Africa USA**, a unique, hands-on wildlife park across the bay in Vallejo. The hour-long passenger-ferry ride provides incredible views of the city, Alcatraz, Angel Island, four bridges, and many tiny islets, some with lighthouses. One of the most popular park features is its spectacular whale and dolphin show—where kids love getting splashed by giant killer whales—but there are plenty of other fine entertainers among its sea lions, walruses, lions and tigers, primates, and exotic and predatory birds. You can ride elephants, feed giraffes, walk though a glass atrium filled with butterflies from all over the world, or roam through a "walkabout" with kangaroos, wallaroos, wallabies, and an occasional emu.

Urban ferry tales... There are plenty of bay cruises that pick up tourists at Fisherman's Wharf and Pier 39, but it's more fun to go to the Ferry Building at the foot of Market Street and ride with the locals on an afternoon **Golden Gate Ferry** to the seaside village of Sausalito. You can do a one-hour round-tripper or stop to explore Sausalito. There is really just one main street—Bridgeway—so it's easy to walk around the yuppie/nautical/ex-Bohemian enclave and find a perfect spot to watch the sun set behind the San Francisco skyline. **Cafe Sausalito**, on the top floor of the Village Fair Building, is a good vantage point, and relatively inexpensive. If sunsets aren't your thing, and you'd sooner toss back a pint at a rowdy tavern full of live music and boisterous baby boomers, try the **No Name Bar**, but don't drink too many happy-hour specials unless you intend to spend the night—the last ferry departs for San Francisco just after 7.

Cruising Golden Gate Park... The city's reigning playground, Golden Gate Park has been home to the 49ers football team and all the city's major hippie happenings (including Jerry Garcia's memorial service in 1995); it still is home to Sunday strollers, skaters, and joggers, to museums, to free operas, even to a herd of buffalo. Most of the park's recreational facilities are covered in the "Getting Outside" chapter, but Golden Gate also probably has more museums than any other urban oasis in the world. The **Asian Art Museum** (John F. Kennedy Dr., opposite 11th Ave.) is the largest museum outside of Asia devoted exclusively to Asian art (more than 12,000 pieces in the permanent collection). There are more than 500 Korean and Chinese masterpieces on display—including the world's oldest-dated Chinese Buddha—plus hundreds of exquisite works from India, Tibet, Nepal, Pakistan, and Southeast Asia. The massive **California Academy of Sciences** complex (off Martin Luther King Jr. Dr., opposite 9th Ave.) is a great place to take your kids, but be sure to allow plenty of time—it includes the Natural History Museum, the Steinhart Aquarium, and the Morrison Planetarium. The most fun shows at the Natural History Museum are in the Earth and Space Hall, which features a simulated earthquake and has lots of good "Star Trek" souvenirs in the gift shop. The planetarium's 50-minute sky shows—projected on a huge domed ceiling—are a hit with adults, but young children tend to get bored and restless. Teenagers love the nighttime laser shows at the planetarium, which feature the recorded works of bands like Metallica and Pink Floyd. The **M. H. de Young Memorial Museum** (next to the Asian Art Museum) is San Francisco's scaled-down, unobtrusive answer to New York's Metropolitan Museum of Art. The major international exhibits bring art-lovers from miles around, but it is the museum's exhaustive collection of American art—from Paul Revere to Georgia O'Keeffe—that puts it on the museum map. There is also a magnificent textile collection, including rugs to die for. While you're there, be sure to stop by the garden cafe for the yummy daily specials.

Then there are the gardens. The 5-acre **Japanese Tea Garden** (adjacent to the Asian Art Museum) is the oldest in America. When you enter through the hand-carved gate, you really feel as though you are in Japan. The bamboo-lined footpaths and bridges pass ponds full of koi fish, tiny Bonsai trees, stone lanterns, Shinto shrines, and a serene 18th-century Buddha. In early spring, the garden is ablaze with cherry blossoms. (Go early in the morning to avoid crowds.) Cap your visit with a rest stop at the tea pavilion for a fortune cookie (they were first introduced there) and a relaxing cup of green tea served by women in traditional Japanese costume. The **Conservatory of Flowers** (on Conservatory Way, near Arguello Blvd.) is a massive glass Victorian greenhouse that was built in Ireland and shipped to San Francisco piece by piece. It is stunning from the outside, and utterly magnificent on the inside, where beautiful exotic flowers and tropical trees are always in season. We suspect the orchids possess magic restorative powers—especially on drab, foggy days.

Museum meccas outside Golden Gate Park...

From a half-block away, the huge circular skylight atop Swiss architect Mario Botta's **Museum of Modern Art** (South of Market) looks like some sort of signaling device for extraterrestrial art collectors. Inside, earthlings have been known to be utterly dazzled by the West Coast's most extensive collection of 20th-century art, which fills 50,000 square feet of gallery space. Botta's magnificent structure is a work of art in itself, and one of the primary reasons to visit.

The city's ethnic diversity and social compassion fuel most of the art displayed in the celebrated **Center for the Arts at Yerba Buena Gardens,** a multi-gallery center adjacent to the new Museum of Modern Art. Exhibits have included panels from the NAMES Project Memorial Quilt and works by prison inmates and residents of local halfway houses. There is also a theater, which hosts a variety of local performances from multicultural groups, and is one of the sites used by the San Francisco Ballet while the city's opera house is undergoing repairs.

The **Palace of Fine Arts** is a must-see, not just because it houses the Exploratorium, but because it looks just like an ancient Roman temple—where's Nero when we really need him?—and it's the only building that remains from the 1915 Panama Pacific Exposition (held to celebrate the opening of the Panama Canal). A trip to the **Exploratorium** is also mandatory. (If you brought your kids, it is a ticket to heaven.) Seasoned locals will assure you it's the most fun you can have without hallucinogenic drugs, especially if you crawl through the dark, sensual Tactile Dome or try any of the other hands-on games designed to totally twist your mind. You never know what the mad scientists will have in store for you at this wonderfully fun, interactive science museum—and the gift shop is the best of any museum in the galaxy.

San Francisco's cable-car system is still run out of a 3-story red-brick barn, and you can watch it in action from several special spectator galleries. The **Cable Car Barn and Museum** includes the original prototype cable car (1873) along with other cars and models. Yes, there is a gift shop full of cable-car souvenirs.

The literally ship-shape **Maritime Museum** looks like a set for an old Hollywood romantic-cruise movie. Nautical types will go nuts when they see all the ship models, relics, figureheads, photographs, scrimshaw—you know, your basic sailor stuff.

Freebies at the major museums... Most major museums set aside special free-admission days; some are free year-round. The free days tend to occur during the first week of the month, so keep that in mind when planning your trip, and always call for the most current schedule. The **Asian Art Museum** in Golden Gate Park is free the first Wednesday of every month and first Saturday from 10 to noon; the **Cable Car Barn and Museum** is free every day from 10 to 6; the **California Academy of Sciences** in Golden Gate Park is free the first Wednesday of every month; the **Center for the Arts at Yerba Buena Gardens** offers free gallery admission the first Thursday of every month from 6 to 8pm, and to seniors every Thursday from 11 to 3; the **M. H. de Young Memorial Museum** in Golden Gate Park is free the first Wednesday of every month and the first Saturday from 10 to noon; the **Exploratorium** at the Palace of Fine Arts is free the first Wednesday of every month from 10 to 9:30; the **Museum of Modern Art** is free the first Tuesday of every month from 11 to 6; and the **Maritime Museum** at Aquatic Park is free every day from 10 to 5. (See the Index for descriptions of each museum.)

Museums for Special interests... When Pogo would make a more entertaining afternoon companion than Picasso, it's time to quit the cathedrals of culture and head for smaller houses of object worship, like the **Cartoon Art Museum** (814 Mission St.). Once tucked away in a largely ignored warehouse space, the museum is now an esteemed neighbor of the Museum of Modern Art, with thousands of pieces in its permanent collection, from original Krazy Kat watercolors and Pogo comic strips to storyboards from the Disney classic, *Fantasia*. Some of the donors include "Peanuts" artist Charles Schulz and rock star Graham Nash.

If you can't resist penny arcades, you'll love the quirky little **Musée Mecanique** at the Cliff House (1090 Point Lobos Ave.). It's packed with antique mechanical gadgets, from old carnival fortune-tellers to marionette shows and player pianos. Admission is free, which is a good thing because you'll easily drop a small fortune in coins playing with all the doohickeys and thingamabobs. One really strange exhibit is a miniature amusement park made out of toothpicks. The fact that the piece was glued together by prisoners at San Quentin kind of makes you wonder.

Galeria de la Raza (2857 24th St.) and the **Mexican Museum** (Fort Mason, Bldg. D) feature Mexican and Chicano art. The Mexican Museum's permanent collection—more than 9,000 pieces—makes it a "serious" museum, but the atmosphere is as informal and friendly as Mexico itself. It showcases the best in Mexican and Chicano culture, from folk art to Frida Kahlo, and has one of the best gift shops in the city. Be sure to check out the many whimsical Dia de los Muertos (Day of the Dead) objects, including the perfect wedding gift—a skeleton bride-and-groom to top the cake. The Galeria de la Raza was the first Mexican museum in the United States. It is more locally oriented than the Mexican Museum, and often more innovative, presenting fine examples of work by community artists, as well as major national exhibits.

The **Jewish Community Museum** (121 Steuart St.) has two primary focal points—history and art. Exhibits have featured a variety of works by Jewish artists, from emerging current artists to masters like Marc Chagall. The gallery is known for presenting shows that challenge visitors to critically examine what they see.

The West Coast's largest photography collection is housed at the **Ansel Adams Center** (250 Fourth St.). From Annie Liebovitz's irreverent portraits to Ansel Adams' awesome images of the American West, this remarkable museum houses five exhibition halls and extensive bookstore. Exhibits change, but one of the galleries is devoted solely to Adams' own work.

To get a virtually private glimpse of the history of one of San Francisco's most intriguing neighborhoods, go to the **North Beach Museum**, tucked away on the mezzanine of the Eureka Federal Savings Bank (1435 Stockton St.). This delightful little museum traces North Beach's past with photographs and artifacts dating back to the turn of the century. Hardly anybody knows the museum is there, so you may have it all to yourself, but you must go during regular banking hours.

Finally, it ain't Fort Knox, but the **Old Mint Museum** (88 Fifth St.) did survive the 1906 earthquake and it does have an 1869 coin press you can use to strike your own souvenir coin (sorry, it's not legal tender) and minting machines that once churned out more nickels and dimes than we could ever count. The building itself—a National Historic Landmark—is a superb example of Federal classical revival architecture.

Museums for really special interests... Ghia Gallery/ Discount Caskets and Urns (2648 Third St.) is a favorite among necro-kitsch fans, but you don't have to be morbid to like designer coffins. Just ask Cher—she bought two of Ghia's "King Tut" sarcophaguses and turned them into wine bars. Other creative coffins include the all-glass "Here's Lookin' At You" models and a variety of custom designs that have been used as phone booths, vanity tables, and nightstands. Some people have been so inspired by Ghia's furniture for the hereafter, they've staged their own funerals while they were still alive.

For flesh freaks, we have two recommendations: **Lyle Tuttle's Tattoo Museum** (841 Columbus Ave.) and **Good Vibrations** (1210 Valencia St.). Lyle Tuttle, undisputed king of the San Francisco tattoo empire, moved his mini-museum from a seedy location at Seventh and Market streets long after he had already engraved Janis Joplin's flesh, but you can still see his collection of tattoo art—including candid shots of himself, covered head-to-toe with indelible designs—at his tiny little shop in North Beach. More pleasurable pleasures of the flesh are explored at Good Vibrations, where the contraptions in the window display look like old-time hair dryers or permanent-wave doodads, but are actually part of an eclectic collection of sex toys and vibratorana, including the "Queen Victoria," a wooden hand-crank model from turn-of-the-century London. The museum/store—which tends to favor women's interests—is almost cheery; if it weren't for the dozens of plastic penises on the shelves, you'd expect a young Henry Fonda to appear from behind the counter and offer you an ice cream soda.

At the **Keane Eyes Gallery** (651 Market St.), where those tacky bug-eyed waif paintings from the

1960s—portrait after portrait of small children with oversized heads and eyes so huge and round they make Liza Minelli look like a squinter—are celebrated as high kitsch.

Hello Gorgeous!! Anyone who recognizes those words as Barbra Streisand's opening line in *Funny Girl* will be in hog heaven at this combo shrine/store/gallery by the same name. It's high Castro kitsch, and the best part is that almost all of the stuff on display is for sale, including prosthetic Streisand noses for around $80 (such a deal). Serious collectors might be more interested in some of the treasures that have been offered on consignment, such as a hat Streisand wore in *Hello, Dolly!* or a set of the star's dishes snatched from a Christie's auction.

Outlandish out-of-town archives... Heading south from the city, US 101 is dotted with weird little wayside collections. The first stop is the **Burlingame Museum of Pez Memorabilia**, not far from the airport. Remember those tiny little candies spit from the mouths of plastic cartoon characters? Since the first Pez-spitter hit the shelves in 1952, hundreds of models have been issued, and the museum's collection of them is exhaustive. Farther down the road, in Palo Alto, is the 2,000-square-foot **Barbie Hall of Fame**, home to nearly every doll, dress, tiny plastic stiletto-heeled shoe, and weird accessory that ever crossed Mattel's twisted little mind. More than 16,000 items are on display; curator Evelyn Burkhalter claims to have every Barbie doll and accessory, with the exception of a half-dozen outfits from the late 1970s. Moving right along to the Silicon Valley, you'll find the perfect antidote to Apple, Intel, and the rest of the high-tech cathedrals: the **Rosicrucian Egyptian Museum**. One of the mummies on display at this San Jose park was actually a post-mortem hitchhiker discovered by the shippers at Neiman Marcus, who packaged up what was supposed to be a "vacant" case. The store graciously offered to dispose of the uninvited mummy, but the Rosicrucians were delighted to keep it as one of their many permanent guests. Last stop, Surf City. The **Santa Cruz Surfing Museum** is as close as you can get to a surfin' safari without climbing on a board and catching a wave. The museum itself overlooks Steamer Lane, time-honored haunt of inveterate Santa Cruz surfers and home to many championship surfing contests. The view is spectacular, and the exhibits inside are totally awesome, dude.

The Bongo-Rama Beatnik tour... Bohemian-history buffs won't want to leave San Francisco without paying homage to some of the hallowed grounds that have made the city a capital of late 20th-century counterculture. One might say the beat movement, for instance, was born in 1953, when Allen Ginsberg moved to San Francisco and Lawrence Ferlinghetti opened **City Lights Bookstore** at 261 Columbus Avenue, even though Neal Cassady and Jack Kerouac already lived in the city at **29 Russell Street** (a small alley off Hyde Street between Union and Grand streets). One weekend in 1955, stoned to the gills, Ginsberg wrote his magnum opus, "Howl," in his apartment at **1214 Polk Street** (between Bush and Sutter streets), and read it for the first time two weeks later to a spellbound audience at the tiny **Six Gallery** at 3119 Fillmore Street (between Filbert and Greenwich streets). City Lights published the poem in 1956, and the police immediately declared it obscene, focusing national attention on North Beach. *Chronicle* columnist Herb Caen coined the term "beatnik" to describe the disheveled literati, who dug poetry and jazz at places like **Vesuvio's** (255 Columbus Ave.), on the corner of what is now Jack Kerouac Alley; **The Place** (1546 Grant Ave.), which Jack Kerouac described in *The Dharma Bums* as "the favorite bar of the hepcats around the Beach"; the **Cellar** (576 Green St.); and **Specs** (12 Adler Place). In 1958, after Kerouac's *On the Road* became a best-seller and Hollywood producers came up with the watered-down TV series "Route 66" to exploit the theme, tour-bus gawkers descended on North Beach to stare at the beatniks, making popular hangouts like **Caffe Trieste** (601 Vallejo St.), the now defunct **Co-Existence Bagel Shop** (1398 Grant Ave.), and **Enrico's** (504 Broadway) feel like zoos for the caged poets. In 1960, The Place and the Co-Existence Bagel Shop closed, and the fuss over beatniks died for a while.

Tune in, turn on, drop out... Just a few years later, the city was the center of a cultural convulsion of a more Day-Glo shade. By the time the infamous Summer of

Love rolled around in 1967, San Francisco's psychedelic scene had actually been in full swing for more than two years, since *One Flew Over the Cuckoo's Nest* author Ken Kesey introduced Owsley acid (known as the "cadillac of LSD") to the Grateful Dead, and acid rock was born. Another acid-powered band, the Jefferson Airplane, first played at a little club called the **Matrix** (3138 Fillmore St., near Union St.) in August 1965, but the club got too loud for the neighbors, so the acidheads moved on and it evolved into a rowdy singles bar still doing business as **Pierce Street Annex**.

Examiner writer Michael Fallon coined the term "hippie" to distinguish the new hipsters from their beatnik predecessors shortly before the first big psychedelic concert was staged in October 1965 at **Longshoreman's Hall** in Fisherman's Wharf (400 North Point) by Chet Helms and his production company, the Family Dog. Later, the Family Dog moved its gigs to the **Avalon Ballroom** at 1268 Sutter Street (near Van Ness Avenue), now a multiplex movie theater. Meanwhile, Bill Graham entered the scene with a benefit for the San Francisco Mime Troupe (December 1965) at the **Fillmore Auditorium** (1805 Geary Blvd., at the corner of Fillmore Street), which would become his virtual kingdom and the undisputed center of the psychedelic rock universe.

In January 1967, 20,000 people showed up for the first "Human Be-In" at the **Polo Field** (just off Middle Drive between 30th and 36th avenues in Golden Gate Park) covered in luminous detail by the *Oracle*, a popular underground newspaper headquartered at **1371 Haight Street**. The Haight had become the center of hippie culture—Janis Joplin lived at **112 Lyon Street** (corner of Oak Street), the Grateful Dead around the corner at **710 Ashbury Street** (near Haight Street), and the Jefferson Airplane at **2400 Fulton Street** (closer to the park). By the summer of 1967, the whole world was watching the Haight, especially when Rudolf Nureyev and Margot Fonteyn were arrested at a pot party at **42 Belvedere Street** (near Haight Street). Drug busts became a priority—if not a sport—for San Francisco's Finest, and the October 1967 raid of the Dead house was the top feature of the premiere issue of **Rolling Stone**, which was produced in a small loft at 746 Brannan Street, South of Market. Drug busts and a massive influx of unenlightened strangers were ruining the scene; that same month, the **Psychedelic Shop** (1535 Haight St.) closed its doors and a march through the neighborhood declared the death of the true hippie movement. The party was over.

The last-call saloon crawl... The party is never over at some good old watering holes—these historic saloons are still full of characters and stories. There are at least a half-dozen classic booze joints in North Beach, from beatnik haunts that orbit City Lights—**Specs**, **Tosca**, and **Vesuvio's**—to beloved neighborhood dives like **Gino and Carlo** and literary hangouts like **Washington Square Bar & Grill**. Many of the best old downtown retreats, like the Templebar (1 Tillman Place, now a popular restaurant called Rumpus), have given way to more stylish ventures, but a few remnants of Old San Francisco remain, the best of which is **Harrington's**, a landmark Irish bar that has never been tamed by the genteel Financial District that surrounds it.

Painted ladies... Some 14,000 Victorian buildings—mostly private homes—are scattered throughout San Francisco, but the ones you usually see on the postcards (the 700 block of Steiner Street) are lined up around Alamo Square, the center of a small, wealthy neighborhood bordered by Golden Gate Avenue on the north, Fell Street on the south, Webster Street on the east, and Divisadero Street on the west. These ornate wooden homes range from gracious to almost garish, depending upon how much gingerbread is involved and who has been choosing the color scheme, but most of them have been meticulously restored. For a famous view, with the painted ladies in the foreground and the city and bay in the background, find a high spot anywhere in **Alamo Square** and face due east (toward Steiner Street), or stand on the corner of Hayes and Steiner streets. The **Archbishop's Mansion** (1000 Fell St., see Accommodations), now an exclusive bed-and-breakfast inn, is a huge blue Victorian mansion right at the northern edge of the Painted Ladies postcard block. (A word of caution: This affluent area is the southwestern neighbor of the Western Addition, which can be dangerous near the public-housing projects, especially at night. If you're not familiar with the area, you may prefer to take a bus or a cab instead of walking.)

DIVERSIONS | THE LOWDOWN

If picture-pretty private residences are less intriguing to you than time-worn structures in a working-class neighborhood, head over to the inner Mission District, where several types of the city's oldest Victorians—stick, Italianate, and Queen Anne—can be found on or near **Liberty Street**, a small side street between 20th and 21st streets. These structures survived the 1906 earthquake because the fires stopped at 20th Street. An 1878 stick-style building, characterized by square bay windows with flat wooden "sticks" that have carved scrolls, leaves, and flowers, stands at 956 Valencia Street, on the corner of Liberty. Head north on Liberty, and you'll see rows of Victorians built between 1870 and 1894. At least five of them (19, 23, 35, 43, and 77) are Italianate style, distinguished by ornate porticos, façades above the rooflines, and slanted bay windows designed to bring in more light on foggy San Francisco days. The house at 27 Liberty is a local adaptation of a Queen Anne, identifiable primarily because of the shingled walls (most Queen Annes have rounded corner towers, but there are many variations on this theme). Some of the most interesting houses in the Mission District combined several architectural styles to get just the right amount of gewgaw and curlicues—the house at 827 Guerrero Street (corner of Liberty Street) has a Queen Anne tower, a Gothic front window, and a Moorish doorway. The Mission is full of wonderful houses. Walk around and explore for yourself, or get a little scholarly advice from Judith Waldhorn's *Take a Walk Through Mission History*, available for $1 from the Stanford Research Institute along with a free 11-page reading list about San Francisco Victorians (Victorian Booklets, M2308, Stanford Research Institute, Menlo Park, CA 94025, tel 415/326–6200).

Mural, mural on the wall... The 200 or so brilliant murals painted on the walls, fences, and sides of buildings in the Mission District are famous around the world, but often overlooked by visitors and locals alike. There are at least 250 more murals in other neighborhoods around the city—including the stunning Depression-era murals that cover the interior walls of the base of **Coit Tower**. Keep your eyes open wherever you venture, but here's a tip for quick total immersion in the art of the streets: Take BART to the 24th Street station and head up 24th toward Potrero Hill—you'll see it looming in front of you—until you come to **Balmy Alley**, nestled between Treat Avenue and Harrison Street. This one-block lane has one of the most dense collections of murals anywhere in the world—practically every inch of every fence, wall, and garage door is covered with color. Many of the alley's most cherished murals were defaced or destroyed by vandals in the past, but local muralists have painted new images and restored old ones. After you've marveled at Balmy Alley, go back out to 24th Street and head farther toward the hill until you reach **York Street**, about four blocks away. Again you will be treated to a marvelous assortment of brilliantly colored murals. **Precita Eyes Mural Center**, a community resource center, hosts a tour of this area that will show you at least 60 Mission District murals in one eight-block stretch.

Are we there yet? (Fun with the kids)... The top family attractions besides Fisherman's Wharf and Pier 39 (sorry) are the **Exploratorium**, Alcatraz, the Zoo (**San Francisco Zoological Gardens and Children's Zoo**), and the **Steinhart Aquarium**. You simply cannot escape these places if your kids are even slightly persuasive. But there are other places they're likely to enjoy as well, depending on their ages. Youngsters love the Children's Playground in Golden Gate Park, just off Waller Street, opposite Arguello Boulevard, with all the requisite paraphernalia, plus wheelchair-accessible equipment. If they get bored with the slides/swings/sandbox routine, there is a restored 1912 carousel right next door (tel 415/666–7201). Other options for the under-14 set include **The Jungle**, 15,000 square feet of crawling, jumping, and climbing. The last thing most teenagers want to do is go *anywhere* with their parents, but if you promise to hide across the room and pretend not to know them, they might just love you for taking them to the **Hard Rock Cafe**, where you'll need earplugs and they'll need enough money to buy expensive souvenir T-shirts.

Fabulous footsteps... Hills, schmills. Don't let a few slopes here and there deter you from one of San Francisco's greatest pleasures—walking around the neighborhoods and exploring the city for yourself. Before you set out on your own, however, pick up some free walking-tour guides from the Visitor Information Center

DIVERSIONS | THE LOWDOWN

(Hallidie Plaza, Powell St. BART/MUNI Metro stop, tel 415/391–2000). The public library also offers about 20 free walking tours led by **City Guides**, volunteers who have completed an exhaustive training program in San Franciscan history, art, and architecture. Tours range from hidden rooftop gardens to brothels and boarding-houses. Some of the city's most unusual tours are orga-nized by local individuals who love to show off their favorite parts of San Francisco. Rachel Heller leads the **Flower Power** Haight Ashbury tour, with stops at erst-while crash pads of famous hippies (Janis Joplin and the Grateful Dead) and other lost psychedelic ports of call, such as the Straight Theater, where Bill Graham first staged his dance concerts. Host Trevor Hailey, a beloved—and very friendly—local historian, will take you **Cruisin' the Castro**, where you'll visit only-in-San-Francisco businesses, chat with the shopkeepers, enjoy brunch in a local hot spot, and discover why gay men have been migrating to San Francisco since the Gold Rush. Television chef and cookbook author Shirley Fong-Torres is the mastermind of the **I Can't Believe I Ate My Way Through Chinatown** tour, which treats walkers to a private tea ceremony, snacks, a visit to a rice-noodle factory, more snacks, visits with local food mer-chants, just one last snack, and a full Chinese luncheon. There are no hills to climb in Elaine Sosa's **Javawalk**, a 2-hour jaunt through Union Square, Chinatown, Jackson Square, and North Beach, with pit stops along the way for—what else?—cups of joe. A multi-course lunch at Enrico's Sidewalk Cafe is the highlight of *Chronicle* food writer GraceAnn Walden's tour that goes behind the scenes at brick-oven bakeries, delis, and sausage makers to show what life is like for **The Italians of North Beach**. For lust and crime, get up early and join author John McCarroll on his **A.M. Walks** through the Barbary Coast, Chinatown, and Union Square, where gold rush-ers found "the best bad things obtainable in America." Then hook up with another local author, Mark Gordon, on his **Frisco Productions Crime Tour**, where you'll visit infamous crime scenes like the Hibernia Bank, robbed by Patty Hearst and the Symbionese Liberation Army in the mid-1970s.

The Index

A.M. Walks. You've got to get up at about 8am to find a little peace and quiet while you roam Chinatown, Union Square, and the Barbary Coast as author John McCarroll recounts tales of unbridled lust, scandal, and crime.... *Tel 415/928–5965. Admission charged.* **(see p. 116)**

Ansel Adams Center for Photography. The largest collection of photography on the West Coast, with one gallery devoted solely to Adams' work.... *Tel 415/495–7000. 250 Fourth St., Powell St. BART/MUNI Metro station; 30, 45, or 76 MUNI bus. Open Tue–Sun 11–5, first Thur of every month until 8. Admission charged.* **(see p. 108)**

Asian Art Museum. Asiaphiles take note: Do not miss this under any circumstances. It is the largest museum outside of Asia devoted exclusively to Asian art.... *Tel 415/668–8921 or 415/668–7855; TDD 415/752–2635. Golden Gate Park, next to the de Young Museum and the Japanese Tea Garden, near Tenth Ave. and Fulton St., 44 MUNI bus. Open Wed–Sun 10–5, first Thur of each month until 8. Admission charged.* **(see pp. 104, 107)**

Barbie Hall of Fame. A small museum stuffed with Barbie everything. Now that her measurements are being cut down to "normal" size, these tall, buxom vintage models should be even more popular.... *Tel 415/326–5841, 460 Waverly Street, Palo Alto. Closed Sun, Mon. Admission charged.* **(see p. 110)**

Boudin Sourdough Bakery. When you're at Fisherman's Wharf or Pier 39, nothing tastes better than a San Francisco–style round sourdough bread from Boudin's.... *Tel 415/928–1849. 156 Jefferson St., 32 MUNI bus. Open weekdays until 8, weekends until 9.* **(see p. 103)**

DIVERSIONS | THE INDEX

Burlingame Museum of Pez Memorabilia. One of the world's most exhaustive collections of Pez dispensers.... *Tel 415/347–2301. 214 California Dr., Burlingame. Closed Sun, Mon. Admission free.* **(see p. 110)**

Cable Car Barn and Museum. San Francisco's cable-car system is still run out of this museum, which also houses the original prototype cable car.... *Tel 415/474–1887. 1201 Mason St., Powell-Hyde or Powell-Mason cable car. Open daily 10–6, Nov–Mar 10–5. Admission free.* **(see pp. 106, 107)**

Cafe Sausalito. For a beautiful sunset view of San Francisco, take a ferry to the seaside village of Sausalito and settle in at this inexpensive cafe.... *Tel 415/332–6579. 777 Bridgeway, Fourth Floor, Sausalito.* **(see p. 104)**

California Academy of Sciences. This huge science museum complex is a major kid-pleaser. The fish roundabout at Steinhart Aquarium puts you inside an enormous tank; the Earth and Space Hall at the Natural History Museum lets you experience a fake earthquake; and the Morrison Planetarium turns almost psychedelic at night with Laserium displays set to the tunes of bands like Metallica.... *Tel 415/221–5610 or 415/750–7145 (recorded message); 415/750–7138 for Laserium. Golden Gate Park, near Eighth Ave. and Lincoln Way, 44 MUNI bus. Open 10–5. Admission charged.*
(see pp. 105, 107)

Cartoon Art Museum. In fancy new digs near the Museum of Modern Art, cartoon artists are taken seriously. This is one of the few art museums where your kids will have as much fun as you will.... *Tel 415/CARTOON (227–8666) or 415/456–3922. 814 Mission St., Montgomery St. BART/MUNI Metro stop; 15, 30, or 45 MUNI bus. Open Wed–Fri 11–5, Sat 10–5, Sun 1–5. Admission charged.*
(see p. 107)

Center for the Arts at Yerba Buena Gardens. This dynamic multi-gallery center focuses on emerging local and regional artists. *Tel 415/978–2700. 701 Mission St., Montgomery St. BART/MUNI Metro station, 14, 15, 30, or 45 MUNI bus. Open Tue–Sun 11–6. Gallery admission charged.* **(see pp. 106, 107)**

City Guides. Free walking tours offered by the public library range from Mission murals, hidden rooftop gardens, and Pacific Heights mansions to brothels, boardinghouses, and bawds.... *Tel 415/557–4266.* **(see p. 116)**

Coit Tower. Depression-era murals cover the interior walls at the base of the tower, while the top offers a 360-degree view.... *Tel 415/362–0808. 39 MUNI bus. Open daily 10–6:30. Base admission free, elevator $3.* **(see pp. 99, 114)**

Cruisin' the Castro. Walk through the city's gay mecca with a local historian who knows every nook and cranny. Brunch at a popular cafe included. Host: Trevor Hailey.... *Tel 415/550–8110. Admission charged.* **(see p. 116)**

Exploratorium. Kids love this wacky, blow-your-mind science circus—especially the dark and often creepy crawl-through Tactile Dome. The gift shop, by the way, is probably the best you'll ever encounter at a museum. (Don't miss the Einstein relativity theory wristwatches.).... *Tel 415/561–0360. Palace of Fine Arts, 3601 Lyon St., 30 MUNI bus. Open Tue–Sun 10–5. Admission charged.* **(see pp. 106, 107, 115)**

Fisherman's Wharf. It's a tacky tourist trap, but if you have to go there, try to save your sanity by feasting on some fresh crab from a sidewalk stall and remembering that it used to be a real fishing port. Your kids may want to hit the Wax Museum and the Ripley's Believe It or Not Museum. To get to the wharf, take any Powell Street cable car or the 15, 30, or 42 MUNI bus. **(see p. 103)**

Flower Power. Take a walking tour through Haight Ashbury, check out the crash pads, concert halls, and psychedelic shops that gave birth to the Hippie era. Host: Rachel Heller.... *Tel 415/221–8442. Admission charged.* **(see p. 116)**

Frisco Productions Crime Tour. Get a vicarious thrill as you visit infamous crime scenes—real and fictional—with local author Mark Gordon, who also offers a Bar Crawl tour, a Sentimental Journey Nostalgia tour, and a Hollywood in San Francisco tour.... *Tel 415/681–5555.* **(see p. 116)**

Galeria de la Raza. The first Mexican museum in the United States, it is still a major art and cultural center in the Latino community.... *Tel 415/826–8009. 2857 24th St., 24th St. at Bryant St. BART station, 48 or 67 MUNI bus. Open Tue–Sat noon–6. Admission free.* **(see p. 108)**

Ghia Gallery/Discount Caskets and Urns. If the Addams Family had an art gallery, there's no question this would be it. Not only is the gallows humor good-natured, the coffins are actually fun to look at. (Cher is a customer—is that a surprise?).... *Tel 415/282–2832. 2648 Third St., 15, 30, or 45 MUNI bus. Admission free.* **(see p. 109)**

Gino and Carlo. No bar in North Beach has more loyal regulars than this classic neighborhood dive almost invariably free of tourists. Venture through the double doors, be prepared for spirited arguments (mostly about sports) and patrons who will undoubtedly retell at least one episode from the bar's long history.... *Tel 415/421–0896. 548 Green St.* **(see p. 113)**

Glide Memorial Church. Charismatic civic leader Reverend Cecil Williams and his gospel choir host services every Sunday morning that seem to lift the spirits of the whole city.... *Tel 415/771–6300. 330 Ellis St. Services Sun at 9 and 11.* **(see p. 102)**

Golden Gate Ferry. Join the locals who ride from San Francisco's Ferry Building at the foot of Market Street to downtown Sausalito, a scenic seaside village with lots of expensive stores, expensive restaurants, expensive real estate, expensive boats—and gorgeous sunsets. The ride takes about a half-hour. Fare is $4.25 each way for adults, $3.20 for children, and $2.10 for seniors. Call for schedule.... *Tel 415/923–2000, TDD 415/257–4554. Embarcadero BART/MUNI Metro stop.* **(see p. 104)**

Good Vibrations. An eclectic collection of sex toys and vibrators. Workshops offered after hours range from safer-sex education (led by the Safer Sex Sluts) to erotic reading circles.... *Tel 415/ 974–8980. 1210 Valencia St. 25th St., BART station 26, MUNI bus. Open daily 11–7. Admission free.* **(see p. 109)**

Grizzly Peak. A popular Berkeley Hills perch for a great sunset vista of the entire bay. From San Francisco: Drive across the Oakland–San Francisco Bay Bridge, follow the signs to Highway 24 toward Walnut Creek (via Interstate 580), go through the Caldecott Tunnel (stay to the far right), and exit immediately after the tunnel at Fish Ranch Road. (The exit turns sharply right, then right again over the freeway.) Drive up to the top of the hill on Fish Ranch Road, turn right at the stop sign onto Grizzly Peak Boulevard, and drive about a half-mile or so until you find a turnout that appeals to you (the view parking spots will be on your left). **(see p. 102)**

Hard Rock Cafe. Teenagers love the super-loud rock music, juicy hamburgers, and T-shirts that prove they've been there.... *Tel 415/885–1699. 1699 Van Ness Ave. (at Sacramento St.), California St. cable car, 1 MUNI bus. Reservations not accepted.* **(see p. 115)**

Harrington's. When original owner Leo Harrington died in 1959, a procession of motorcycle police led a mile-long cortege in his honor—that's how beloved this Irish bar is. The old building is wonderfully creaky and the floors have been known to get ankle-deep in green beer on St. Patrick's Day.... *Tel 415/392–7595. 245 Front St., California St. cable car.* **(see p. 113)**

Hello Gorgeous!! Streisand kitsch a-go-go, and all for sale.... *Tel 415/864–2678. 549 Castro St., Castro St., MUNI Metro stop. Admission charged.* **(see p. 110)**

I Can't Believe I Ate My Way Through Chinatown. Shirley Fong-Torres lets you in on a private tea ceremony, among other gustatory delights, before you reach your final destination: a huge Chinese luncheon.... *Tel 415/355–9657 or 800/281–9255. Admission charged.* **(see p. 116)**

The Italians of North Beach. This 4-hour tour is worth taking for one simple reason: It ends up with a full, multi-course lunch at Enrico's Sidewalk Cafe (see Dining). Host: GraceAnn Walden.... *Tel 415/397–8530. Saturdays only; during the week by prior arrangement. Admission charged.* **(see p. 116)**

Javawalk. Walk the coffee trail in Chinatown, Jackson Square, and North Beach with Elaine Sosa.... *Tel 415/673–9255. Admission charged.* **(see p. 116)**

Jewish Community Museum. This fine museum highlights important events in Jewish history, including the works of Jewish artists.... *Tel 415/543–2090 or 415/543–8880* *(recording). 121 Steuart St., Embarcadero BART/MUNI Metro station. Open Sun–Wed 11–5, Thur until 7 (closed on all Jewish holidays). Admission charged.* **(see p. 108)**

The Jungle. A huge indoor playground (15,000 square feet) where kids can crawl, jump, climb, and basically be kids.... *Tel 415/552–4386. 555 Ninth St. (above Toys R Us), Civic Center BART/MUNI Metro station. Open 10–9, Sat 9–9, Sun 10–8. Admission charged.* **(see p. 115)**

Keane Eyes Gallery. Portraits of small children with oversized heads and huge waifish eyes.... *Tel 415/922–9309. 651 Market St., 6, 7, 8, 9, 21, or 66 MUNI bus. Open Mon–Fri 10–6, Sat until 4. Admission free.* **(see p. 109)**

Lyle Tuttle's Tattoo Museum. Lyle Tuttle is the undisputed king of the San Francisco tattoo empire.His list of satisfied clients includes Gregg Allman, Cher, Joan Baez, and Peter Fonda.... *Tel 415/775–4991. 841 Columbus Ave., 15 or 30 MUNI bus. Open Mon–Thur noon–9, Fri and Sat until 10, Sun until 8. Admission free.* **(see p. 109)**

M. H. de Young Memorial Museum. This beautiful Golden Gate Park art museum hosts most of the major international shows that come to town, but is best known for an impressive collection of American art that dates back to the 1600s.... *Tel 415/750–3600 or 415/863–3330 (recording). Golden Gate Park, near Tenth Ave. and Fulton St., 44 MUNI bus. Open Thur–Sun 10–5, Wed until 8:45. Admission charged.* **(see pp. 105, 107)**

Marine World/Africa USA. Kiss a whale, let an exotic butterfly land on your nose, ride an elephant, feed a giraffe, or get soaked by a mighty splash from the tail of a gigantic killer whale in a million-gallon pool. The wildlife park is an hour from the city via high-speed Blue & Gold ferry from Pier 39; the fleet's package deal—round-trip ferry transportation, shuttle to the park, and all-day park admission—costs $36 adults, $30 seniors and ages 13–18, $20.50 ages 5–12, under 5 free. Reservations recommended.... *Tel 415/707–5555 (ferry information), 707/643–6722 (park information, including driving directions).* **(see p. 104)**

Maritime Museum. Kids like it because it looks like a life-size plaster model of a ship. Inside, the nautical exhibits—

models, relics, and other inanimate sailor stuff—might bore the youngsters, but the macramé knots are kind of fun for parents with a twinge of 1970s arts-and-crafts nostalgia.... *Tel 415/929–0202. Fisherman's Wharf, 901 Beach St., Powell-Hyde cable car, 15, 30, 42, or 69 MUNI bus. Open daily 10–5. Admission free.* **(see p. 107)**

Mexican Museum. Some people go for the huge permanent collection, others go for the changing exhibits that range from Diego Rivera to graffiti art. We go for the gift shop.... *Tel 415/441–0404. Fort Mason Center, Bldg. D, 28 MUNI bus. Open Wed–Sun noon–5. Admission charged.* **(see p. 108)**

Musée Mecanique. This ingenious little museum inside the Cliff House restaurant is full of mechanical gadgets you can actually play with, from player pianos and old carnival fortune-tellers to an entire miniature amusement park. Bring your own quarters.... *Tel 415/386–1170. 1090 Point Lobos Ave.; 18 or 38 MUNI bus. Open Mon–Fri 11–7, weekends 10–8. Admission free.* **(see p. 107)**

Museum of Modern Art. Opened in 1995, this ultramodern skylit structure set in the middle of the city's art center, South of Market, features major modern and postmodern artists, but the best part is its huge collection of art photography.... *Tel 415/357–4000. 151 Third St., Montgomery St. BART/MUNI Metro station, 15, 30, or 45 MUNI bus. Open Tue–Sun 11–6, Thur until 9. Admission charged.*
(see p. 106, 107)

Nick's. Located right on Fisherman's Wharf, Nick's funky sidewalk seafood stall recalls the way things used to be when the area was still a bustling wharf.... *Tel 415/929–1300. Fisherman's Wharf (Jefferson St.), 32 MUNI bus.* **(see p. 103)**

No Name Bar. The music is live (blues and jazz) and the rowdy baby boomers are always in the mood to dance, 7 nights a week.... *Tel 415/332–1392. 757 Bridgeway, Sausalito.*
(see p. 104)

North Beach Museum. Tucked away on the mezzanine of a small bank, this delightful little museum traces North Beach's history with photographs and artifacts dating back to the turn of the century. Call for schedule.... *Tel 415/ 391–6210. Eureka Federal Savings, 1435 Stockton St. (at*

Columbus Ave.); 15, 30, or 45 MUNI bus. Closed week-ends. Admission free. **(see p. 108)**

Old Mint Museum. The city's second mint is now a National Historic Landmark.... *Tel 415/744–6830. 88 Fifth St., Powell St. BART/MUNI Metro station. Open Mon–Fri 10–4. Admission free.* **(see p. 109)**

Palace of Fine Arts. This wonderful old building resembling a Roman ruin is home of the **Exploratorium** (see above) and the sole surviving structure from the 1915 Panama Pacific Exposition.... *Tel 415/567–6642. 3601 Lyon St., 30 MUNI bus. Open Tue–Sun 10–5.* **(see p. 106)**

Pier 23 Cafe. Great views of the bay and live jazz with no cover (5–8pm every night except Friday).... *Tel 415/362–5125. Pier 23 (the Embarcadero), 32 MUNI bus.* **(see p. 103)**

Pier 39. Basically a glorified shopping mall/carnival, but not so bad if you steer toward the sea lions (K-dock).... *Tel 415/705–5500; 15, 30, or 42 MUNI bus. Open Mon–Fri 9–5, longer on weekends.* **(see p. 103)**

Precita Eyes Mural Center. This community resource center for murals and muralists offers information, tours, and workshops.... *Tel 415/285–2287. 348 Precita Ave. (near Folsom St.), 27 MUNI bus. Tours Sat 1:30pm. Admission charged.* **(see p. 115)**

Rosicrucian Egyptian Museum. The West Coast's largest collection of Egyptian, Babylonian, and Assyrian antiquities: jewelry, pottery, tools, textiles, mummies, and funerary exotica....*Tel 408/947–3636. Park and Naglee Aves., San Jose. Admission charged.* **(see p. 110)**

San Francisco Zoological Gardens and Children's Zoo. At this 65-acre zoo, nothing can top Gorilla World, one of the world's largest assortments of the big guys. Other delights include the Children's Zoo, adjacent to the main park, where kids can pet baby animals in the zoo nursery or visit the Insect Zoo (more than 6,000 specimens).... *Tel 415/753–7080, 415/753–7083 (recording); Sloat Blvd. and 45th Ave., L Taraval MUNI Metro streetcar to the end of the line. Open daily 10–5, children's zoo 11–4.*

Admission charged, under 5 free; children's zoo, admission charged, under 3 free. Free first Wed of every month.

(see p. 115)

Santa Cruz Surfing Museum. Cowabunga! This beachside museum features surfboards (from the old redwood "planks" to today's high-tech designs), ancient wetsuits, photos, and other artifacts from 100 years of surfing.... *Tel 408/429–3429. Mark Abbott Memorial Lighthouse, West Cliff Dr., Santa Cruz. Admission charged.* **(see p. 110)**

Specs. This tiny brick-walled bar, a beatnik landmark, is cluttered with mementos including a whale's penis bone that hangs over the bar.... *Tel 415/421–4112. 12 Adler Place.* **(see p. 113)**

Steinhart Aquarium. Part of the California Academy of Sciences, the aquarium is one of the largest in the United States—more than 14,000 species. It's tough to say which is most popular with kids—the 10,000-gallon fish roundabout (a miniature ocean that surrounds you) or the feeding of the dolphins, seals, and penguins. There are also tidepools and a living coral reef.... *Tel 415/221–5100, 415/750–7145 for recorded information. California Academy of Sciences, Golden Gate Park, near Eighth Ave. and Lincoln Way, 44 MUNI bus. Open 10–5. Admission charged.* **(see p. 115)**

Tosca. Everyone who stays in San Francisco long enough eventually ends up at Tosca, where the jukebox plays Pavarotti and the cappuccino automatically comes with a shot of booze.... *Tel 415/986–9651 (pay phone). 252 Columbus Ave.; 15, 30 MUNI bus.* **(see p. 113)**

Vesuvio's. The list of poets who have spent hours at Vesuvio's getting anywhere from pleasantly buzzed to totally soused stretches from Dylan Thomas (soused) and his namesake Bob Dylan (buzzed) to Jack Kerouac (soused) and Allen Ginsberg (soused and buzzed).... *Tel 415/362–3370. 255 Columbus Ave.; 15, 30 MUNI bus.* **(see p. 113)**

Washington Square Bar & Grill. Whatever it is, it's already been done at the "Washbag"—weddings, wakes, funerals, deals, scandals—during the past quarter-century.... *Tel 415/982–8123. 1707 Powell St., 15, 30 MUNI bus.* **(see p. 113)**

getting

4

outside

At first glance, it
might seem that
San Franciscans'
favorite outdoor
activity is loung-
ing at sidewalk
cafes—a

respectable pastime, to be sure, though hardly a hallmark of physical fitness. But very little is as it seems in this unortho-dox city. A magnificent natural environment distinguishes it from most others, and even the most impassive urbanites eagerly embrace any diversion that takes place outdoors, from picnics to surfing. San Francisco may not be Montana or Wyoming, but there's still so much open space around it that cattle ranching remains a major industry in the East Bay. The Bay Area's public greenbelt—more than 860,000 acres of open land and watershed—is probably the largest of any major metropolitan center in the country, according to Greenbelt Alliance, a regional land conservation organiza-tion. Add undeveloped private land and there is easily more than 1,000,000 acres of open space in and around the city, with almost a third of that set aside as public park and recre-ation areas, including such huge, inviting parks as Golden Gate Park and the Presidio. There's a lot of fun stuff off-shore, too, on the islands that dot San Francisco Bay, some of which are just a short ferry ride from the heart of the city, and a great escape—so to speak—from the hubbub. And, of course, there is the spectacular **Golden Gate Bridge**, which you must walk across before you can truly claim to have seen San Francisco.

The Lowdown

Parks... Two dozen neighborhood parks within the city lim-its include facilities for baseball, basketball, barbecues, boating, bird-watching, bocce, bicycling, cricket, jogging, football, fishing, picnics, swimming, tennis, golf, soccer, volleyball, windsurfing, handball, and lawn bowling. Some even have gyms. **Golden Gate Park** covers 1,000 acres stretching from the Panhandle to the beach. Besides various major attractions covered in the Diversions chap-ter, it has 11 lakes, 2 waterfalls, 21 tennis courts, horse-back-riding stables (tel 415/668–7360, Kennedy Dr. and 36th Ave.), horseshoe pits (off Conservatory Way near Grove St.; bring your own horseshoes), a nine-hole golf course, fly-casting pools, a miniature yacht club, a 5-acre Japanese tea garden, a primitive garden featuring plants from the dinosaur era, and the very same polo grounds where Allen Ginsberg and Timothy Leary ushered in the Summer of Love at the first "Human Be-In" in 1967. If that's not enough, there's even a resident herd of bison at the Buffalo Paddock on John F. Kennedy Drive (parallel to 38th Avenue), adjacent to the Chain of Lakes. The breeding herd of *Bison bison* are particularly fond of stale bread tossed to them by passersby. The animals are the progeny of two cows, Sarah Bernhardt and Princess, and a bull named Ben Harrison, who were purchased by the city in 1890 and brought down from the Montana plains. Not far from the buffalo paddock is the Model Yacht Club Boat House, where miniature yachts are prepared for racing on Spreckels Lake by the second-oldest miniature yacht club in America, founded in 1901. Another goofy little wonder in the park is near the M. H. de Young Museum, off Tenth Avenue and Fulton Street. Called the Forgotten Works, it's a field of carved rocks (some hidden beneath the grass) which are actually part of the ruins of El Monasterio de Santa Maria de Avila, a monastery near Madrid, Spain, part of which was reassembled in the museum nearby. Another fun spot is **Marina Green**, a bayshore strip of park where you can listen to the **Wave Organ**, a bizarre contrivance made of different lengths of pipes that extend into the bay and resonate to the motion of the waves. (To reach the green from the Golden Gate Promenade, turn off at the St. Francis Yacht Club and take a short walk east past the lighthouse and the Golden Gate Yacht Club.) Sometimes it's so quiet you can barely hear it; other times it's like a soothing liquid mantra. Just west of Marina Green, the **Presidio**—where the city was originally founded as Yerba Buena in 1776—is now a national park, with spectacular views of the Golden Gate Bridge, beautiful hiking and biking trails, a fishing stream, and other diversions, not the least of which is the city's pet cemetery. At Crissy Field, at the west end of the Golden Gate Promenade in the Presidio, you can watch kite-flyers strut their stuff or windsurfers whizzing around on the bay. **Mountain Lake Park**, at the edge of the Presidio, has great running trails, four tennis courts, and fishing; **Lake Merced Park**, near the zoo and Fort Funston, has all the water sports you can imagine, plus two golf courses and lots of jogging trails. It's also the city's best park for bird-watching.

Stretching your legs... Some of the most beautiful—and least hilly—places to jog or walk in San Francisco are its promenades, which trace the shoreline of the bay from the Embarcadero's South Beach area to the foot of the Golden Gate Bridge at Fort Point. The 42 MUNI bus will drop you off near China Basin, a block from King Street and the Embarcadero, which is a good place to start your trek along the **South Promenade**. Heading north, you'll experience a stunning perspective change as you approach and then pass directly under the Oakland–San Francisco Bay Bridge. On your left, across the street, you'll see tempting sidewalk cafes and lush palm trees. On your right, nothing but a railing separates you from the bay itself. It's the most spectacular sea-level view in the city. At Pier 24, the **Waterfront Promenade** features a nearly mile-long staircase that leads down into the water and continues to the Ferry Building. On Saturdays, you may want to stop there and wander through the outdoor farmer's market at the Ferry Plaza (across from the Embarcadero, at the end of Market Street). If you continue along the Embarcadero, you'll pass Pier 39 on your right and end up at Fisherman's Wharf within $1\frac{1}{2}$ miles. **Golden Gate Promenade** starts at Aquatic Park/Fort Mason at the western edge of Fisherman's Wharf—the 28 MUNI bus route runs near the trail, so you can go one-way or round-trip, or stop anywhere along the way. The Golden Gate Promenade, which is marked by blue-and-white signs, ends at Fort Point, where steps lead up to the Golden Gate Bridge's pedestrian walkway; the entire route is less than 4 miles long (not counting the walk across the bridge), and is popular with cyclists, because of the beautiful views, varied terrain, and decided lack of automobile traffic. Heading west, there's a $2\frac{1}{2}$-mile parcourse loop for fitness buffs who aren't satisfied with a simple walk or jog, as the trail follows the seawall along the Marina Green. Look over your left shoulder and you'll see the Marin Headlands, Mount Tamalpais, Angel Island, and Alcatraz. When you get to the Palace of Fine Arts, you will have gone a bit more than $1\frac{1}{2}$ miles. Continue along the promenade to the St. Francis Yacht Club, where, if you want to distract yourself for a quiet moment, you can go east past the lighthouse and the Golden Gate Yacht Club to find the Wave Organ (see Parks, above). Head back out to the promenade, pass Crissy Field, and you'll have another mile to your credit.

From there, it's about 1 more mile to Fort Point; on a windy day, the ocean may spray its mist onto your face as you pass. On Sundays and holidays, **Golden Gate Park** is great for jogging; John F. Kennedy Drive is closed to vehicular traffic from 19th Avenue to Kezar Stadium—about $2^{1}/_{2}$–3 miles. To get there, take the N. Judah MUNI Metro streetcar or the 7 MUNI bus to Kezar, or the 5 MUNI bus to Park Presidio and Fulton Street, then walk into the park to John F. Kennedy Drive. You'll pass many potential diversions along the way, so just pretend it's a form of interval training and stop often to indulge yourself. Neighborhood parks with running trails include the 700-acre **Lake Merced** (tel 415/753–1101) at Harding Road off Skyline Boulevard, and the 15-acre **Mountain Lake Park** (tel 415/666–7005) at Lake Street and 12th Avenue. Slightly wacky joggers and walkers—two-, four-, or many-legged—are always welcome to join the **Bay to Breakers** in May, one of America's favorite footraces, when more than 100,000 revelers in goofy costumes make their way from the Embarcadero to the ocean. If you aren't in shape to run the distance (7.5 miles), you'll have plenty of company—most people walk, trot, dance, or just sort of drift along with the crowd. It's a popular race; register well in advance (call 415/296–7111 for info) to ensure getting your T-shirt at the finish line. There is no more intimate view of the city than the fantastic scenery along the route of the **San Francisco Marathon**, run in early July (register by June—call 415/3391–2123 or 800/722–3466), a time of year when the oddball weather here is generally pleasantly cool. The 26.2-mile race starts on the Golden Gate Bridge and winds past the Palace of Fine Arts and the Embarcadero, through Chinatown and Haight Ashbury, ending up at Kezar Stadium in Golden Gate Park.

Pedal pushing... There are two basic ways to ride a bicycle in San Francisco—laboring up the hills and coasting swiftly down the hills. Don't give up the idea, though. There are exceptions—most notably Golden Gate Park, the Great Highway, the Golden Gate Promenade, and the Golden Gate Bridge—which are relatively easy to ride and absolutely gorgeous to behold. The best time to ride in **Golden Gate Park** is ostensibly on Sunday, when John F. Kennedy Drive (7.5 miles) is closed to automobile traffic, but since that fact is well known to every cyclist, in-line skater, jogger, and baby stroller in the city, congestion can be a bit of a nuisance for cyclists, even without cars. A good alternative is to use the park during the week and steer clear of the area between Arguello Street and 19th Avenue, where most of the museums and other popular attractions are located. The **Great Highway**, from Ocean Beach (at the end of Golden Gate Park) to Lake Merced (turn right on Sloat Boulevard), is an easy 3-mile ride along the ocean on a flat sidewalk with three bike lanes. Add-ons: a 5-mile ride around Lake Merced or a 200-foot ascent on Point Lobos Avenue (near the Cliff House) on your return trip to the park. The most convenient bike rentals for these rides are at **Lincoln Cyclery** (tel 415/221–2415, 772 Stanyan St.) and **Park Cyclery** (tel 415/221–3777, 1749 Waller St.). The **Golden Gate Promenade**, from Aquatic Park/Fort Mason to Fort Point, is less than 4 miles of relatively easy riding if you don't give in to the temptation of the **Presidio**'s more challenging forest trails (15 miles) or the $1^{1}/_{2}$-mile ride across the **Golden Gate Bridge**, often against heavy winds. If you do cross the bridge—and you're still optimistic about developing thighs of steel—take the bike lane (parallel to Highway 101) from the Vista Point parking lot and turn off onto Alexander Avenue for a downhill jaunt to Sausalito, another 2 miles. Just remember: What goes down, must come up. You can rent bikes for these rides at **American Bicycle Rental** (tel 415/931–0234, 2715 Hyde St.). **Angel Island** is a good place to explore on two wheels. Take a ferry (see "Islands with a past" below) to the state park, then rent a mountain bike at Ayala Cove for $12–$17 per hour or $25–$40 per day (helmet included). There are about 8 miles of beginning and intermediate trails and many steeper advanced trails. If you decide to get around—or out of—the city on a bicycle, BART is a good option, since it allows cyclists to board on off-peak hours. Bike route maps and information are available from the **San Francisco Recreation and Park Department** (tel 415/831–2700) and the **East Bay Regional Park District** (tel 510/635–0135).

Working up a sweat... If you're staying at any of the city's major hotels, you're probably eligible for the special $10 daily guest package (regularly $15) at the state-of-the-art **Pinnacle Fitness Club**, voted best in the Bay Area by the

San Francisco Bay Guardian. This immaculate club with new and perfectly maintained equipment is frequented by locals as well as hotel guests; the majority tend be young (20–35), fitness-conscious professional types rather than bulky bodybuilders. The price is fantastic, but the only pool is a small lap pool at the Post Street location. The list of participating hotels is far too long to give here; ask your concierge or call one of the three facilities (tel 415/495–1939, 345 Spear St., near Embarcadero BART or MUNI Metro stops; tel 415/781–6400, 1 Post St., or tel 415/543–1110, 61 New Montgomery St., both near Montgomery St. BART or MUNI Metro stops). **North Point Health Club** (tel 415/989–1445, 2310 Powell St., near Fisherman's Wharf), a small, no-frills neighborhood gym with no pool, also welcomes drop-in visitors for $5 a day; separate hours for men and women. If you get the urge to pump iron in the middle of the night, there's always **24 Hour Fitness**, with five huge facilities in the city. You won't find many "gym rats" there, nor will you find many women in the middle of the night, but at other hours there's a fairly even mix of men and women, varied according to the neighborhood. Daily fee is $15 (tel 415/776–2200, 1200 Van Ness Ave.; tel 415/395–9595, 350 Bay St.; tel 415/543–7808, 2nd and Folsom Sts.; tel 415/334–1400, 1850 Ocean Ave.; and tel 415/434–5080, 100 California St.). The **Jewish Community Center** (tel 415/292–1220, 3200 California St. at Park Presidio) charges $10 a day at its facility, which has a pool and all the requisite exercise equipment—plus handball courts—but unfortunately exudes a funky chlorine-and-sweat smell. Of the city's four YMCA health clubs, the cream of the crop is the **Embarcadero YMCA** (tel 415/957–9622, 169 Steuart St., $12 a day), with a sparkling pool, state-of-the-art exercise equipment, and a spectacular view of the bay from the Lifecycle machines. During the week, the club is filled with financial district types—especially at lunchtime—but on weekends, you're likely to see locals just in from their morning espresso at a North Beach cafe.

Hitting the beach... Can we talk? Northern California ain't Hawaii, kids. The water is usually as cold as ice, the wind can be fierce enough to blow your tuna sandwich into the next person's picnic basket, and the summer sky is generally overcast—though it will give you a dreadful sunburn if you don't wear industrial-strength sunblock. So forget the idea of swaying palms and white-sand beaches. That's a different California. The rugged, cliffside beaches in San Francisco are some of the most spectacular in the world to look at. Huge waves crash against sheer walls of rock, but a treacherous undertow and unpredictable surf conditions make them dangerous for swimming.

Ocean Beach (at the end of Golden Gate Park, near the Cliff House) is surely the most dramatic seaside vista in the city—at least the sea lions that gather on Seal Rocks seem to think so—but it is absolutely forbidden to swim there. You can enjoy sunbathing, beachcombing, hiking, sipping a drink at the **Cliff House** (tel 415/386–3330, 1090 Pt. Lobos Ave.), but don't even think about dipping your little toe in the water. Swimming is also prohibited at **Land's End Beach** (north of the Cliff House), **Kirby Beach** (below the northern end of the Golden Gate Bridge), **Rodeo Beach** (at Fort Cronkite, Marin Headlands), and **Tennessee Beach** (north of Rodeo Beach), though beachcombing can be fun if you stay a safe distance from the water. There are safe swimming beaches in the city, if you can stand the cold water: **China Beach** (28th Ave. and Sea Cliff Dr.) and **Aquatic Park** (end of Hyde Street). Both are sandy coves where lifeguards are on duty during the summer; they're open April 15–October 15, 7am–dusk. More popular with adventurous locals is **Baker Beach**, where nude sunbathing is fashionable for both gay and straight sunbathers. Officially designated clothing-optional by the city, it's easily reached by public transportation (you might want to keep your clothes on while you're riding the bus). The truly gay men's section, according to that indispensable, outrageous local guide *Betty and Pansy's Severe Queer Review*, is beyond the large rock formations, which are most easily navigated at low tide. That part of the beach is definitely a cruise scene. The rest of the beach, however, has a predominant atmosphere of comfortable indifference to the fact that many people are not wearing clothes. Swimming is not prohibited but is definitely very dangerous and should be avoided. No lifeguards are on duty; there are changing rooms, which seem rather pointless when no one's wearing clothes anyway. The beach is open April 15–October 15, 7am–9pm. If you're around in September and want to meet some real-live local maniacs, get out your wetsuit and join in the 8am **Alcatraz Shark Fest**, a 1.5-mile swim from the Rock to the city shore. Believe it or not, it's a relatively popular event, so preregister (tel 415/868–1829). For beachcombing, tide-pool exploring, hiking, camping, or romantic bed-and-breakfast get-aways, a trip to **Point Reyes National Seashore** is without equal. At 65,000 acres, it's the largest and wildest section of the Bay Area's greenbelt—32,000 acres of designated wilderness. You may even be lucky enough to spot a great white shark out in the water. Point Reyes' beaches and tiny villages are accessible by Golden Gate Transit public transportation (tel 415/332–6600, TDD 415/257–4554), but are much easier to reach by car, less than an hour from the city.

Bathing in the buff: Beyond Baker Beach... While **Baker Beach** (see "Hitting the beach," above) is the most popular, three other city beaches are also clothing-optional—**Land's End**, **Fort Funston Beach**, and **Golden Gate Bridge Beach**—and bare-butt bathing is allowed at all Golden Gate National Recreation Area beaches as long as nobody complains (which they rarely do). Marin County's nude beaches are generally sunnier and less crowded than those in the city. The best is **Muir Beach** (Pacific Way, off US 1), where there is plenty of sand and privacy, but no cops or poison oak. The crowd is mixed—gay, straight, singles, families. Get there before 11:30 on weekends to find a parking lot space. On the other side of San Francisco, head south on US 1 past the town of Pacifica to **Devil's Slide**. Turn left onto the unmarked road 3 miles south of the Denny's restaurant in Linda Mar and you'll find an immaculate, privately operated beach. Gays, straights, singles, and families flock to this little cove, even though swimming in the freezing-cold water is dangerous and sharks occasionally have been spotted offshore. For weather conditions, call 415/728–5336. Privately operated **San Gregorio Beach** (about an hour south of San Francisco, near the junction of US 84 and US 101) claims to have been the first nude beach in America, established as clothing-optional in the 1930s. It's warm enough here to run around naked on the 2 miles of rolling sand as early as February, but it's often very windy with water usually too cold and dangerous for swimming. For details on these and other spots, consult the Northern California Nude beaches website (http://www.sfbg.com/Nude/nocal.html) or call 800/2BE–NUDE for the Western Sunbathing Region.

GETTING OUTSIDE | THE LOWDOWN

Poolside plunges... OK, the beaches weren't made for swimming, and not many of the hotels have pools, but if you really want to take off your summer cold-weather gear and dive in, the best poolside scene in the city is at **The Phoenix** (tel. 415/776–1380, 601 Eddy St.), where rock stars and their attendant groupies lounge, socialize, sip cocktails, and sometimes even swim—but you must be a hotel guest (or invited by one) to join in. The abstract mural on the bottom of the pool—painted by New York artist Francis Forienza—was almost outlawed by state inspectors, who insisted it was a hazard and claimed: "People have been hurt by art before." Ultimately the governor of California enacted a bill exempting the mural from an antiquated law that requires all pool bottoms to be painted white.

Water sports... You won't have to worry about dangerous murals lurking at the bottom of the bay when you go sea kayaking, windsurfing, sailing, or fishing. Watching the windsurfers on the bay just off Crissy Field, it's easy to forget there are skyscrapers a few minutes away. On an ideal day, the waves are high and the wind is strong enough to give advanced windsurfers a ride that would make anyone forget the stress of urban life; beginners should definitely stick with calmer waters. **Lake Merced** offers lessons and rentals through the **San Francisco School of Windsurfing** (tel 415/753–3235, 1 Harding Rd., Lake Merced and Candlestick State Park). All-day kayaking trips (weekends only) are definitely the up-close-and-personal way to enjoy the dramatic cliffs, secluded beaches, and unbelievable views on **Angel Island**—and you don't even have to know how to paddle. All trips are led by expert naturalists and require specific advance reservations; the $100 fee includes lunch. Paddlers may rent single kayaks for $15 the first hour and $10 per each additional hour; doubles rent for $30 the first hour and $10 per each additional hour. Contact **Sea Trek Ocean Kayaking Center** (tel 415/488–1000; fax 415/488–1707). Sailing is kind of a misnomer for what one does in a rented boat on **Stow Lake** in Golden Gate Park (tel 415/752–0347), but few things in life are more fun than getting in a pedal boat with someone else and simply pretending to pedal while your friend does all the work. At Stow Lake, you can also rent rowboats, which are especially suitable for afternoon trysts or for dressing up fancy and pretending you're in an Impressionist painting. If you're feeling sort of Hemingway-esque and you just have to get out on the bay in a real boat, both **Spinnaker Sailing** (tel 415/543–7333, Pier 40, South Beach Harbor) and **A Day on the Bay** (tel 415/922–0227, San Francisco Marina) offer sailing instruction and rentals. If you'd rather sip cocktails and let the captain sail the ship, there are dozens of charters, from dinner cruises to overnighters aboard yachts (see Diversions).

Reeling them in... If that Hemingway thing just won't go away, you could always pay your money and take your chances on a fishing boat. There are dozens of charters, but only one is owned and operated by a woman: **Wacky Jacky** (tel 415/586–9800). Skipper Jacky has been having a great time on the bay for 23 years, and her sense of humor makes even the most inexperienced angler have fun—and catch fish. A day on Jacky's sleek, fast 50-footer (board at Fisherman's Wharf at 5:30am, depart 6am, return 3pm) will cost around $75, including license, rod, tackle, and anything else you'll need to land a big fish. Here's an inside tip: When you choose a rod, ask for the Green Weenie. It has brought in so many big ones, Jacky is considering retiring it for good behavior.

For tasty little trout, **Lake Merced** is a good stop. The **Lake Merced Boating and Fishing Company** (tel 415/753–1101) can set you up with boats, rods and reels, bait, and licenses (California requires a state fishing license that costs $9.45 a day or $26.50 annually; Lake Merced charges an additional $4 for a daily use permit). And if the swoosh-swoosh-plop of a perfect flycast is your cup of tea, bring your own rod to the **Golden Gate Park Fly Casting Pools** (tel 415/386–2630, opposite the Buffalo Paddock off John F. Kennedy Drive), where tournament-level fly casters can be found practicing (ask them for pointers). Tuesdays, Saturdays, and Sundays are the best days; there's no fee, but then there are no fish here either—it's strictly for practice.

Par for the course... If you suddenly get the urge to sink one but you didn't bring your clubs, don't worry. The **Lincoln Park Golf Course** (tel 415/221–9911, 34th Ave. and Clement St., near the California Palace of the Legion of Honor) will rent you a set of clubs for $10 and send you out to try your luck on this 18-hole, par-68 course, where you may get distracted by the vista of the Pacific Ocean and the Golden Gate Bridge. Greens fees are $21 weekdays, $25 weekends; golf carts are $20. The **Golden Gate Park Course** (tel 415/221–9911, 47th Ave. and Fulton St.) is less challenging—9 holes, par 27, and 1,357 yards—but it's three blocks from the Pacific Ocean and is a great place to practice your swing and stay in shape without spending a fortune. Greens fees are just $8 weekdays, $11 weekends.

Lawn bowling... At the opposite end of the park, you'll find another delightfully peculiar sport—lawn bowling. Free lessons are offered at the **Golden Gate Park Bowling Green** (tel. 415/753–9298, just south of the tennis courts on Bowling Green Drive).

Islands with a past... Alcatraz is certainly the most commemorated of the San Francisco Bay's 14 islands—virtually every souvenir stand in the city sells a variety of tacky T-shirts proclaiming the wearer to be an inmate, escapee, or survivor of the notorious island prison, once home to folks like Al Capone and Machine Gun Kelly. But far from being a tourist trap, it's more like a set for a nightmarish Fellini movie co-authored by Stephen King—part bucolic Mediterranean island, part claustrophobic cell-block nightmare. Truly masochistic visitors can ask to be enclosed in deep six, a solitary confinement cell. After the prison was closed down, fitness guru Jack LaLanne once swam from Alcatraz to the city's shore handcuffed or blindfolded or both (who can remember?), perhaps inspiring today's Escape from Alcatraz triathlon, which originally included a bicycle ride to Marin County and a brutal Double Dipsea run over a twisted, mountainous course—better designed for billy goats—from Stinson Beach to Mill Valley and back. The race now finishes with a 12-mile run through the Golden Gate National Recreation Area, and has 500 competitors. Aside from morbid and/or historical fascination, however, the jagged island, 135 feet above the bay, is a surprisingly lovely spot for walking, with views of the city's skyline and the Golden Gate Bridge that are worth every penny of the $10 round-trip ferry ride (children $4.75, seniors

$8.25; ferries operated by Red & White Fleet, tel 800/ 229–2784 or 415/546–2700). Admission to the island park is free. Ferry reservations are suggested at least two weeks in advance during the summer.

Angel Island—a 640-acre state park with a 360-degree view of the bay from atop Mount Livermore (781 feet)—is a favorite with locals for cycling, hiking, sea-kayaking, and overnight camping, but, besides being a quarantine station and a Nike missile base, it was once a detention center for more than 175,000 Chinese and other Pacific Rim immigrants (1910–1940). It used to be nearly impossible to explore that immigration station, but now the park offers an open-air TramTour through the area, with a narrated history and aerial views that evoke audible sighs from passengers. The tram departs the Cove Cafe weekdays at 11, 12:30, and 2; weekends and holidays at 10:45, 11:15, noon, 12:30, 1:30, 2, 2:45, and 3:15. Fare is $9, $5 for children 5–12, $8 for seniors. Ferries to Angel Island, operated by Red & White Fleet (tel 800/229–2784 or 415/546–2700), cost $9 round-trip, $4.50 for children. For cycling information, see "Pedal pushing"; for kayaking, see "Water sports."

Fantasy islands... It takes a little more work to get to the bay's undiscovered islets, but if you want to see a part of outdoor San Francisco rarely experienced even by locals, it's worth the effort. **Brooks Island** is tough to get to; it is accessible only at high tide, and most people sail their own boats, though boatless travelers can make the trip with **California Canoe and Kayak** (tel 510/893–7833) for $89 per person (group of six or more; make reservations at least two weeks in advance). Why bother? Because it is a rare remaining example of a bay habitat, home to more than 100 species of birds. Views from a single picnic table at the 163-foot summit easily rival those of Angel Island. And you certainly won't have to stand in line with anyone wearing a My-Mom-Went-to-Frisco-and-All-I-Got-Was-This-Lousy-T-Shirt tank top. The bed-and-breakfast innkeepers on **East Brother Island** ferry visitors to the island in a tiny boat, but you have to go to the San Pablo Yacht Harbor (Point Molate exit off Highway 580, east of the Richmond–San Rafael Bridge) to catch it. A defunct lighthouse station (1874–1969) has now been replaced with an automated signal, and the elegant Victorian structures that once served as the light tower and signal building have been converted into a four-bedroom bed-and-breakfast. It's a wonderfully quiet (and often sunny) retreat from the city during the summer, but be warned: from October 1 to April 1, the foghorn sounds every 30 seconds. Day visits, 11–3:30, cost just $10 (bring your own picnic lunch). Reservations should be made a month in advance for day visits and six months in advance for overnight stays (tel 510/233–2385).

Day trips... You'll need a car to get to **Mount Diablo State Park** (tel 510/837–2525), but on a clear day you can see (almost) forever from the summit. It's not that high— 3,849 feet—but because of its positioning, you can see more of the earth's surface from there than from anywhere else in North America. It's not unusual to spot Mount Lassen, an active volcano more than 200 miles north, or towering Mount Shasta toward the Oregon border. You'll almost certainly be able to pick out San Francisco landmarks and all of the bridges that cross the bay, as well as the Farallone Islands afloat in the Pacific. The weather on inland Mount Diablo is more extreme than San Francisco's temperate coastal climate; in summer temperatures often hover in the 90-degree range, and in winter the mountain almost always gets a snowcap. Hike, picnic, or camp overnight if you want, but start off with this incredible summit view. The easiest way to get there from San Francisco is by car. Cross the Oakland– San Francisco Bay Bridge, then follow the signs to Walnut Creek (through the Caldecott Tunnel) and proceed on Highway 24 to Highway 680 north. Take the first exit—Ygnacio Valley Road—and turn right at the end of the exit onto Ygnacio Valley Road. You'll be in the middle of suburbia, but don't give up. Drive 1 1/2 miles and turn right onto Walnut Avenue, which runs into North Gate Road after 1 more mile. From there on, the drive is absolutely bucolic. Follow North Gate Road 7 windy miles up the side of the mountain to the park headquarters, where you will pay a $5 day use fee. From there it's a 4 1/2-mile drive to the summit parking lot and visitor information center. There are small telescopes on the summit tower's viewing deck.

On the other side of the bay, and only about half an hour from San Francisco, is another amazing natural wonder that shouldn't be missed—**Muir Woods National Monument** (tel 415/388–2595), an expanse of virgin redwood forest so beautiful and so quiet that you may never want to go back to the city. Some of the trees are more than 250 feet tall and many of them are 1,000 years old. When Ronald Reagan—a Southern California denizen—was governor of the state, he made redwood trees famous by declaring, "When you've seen one, you've seen 'em all." But the fact is, you'll never see even one unless you're in Northern California. They don't grow anywhere else, and they are unimaginably beautiful—towering, majestic, and as green as green ever gets. Muir Woods is accessible by Golden Gate Transit bus (tel 415/923–2000, TDD 415/257–4554) or by car. To drive there from San Francisco, cross the Golden Gate Bridge and continue on Highway 101 north to the Stinson Beach/Highway 1 exit. Follow Highway 1 for 3 miles to Panoramic Highway, then drive 1 more mile and turn left on Muir Woods Road. The parking lot is another 1½ miles down the road.

Point Reyes National Seashore (tel 415/663–1092), one of the most pristine coastal wilderness areas in California with more than a dozen beaches in 65,000 acres, is less than an hour's drive from San Francisco. It's separated from the mainland by the famous San Andreas Fault, the primary source of San Francisco's powerful earthquakes. Don't let that scare you, though; the epicenter of the last big tremor in 1989 was about 100 miles southeast. Still, it's fascinating to take the ¾-mile Earthquake Walk along the fault line when you first enter the 65,000-acre park (at Bear Valley). You can also wade while you watch hundreds of species of birds at Limantour Beach; swim, hike, and picnic at Tomales Bay; canoe at Abbotts Lagoon, where you may spot a herd of tule elk; picnic at Point Reyes North and South Beaches (the undertow and hammering surf make it too dangerous to swim there); picnic, sunbathe, and wade at Drake's Beach; walk down 300 steps to the Point Reyes Lighthouse for a close-up view of seals and sea lions; and hike the many beautiful trails that traverse the area. A word to the wise: High tides, pounding surf, and treacherous rip currents can make the ocean beaches extremely dangerous; get a map and a tide table from the visitors' center before you set out. Tomales Bay is definitely the best area for swimming, a protected cove with warmer water that's often sunny when the rest of the area is overcast; Heart's Desire Beach, Pebble Beach, and Indian Beach are also great for swimming. There are about two dozen cozy inns and cottages in the area, in case you decide to stay for dinner and a moonlight walk on the Pacific; **Point Reyes Lodging** (tel 415/663–1872) can set you up in any of them.

Soothing spas and marvelous massages... After all this energetic outdoor activity, you may have a sore muscle or two. If so, you couldn't be in a better place— one of the more pleasant aspects of San Francisco's health-conscious lifestyle is an abundance of certified massage therapists (licensed by the state) whose healing hands definitely outclass those magic fingers motel beds. Therapeutic massage is so popular in the Bay Area that many hotels, such as the **Miyako** in Japantown, offer it as part of their service packages. If your hotel isn't one of these, get thee to a spa and find out why Californians rave about hot tubs and aromatherapy and all those other things that Europeans and Asians brought to the Left Coast. A typical therapeutic massage incorporates Swedish, Shiatsu, reflexology, and sports techniques in a half-hour or hour session. The spa that's probably most recommended by locals to their out-of-town guests—but not yet discovered by throngs of weary tourists—is **Kabuki Hot Springs Spa and Shiatsu Center** (tel 415/922–6002 or 415/922–6000, 1750 Geary Blvd.) in Japantown. There are few—if any—misfortunes that a Kabuki back scrub, massage, and hot-tub soak can't cure. The ultimate San Francisco indulgence—at a very reasonable price—it has separate days for men and women (women's days are Sunday, Wednesday, and Friday; men are welcome Monday, Tuesday, Thursday, and Saturday). Their many packages range from $12 for hot-tub soaks and use of the communal spa facilities to $69 for back scrub, hot soak, sauna, steam room, 55-minute private Shiatsu massage, and full use of all spa facilities, which also include a cool plunge. If you want all of these spa services *and* one of the most beautiful urban resort settings in America, take BART just four stops across the bay to Rockridge and have a cab drop you off at the **Claremont Resort Hotel, Spa & Tennis Club** (tel 510/549–8566 for reservations, 510/843–3000 for information; Ashby and Domingo Aves., Oakland). This spectacular Victorian landmark hotel, nestled in 22 lush acres at the foot of the Oakland/Berkeley hills, is especially lovely during the summer—when San Francisco is foggy and cold, the Claremont is sunny and warm. The full-service European spa here offers nine different types of massage, seven body-care treatment packages (wraps, masks, scrubs, massages, Swiss showers, whirlpool baths), and many varieties of facials, skin-care and salon treatments, and fitness therapies, as well as packages that include use of the health club, swimming pools (huge, outdoors), and a spa lunch at their award-winning restaurant. As a bonus, tennis players who have scheduled spa treatments are allowed to use the tennis courts on an as-available basis. Reservations are a must—one to two weeks in advance for weekend visits—but midweek visits can often be arranged on the same day. The best package deal is the $99 Refresher, which includes an aroma bath, neck and shoulder massage, manicure or shampoo/blow dry, gift, lunch, and use of all facilities. On the north side of the bay, just 12 miles from the city, is **Tea Garden Springs** (tel 415/389–7123, 338 Miller Ave., Mill Valley), a holistic spa with a Chinese tea garden, where visitors are invited to sip a cup of calming tea or enjoy a vitalizing elixir before receiving massages or other treatments. The spa, designed in accordance with Feng Shui—the Chinese science of aesthetically and spiritually favorable architectural placement—is at the foot of Mount Tamalpais in Mill Valley, a sequoia-ringed village with more filmmakers and screenwriters per square inch than Hollywood. Even the most stressed-out movie producer would turn to putty after one of the Tea Garden Springs' 10 different types of Eastern and Western massages. What really sets this spa apart from the others is its many ancient Chinese practices and meticulous attention to aesthetic detail. Day visitors are welcome on a same-day basis, but reservations are recommended. Massages cost $40 to $78, depending upon the technique and duration; half-day retreats including several services and a meal are also available. If you don't want to go to a spa but would still like to experience the benefits of a therapeutic massage, don't call an escort service, where a massage generally means something quite different—instead, get a reliable referral from the American Massage Therapy Association (tel 800/696–2682).

5

ping

In San Francisco's
neighborhood
boutiques, the
glorious hodgepodge
of goods ranges
from merely wacky
to utterly

bizarre. Here lies the Bay Area's most memorable shopping. Vintage clothing, countercultural accoutrements, New Age paraphernalia, and all kinds of obscure books are the city's stock in trade, living up to San Francisco's reputation for the offbeat.

Then, of course, there's Union Square, where the city's conservative and classic side asserts itself with tiny department stores and designer boutiques. Refined little old ladies in prim white gloves still bemoan the loss of the landmark City of Paris building, on the corner of Stockton and Geary streets, which has been replaced by the modern Nieman Marcus store, but tradition is hardly threatened in this neighborhood.

Not much can be said for San Francisco's shopping centers and malls. With few exceptions, an afternoon at the Anchorage, the Cannery, the Crocker Galleria, or Pier 39 isn't all that different from an afternoon in any other well-groomed mall. Some of the stores are housed in historic buildings—just as they are in Denver, Seattle, Sacramento, and dozens of other cities' old-town areas—but the intrigue tends to end with the architecture.

Target Zones

Union Square (bordered by Kearny and Mason streets, from Market Street to Bush Street) is the stop for department stores and exclusive designer shops that rival the world's best. Even the larger stores offer courteous personal service and at least a couple of small cafes; Saks and Nieman Marcus still provide elegant lounges where female shoppers can freshen their lipstick and rest on comfy chairs when a quick trip to the toilet just isn't enough. Nearby **Maiden Lane**, a hidden 2-block alley that runs from Kearny Street to Stockton Street (between Geary and Post streets), continues to count Brooks Brothers and Chanel among its many upscale tenants.

Oh-so-prettified **Union Street** (between Van Ness Avenue and Steiner Street) has become rather old-hat and overpriced, a favorite haunt of well-heeled tourists and visiting suburbanites. Union Street's shops seem to sell stuff from everywhere but San Francisco—New York bagels, Seattle coffee, European clothes. It's also a great place to find top-quality children's clothing and toys.

Fillmore Street (between Post and Jackson streets), the nouveau-chic area that proclaims itself a five-star neighborhood on obnoxious yellow banners at every street corner, is on the verge of becoming the next Union Street. A few short years ago, when there were just a handful of interesting little shops and cafes—and **D & M Wine and Liquor Co.** (2200 Fillmore St.), the best wine store in the city, bar none—some of the merchants tried desperately to establish this small patch of real estate as part of wealthy Pacific Heights rather than the notoriously slummy Fillmore District. They succeeded. Now you have to wait in line to get a cup of coffee on a Sunday morning, the bars are jammed with *GQ*-model lookalikes, and the sidewalks are congested with yuppie baby strollers. Locals looking for something truly interesting to do look elsewhere.

Chinatown is one of the most popular neighborhoods among tourists, though the bounty to be found here is often of dubious value—tacky souvenirs made in Taiwan, jade jewelry at a discount, or XXX-rated fortune cookies. Hand-painted signs swear that everybody is going out of business and must sell everything at incredibly low prices right now. Sidewalk stalls are stuffed with every plastic and rubber item ever sold for less than $5. Herbalists sell dragon's blood and other exotic ingredients next to vegetable stands, jewelry stores, banks, and dim sum parlors. There are some fun bazaars, though, and the smells alone are worth the visit.

The **Hayes Valley** (Hayes Street between Franklin and Buchanan streets) is a happy byproduct of the 1989 earthquake, which brought down a nearby freeway and let the sunshine in. It's fun, hip, eclectic, friendly, and not yet full of itself. You can find local clothing designers, bead stores, vintage clothing, African artifacts, Mexican art and knickknacks, collectible furniture, junk stores, and tarot card readers, among other things.

Haight Street ain't what it used to be, but it's still quasi-psychedelic and filled with people and things you certainly won't see in Kansas. Vintage clothing stores are a big thing, but the value ranges from great deals on retro-fashions to ridiculously overpriced castoffs. Don't get caught paying $75 for a used Levi's jacket just because some guy with a mohawk cut the sleeves off it. If you're looking for avant-garde new clothing and shoes, this is the place. And if you're a man looking for a pair of shimmering red cha-cha heels in a perfect size 12, this may be the only place. Most of the shops are between Central and Stanyan streets.

North Beach will never leave you bored, with everything from beatnik bookstores and hippie poster shops to tattoo parlors and record stores. You can buy postcards, wigs, shoestrings, old clothes, new clothes, incense, bells, beads, crystals, jewelry, pasta machines, furniture, focaccia, and anything else you can imagine—even a new set of bocce balls.

The **Mission District** (between 16th and 24th streets) is a weird and wonderful place to shop, if you can handle being on two planets at once. Mission Street has the tightest cocktail dresses and shiniest spiked-heel shoes in town, alongside pure white confirmation and wedding dresses. Valencia Street sells used books and new vibrators, candles for Catholic and other rituals, expensive clothes that look like they've already been through the ringer, antiques, and thrift-shop treasures.

Bargain Hunting

San Francisco is loaded with thrift stores and secondhand clothing stores, which may be good sources for bargains (though prices on vintage clothing, which can be very hip, can also be steep). Haight Street is a prime area for all this. (Also see "Recycled regalia" and "Cheap thrills," below.) For discounts on all kinds of new merchandise, there are more than 40 factory outlets South of Market—you really need a guide to hit them all. It's easier if you take the mall approach—start at **Yerba Buena Square** (tel 415/974–5136, 899 Howard St.; near Montgomery St. BART stop or 15, 30, 45 MUNI buses), the city's largest off-price mall, for another 100,000 square feet of bargains. (Also see "In the outlets" below.)

Trading with the Natives

San Francisco's merchants are by and large well-disposed toward out-of-towners. All major department stores will hold merchandise for a reasonable amount of time and will ship your packages home for you. (If you live out of state you won't have to pay sales tax.) Most will accept your personal check if you have proper identification, such as a driver's license with photo; it is illegal to ask for a credit card as a form of identification. Some small stores may not accept out-of-state checks, but as a rule, paying by check is not a problem in the Bay Area. It's not common practice to negotiate prices unless you're at a flea market, garage sale, or used-car lot, but it's always acceptable to point out a flaw or defect and ask for a reduction in price. (Whether you get it is up to the sales staff.) Most department stores will automatically give you 10 to 20% off for a broken zipper, missing button, or similar problem; smaller stores vary in their policies. Stores are not required to give refunds if you're not satisfied with your purchase—many stores will, though some will offer it only in the form of exchange credit. Stores cannot charge an extra fee for credit-card purchases, but they may offer a discount for cash payment.

Hours of Business
Most stores tend to open around 10 or 11am (noon on Sundays) and close up at times that suit the neighborhood and clientele. Department stores, for instance, usually stay open through early evening, while many neighborhood boutiques and bookstores don't close until 10 or 11 at night. Most are open seven days a week—the Index below notes if they're not.

Sales Tax
A sales tax of 8.5% is added to every purchase unless the store ships it out of state for you. This is a state tax, with a .25% surcharge for rapid-transit subsidy; some outlying areas don't include this surcharge, leaving the tax at 8.25%. To make matters more confusing, some items—including just about anything edible—are not taxable.

The Lowdown

Shopping bags to show off... When shopping in Union Square's exclusive stores, it's always wise to carry a shopping bag that proves you're buying—not just looking—and therefore deserve deferential treatment. Post Street is heaven for bourgeois bags; you can start small, with a cigar from **Alfred Dunhill of London** (250) or a few pieces of candy from **Saks Fifth Avenue** (384), so long as you get a nice big bag to carry it in. Then carry the bag with the logo in full view as you work your way down Post Street, visiting **Tiffany and Co.** (350), **Cartier** (231), **Louis Vuitton** (230), **Burberry's** (225), **Brooks Brothers** (201), **Gump's** (135), or **The Polo Store/Ralph Lauren** (90).

Are you being served?... The best service in town is definitely proffered by **Nordstrom**, in the San Francisco Centre. While you relax in the fitting room, sales assistants will run up and down the store's five floors to find a blouse in the exact shade of ivory that flatters your face and matches the navy skirt you're thinking about buying. They'll keep a customer card on file if you have particular needs and intend to return some other time. If that's not enough to make you feel pampered, Nordstrom's has a full-service European spa and four restaurants.

One-stop shopping... Hit the department stores. There's no shame in shopping at **Macy's**, especially now that it's got an entire building devoted strictly to men. Plus, there are almost always sales and clearance racks in every department. The other big department stores are **Neiman Marcus**, the super-upscale Texas store that's sometimes bigger on price than taste (it does offer a fur salon for those who aren't afraid of being pelted by animal-rights activists); **Saks Fifth Avenue**, where the sales staff can sometimes be a bit too uppity for the rather pedestrian merchandise on display; and, as mentioned above, **Nordstrom**, which is the most fun of any of them.

For foot fetishists... Nordstrom probably has the largest selection of women's and men's shoes in the city, in prices ranging from very reasonable to check-your-credit-limit. If expensive isn't a scary concept to you, head to **Kenneth Cole** (in the San Francisco Centre, the same mall as Nordstrom) for trendy, high-fashion shoes, or to **Stephane Kelian** (Crocker Galleria) for the most popular shoes made in Paris. **Gimme Shoes** on Hayes Street sells funky new designs from Belgium and France. The **Shoe Loft** offers designer shoes at a hefty discount and **McB's Shoes** (which recently moved a few BART stops away, to Oakland) specializes in unusual sizes, from 9 AAAAA to 14 EE (drag queen alert). **East West Leather** in North Beach has cowboy boots galore. And don't forget those sensible shoes: Get 'em at **Ria's**, **Birkenstock Natural Footwear**, and **First Step**.

If it's July, you're going to need a sweater... **Dreamweaver** has fluffy American handknits to die for; **395 Sutter** sells hand-loomed knits; **Tse Cashmere** features rich colors and luxurious 10-ply handknits; **House of Cashmere** is just what its name implies; and **Irish Castle Shop** has fisherman-knit sweaters and the claim to fame of having served Sinead O'Connor in the past.

For men who want to look like Cary Grant... It's tough to go wrong at **Wilkes-Bashford**, whose small line of impeccably tailored clothing has served as a mark of distinction in San Francisco for more than 30 years.

Sulka has been selling its exclusive clothes for 100 years—if you want to out-Cary Cary, snag a pair of gorgeous Sulka pajamas ("pyjamas," as they spell it) and make sure you are seen in them. **Courtoué** features both classic and avant-garde Italian designers and made-to-measure tailoring. If the tailoring idea appeals to you but you're in a rush, try **David Stephen**, a mostly sportswear store that offers same-day alterations.

For men who'd rather look like Lou Reed than Cary Grant... Rolo SF, **Dinostore**, and **Daljeets** will outfit you in off-the-rack alternative styles suitable for clubs, cafes, or taking a little walk on the wild side. **Citizen** is a bit more elegant, but still a good bet for hip men's clothes that you won't find in department stores, including a small selection of shoes. For specially designed clothes from Michael Cronan, stop by **Cronan Artefact** (South of Market), which features what it calls threshold attire. A less pretentious description might be "clothing for both work and play," but you're talking capital-D designer here.

If you can't make it to Hong Kong, but you're into custom-made shirts... The California Gentleman by Astanboos makes dress and casual shirts on the premises; a staff person will come to your hotel if you prefer. They also make suits and ties, and blouses for women. **Patrick James** also does custom shirts and clothing, and offers tailoring and alterations for the lifetime of the garment.

If you simply can't live without a feather boa and a new tiara... Go right to **Piedmont Boutique** in the Haight, where drag queens, strippers, and ultra-hip high-school girls buy their velvet-and-feather bell-bottoms, sequined micro-mini-skirts, and long chartreuse gloves. When you see Piedmont's wall of earrings (more than 18,000 pairs in stock) starting at a mere $2, and racks of fishnets and other outlandish tights, you'll know why Sister Dana van Inquity, one of the drag nuns in the Sisters of Perpetual Indulgence, prays, "Please, God, let only my seams be straight."

Recycled regalia... We're not talking flannel shirts and dirty hair—that's Seattle's fashion problem—we're talking the hottest street couture around. Haight Street is the used-clothing mecca of San Francisco. The best prices are at **Buffalo Exchange** (1555), where you can also sell your clothes for cash or trade. **Aardvark's Odd Ark** (1501) has a huge and fairly boring collection, but it's good for simple items like jeans and vests. **Wasteland** (1660) is staffed by inattentive young hipsters who seem truly impressed with the loud music, high prices, and each other. You can occasionally find something great, but most of the ordinary stuff here is overpriced. Upscale **La Rosa** (1773) is the Saks Fifth Avenue of the Haight Street vintage stores. Meanwhile, in other parts of the city: **American Rag Compagnie** has already sorted through the maybe rack and trimmed its stock down to the most desirable items; **Clothes Contact** sells clothing by the pound, which sounds terrific until you put an old leather jacket on the scale and see how much it weighs; **560 Hayes** sells high-end vintage clothing, much of which was bought from old stores' unsold stock and has never been worn. **Guys and Dolls** is the place to buy a used tuxedo and all the accessories to go with it.

Cheap thrills: nonprofit thrift shops... The trouble with thrift shops is that you could spend your entire vacation combing them and never turn up a thing, or you could spend an hour in one place and come out with the outfit of the century for a couple of dollars. There's no way to predict, but if a scavenger hunt appeals to you, try these favorites: **Goodwill Stores** (nine locations); **Community Thrift Store**; **Repeat Performance**; and **Thrift Town**.

In the outlets... Among the city's many outlet stores, here are three of the best: the **Esprit Outlet Store**, where the bargain bins are not to be missed; **North Face Factory Outlet** store, one of California's top outdoor-gear manufacturers; and **Gunne Sax Discount Outlet**, a gem tucked away in an alley and full of frilly prom dresses and Jessica McClintock designer clothes at prices that tempt you to buy one of each.

Politically correct splurges... If you're ambling along Hayes Street and you come across a store that looks like Martha Stewart's ecologically correct attic, you're probably at **Worldware**, where you can get sheets and towels made from organically grown cotton and linen, as well as housewares made of exotic hardwoods from sustainable forests. The goods are actually very nice, but they're rather expensive, and the atmosphere is a bit contrived. **Global Exchange** is part of a national network that buys crafts from third-world countries and pays the artisans roughly 40% of the retail price—far more than most importers share. Pick up that voodoo wall hanging you've always wanted, and you can sleep well knowing you've helped a Haitian artist pay the rent. **PlaNetweavers Treasure Store**, a UNICEF store in the Haight, also sells crafts made by indigenous people around the world and doesn't rip them off in the process. The prices can be higher than some of the large import chains, but proceeds directly benefit UNICEF's programs to fight hunger and disease among the world's children.

Crystals and other assorted New Age voodoo... What else would you expect from a city with a gigantic pyramid in the middle of its financial district? **Crystal Way** specializes in crystals, and will arrange psychic or tarot card readings for you by appointment. **Lady Luck Candle Shop** will supply you with candles and other ritual objects you might need. **Curios and Candles** caters to middle-aged mystics and adolescent pagans in search of doves' eyes, newt's bones, and other essential spell-casting ingredients. It also offers the usual assortment of New Age aromatherapy oils, candles, incense, herbs, and occult books. Get a tarot reading while you're there.

Baubles, bangles, and beads... Be an artist for a day, or at least a wild-and-crazy jewelry maker. When you visit the **Magical Trinket**, you'll find loads of beads, as well as a staff of artisans willing to help you make your own necklaces and earrings, or even make hand-blown glass beads that are truly works of art. Call far in advance (see Index below) to register for a weekend bead-making class, limited to three students. **The Bead Store** is worth a visit to check out the sacred statues and ethnic jewelry; **African Safari** has beads to use in hair braiding; **Gargoyle Beads** specializes in Czech beads; **General Bead** is huge—3,000 square feet—and offers many closeouts at bargain prices; and **Yone of San Francisco** in North Beach is hailed by locals for its unusual beads.

Goofatoriums... (or is that goofatoria?) San Franciscans pride themselves on being a bit off-center, and many of the city's small stores go out of their way to milk that image. The dusty, doodad-crammed Schlock Shop, a North Beach institution, closed its doors in 1996, but **Quantity Postcards** is still alive and well across the street, still selling just one thing: postcards. This is the largest, goofiest collection you'll find anywhere—more than 10,000 different cards. Don't miss the Swingin' Fifties party cards (great for last-minute invitations) or the ridiculous dirty joke section. Buy a card here, if only to get a close-up look at the funky cash register. Across town in the Haight, **The Mascara Club** also has a cash register worth seeing (a fortune-teller model). The store's main shtick seems to be Mexican Day of the Dead paraphernalia—you're greeted by a 10-foot-tall papier maché skeleton when you enter—but the whimsical merchandise ranges from skull boxes and ash trays to those bob-bob-bobbing hula dolls for the car dashboard. While you're there, check out the shrine to Elvis, Marilyn Monroe, and James Dean. At first, Upper Market's **Paxton Gate** seems to be a high-end gardening store—until you spot the mounted insects and glass eyes used for taxidermy. Then comes the kicker, the collection that recently has made the store a huge favorite among avant-garde gift-givers: stuffed mice (real, dead mice) dressed up in costumes as Hamlet, the Pope, and many other "seasonal favorites." No doubt about it, you're nowhere near Kansas anymore.

Gumby for grown-ups... You don't have to be Jack Nicholson to know that all work and no play makes Jack a dull boy. Toys for adults are a booming business, and San Francisco sells its share. **Uncle Mame** is Upper Market's one-stop shop for everything your parents wouldn't buy you when you were a kid—that bad-ass G.I. Joe with the Kung Fu grip, or "collectible" boxes of sticky sugar-coated cereal. Uncle Mame claims to have the West Coast's largest collection of currently available Pez dispensers; one of the first things you see when you walk in is a miniature football stadium made of hundreds of unwrapped Pez candies. **The Scairy Hairy Toy Company** is actually a Mission District artists' studio with a toy store in front. Co-owner Flower Frankenstein (yes, that really is her name) created one of the store's most popular items, a game called "Voodoo You Love" that was named Best Way to Get Over an Ex by the *San Francisco Bay Guardian*. It comes with, naturally, a voodoo doll and pins. While not technically a toy store, Union Square's **Globetrotter** offers a complete library of beautifully illustrated books about the European comic-book adventurers Tin Tin and Asterix; it's the only official Tin Tin store in the United States. It stocks the books in a variety of language, along with watches, luggage, clocks, and collectibles. The staff is helpful and friendly, and there are bean-bag chairs up front to curl up in as you read.

If you've got an itch for leather... North Beach **Leather** is probably the city's most famous manufacturer of stylish leather clothing for men and women. The quality and prices are high, but the workmanship is unbeatable, and jackets can be custom-made for hard-to-fit customers. If, however, your interests tend toward leather in its more exotic sense, head for **Stormy Leather**, which bills itself as San Francisco's premier erotic-fetish boutique. It never disappoints the whip-and-chain crowd. **A Taste of Leather** deals in adult items including leather toys and body jewelry.

Everything you ever wanted to know about sex... Don't be afraid to ask at **Good Vibrations**, an airy, comfortable bookstore/sex-toy shop owned and run by women. Their mail-order business has become one of the most successful in the country, but this flagship store in the Mission District is still small, personal, and as far from sleazy as you could possibly get. The clientele is primarily women, but the books and toys are for both sexes.

Or sexy underwear... Now that the Wonder Bra has taken the term "flat-chested" out of the popular American dictionary, you can walk into any K-Mart and buy seductive lingerie that once would've been found only at Frederick's of Hollywood. Still, there's something delicious about a small underwear boutique. Some of the city's most conventional-seeming yuppies prefer the more discreet service of **Romantasy**, where sex games, love oils, and other implements of sensual pleasure are sold along with the lace teddies and bustiers. Carol Doda, for years queen of the city's premier strip joint, the Condor, now sells all the expected sexy stuff for women at **Carol Doda's Champagne and Lace Lingerie Boutique**, along with some racier inducements for both sexes, including see-through underwear and G-strings for men, stripper's accouterments, and other fun little objets d'amour. A visit to **Backseat Betty** makes lacy push-up bras seem ho-hum—this store is for people who think sex is fun, and looking sexy even more fun. Yeah, yeah, yeah, there's all the rubber and latex stuff, but the basic mode is Cher, all the way.

Uncommon scents... **Jacqueline Perfumery** has the best selection of scents in the city, including some French perfumes that aren't available anywhere else in the United States. If you don't know what you want, ask her for a suggestion; her olfactory intuition is uncanny. Check your bag when you get back to your hotel—Jacqueline has been known to tuck in samples of expensive and exotic perfumes with customers' purchases.

Sweets to go... At **Joseph Schmidt Confections**, feast your senses on the most delectable chocolate sculptures in the Western world. Buy at least a truffle or two (your taste buds will worship you for it), and do not miss the ever-changing, elaborate window displays. While you're there, step across 16th Street and peek at the outdoor mural entitled *La Madre Tonantsin*, to get in the mood for a trip to the **Pacitas Bakery** for *pan dulce*, sugary pastries in the Central American tradition, and *bolillos*, yummy little torpedo-shaped rolls that are especially wonderful dunked in Mexican hot chocolate. **Just Desserts** is full of fabulous, fattening goodies at all its six locations, including an award-winning chocolate fudge cake that will put you on a sugar-high for hours (especially if you down it with a double cappuccino, as many locals do). For more organic types, Just Desserts also owns **Tassajara Cafe & Bakery**, featuring breads, muffins, and cakes that seem far too delicious to be good for you. A favorite takeout bakery item is the sourdough *batard*, a luscious and tangy French-style round bread.

Italian treats to go... Just about any cafe in North Beach has great pastries, but **Stella Pastry & Caffe** has all that and *La Sacripantina,* too. Owner Frank Santucci will be happy to tell you about the patent he has on this puffy, sweet dessert that's one of Luciano Pavarotti's favorite confections. **Dianda's Italian American Pastry** has the best Italian cakes; **Danilo Bakery** bakes breads, *panettone*, tortes, and cookies for many of the top local restaurants; and **Italian French Baking Co.** still uses a brick oven and makes the best hand-rolled bread sticks you'll ever taste. While you're in North Beach, stop by the landmark deli **Molinari's** for a classic selection of Italian grocery and deli items; the old Italian locals shop there daily. Oddly enough, another great Italian deli is in the Mission District: **Lucca Ravioli Co.**, a traditional full-service deli with good-humored employees in white aprons. Their takeout sandwiches are superb and inexpensive.

The best deal on the best bubbly... Don't even bother shopping around. The staff at **D & M Wine and Liquor Co.** is friendly, funny, and more knowledgeable than all the wine editors in the country combined. They have the largest selection of champagne in the U.S. and will steer you away from overpriced status wines to lesser-known and cheaper ones that will make you think you've died and floated away to heaven. Every wine in the store has been tasted by the staff—all of whom are inveterate oenophiles—and you can be absolutely certain that any bottle they suggest will meet your expectations, and then some. Their latest addition to the gourmet intoxicants repertoire is single-malt Scotch, of which they have the best selection in town.

Kid stuff... You probably won't see Tom Hanks running up and down a gigantic keyboard at **FAO Schwarz** like he did in the movie *Big*, but this branch of the famous New York store is still a fantasyland for toy-lovers. Other great toy spots include **Jeffrey's Toys**, **Kinder Toys**, **Sanrio at Union Square**, and **Basic Brown Bear**, where you can see teddy bears being made and even stuff your own, if you like. If you go in for designer clothing for kids, try **Dottie Doolittle** or **Minis By Profili**.

Words, words, words... A Clean Well-Lighted Place For Books is a favorite of author Armistead Maupin (*Tales of the City*); **The Booksmith** boasts more than 1,000 foreign and domestic magazines and newspapers; **City Lights Bookstore** is Lawrence Ferlinghetti's legendary beatnik haunt; **A Different Light** is the foremost gay and lesbian bookstore in the city, as well as a resource center for gay information. **The Anonymous Place** carries 12-step recovery books; **The Buddhist Bookstore** represents many Buddhist traditions and also offers altar supplies; **Forever After Books** sells used books on spirituality, psychology, health, history, true crime, and other assorted topics. **McDonald's Bookshop** has more than a million used books and can get you a copy of *Life* published when you were born. **Dog Eared Books** is a great place to pick up some reading material—check out the Lust and Desire section before you settle in for an espresso at one of the neighboring cafes; **Argonaut Book Shop** is a rare-book shop that specializes in California history. The **Sierra Club Bookstore** offers field, trail, and travel guides, as well as its collection of environmental books.

In search of 12-inch vinyl... If you're one of those people who understands the magic of a phonograph needle dropping softly into a groove, you're in luck. San Francisco has several record stores that still sell records: **Streetlight Records**; **The Record Finder**; and **Medium Rare Records**.

Music meccas... Every city in America has plenty of stores that sell compact discs and cassette tapes, but San Francisco's music stores boldly go into musical niches that the MTV nation barely dreams of. **Open Mind Music**, for instance, is a clothing/music emporium that features "cool collectibles and the esoteric." **Let It Be** carries Beatles memorabilia, rare and out-of-print records, collectibles, and concert items. For Latin and salsa, **Discolandia** is a good bet—you'll hear the music long before you get close enough to see the Latin/psychedelic/airbrush/jukebox storefront. **Amoeba Music** in Berkeley has more than 30,000 used CDs, plus original Fillmore and Avalon concert posters from the sixties; **Mod Lang**, also in Berkeley, features imports, indies, acid jazz, ambient, trance, and reissues; Oakland's **Saturn Records** has an eclectic collection in one of the most fun walking neighborhoods (Rockridge) in the East Bay; and the **Groove Yard**, also in Oakland, specializes in jazz, blues, and soul. Oakland is the blues capital of the West Coast, so get over there and groove.

The Index

A Clean Well-Lighted Place For Books. This independent bookstore has a very helpful and informed staff; they will ship internationally.... *Tel 415/441–6670. 601 Van Ness Ave., Opera Plaza, Civic Center BART station.***(see p. 157)**

A Different Light. Gay and lesbian literature, magazines, and community resource information are sold here by a friendly staff.... *Tel 415/431–0891. 489 Castro St., Castro St. MUNI Metro station (K,L,M). Open 10am–midnight.* **(see p. 158)**

A Taste of Leather. Adult and custom-leather items.... *Tel 415/252–9166. 317A 10th St. at Folsom St., south of Market St., 42 MUNI bus.* **(see p. 155)**

Aardvark's Odd Ark. This huge store sells used clothing in current styles. It's not as eccentric as some other Haight Street shops.... *Tel 415/621–3141. 1501 Haight St., 7 MUNI bus.* **(see p. 152)**

African Safari. Beads for hair braiding are sold here, wholesale and retail.... *Tel 415/922–2899. 1221 Divisidero St. between Eddy and Ellis Sts., Western Addition, 5, 38 MUNI buses. Closed Sun–Mon.* **(see p. 153)**

Alfred Dunhill of London. Too bad San Francisco is so anti-smoking—there's nothing like a Dunhill lighter to make you feel decadently luxurious.... *Tel 415/781–3368. 250 Post St., Union Square, Powell St. BART station.* **(see p. 149)**

American Rag Compagnie. Stylish, contemporary secondhand and vintage clothing—and not cheap. The staff ranges from friendly to way-too-hip.... *Tel 415/441-0537. 1305 Van Ness St. between Sutter and Bush Sts., 42 MUNI bus, California St. cable car.* **(see p. 152)**

...

Amoeba Music. This Berkeley store—voted best in the Bay Area by the *Guardian*—has a huge selection of used CDs.... *Tel 510/549–1125. 2455 Telegraph Ave., Berkeley, Berkeley BART station.* **(see p. 158)**

The Anonymous Place. The specialty here is 12-step recovery books and gifts—sold by a supportive staff, as one might well imagine.... *Tel 415/923–0248. 1885A Lombard St., 28, 30 MUNI buses. Closed Sun.* **(see p. 158)**

Argonaut Book Shop. Fine and rare books and manuscripts are bought and sold here, especially volumes on California history. Established in 1941.... *Tel 415/474–9067. 786 Sutter St. at Jones St., Union Square, Powell St. BART station. Closed Sun.* **(see p. 158)**

Backseat Betty. Naughty underthings and outerwear for contemporary sex kittens.... *Tel 415/431–8393. 1584 Haight St., 7 MUNI bus.* **(see p. 156)**

Basic Brown Bear. Kids love this teddy-bear factory. Discount prices.... *Tel 415/626–0781, 444 DeHaro, Potrero Hill; 2801 Leavenworth, the Cannery, 30, 42 MUNI buses or Powell-Hyde, Powell-Mason cable cars.* **(see p. 157)**

The Bead Store. Come here for beads, sacred statues, ethnic jewelry.... *Tel 415/861–7332. 417 Castro St. at Market St., Castro St. MUNI Metro station.* **(see p. 153)**

Birkenstock Natural Footwear. Comfort shoes, California-style.... *Tel 415/776–5225. 1815 Polk St. at Washington St., 42 MUNI bus or Powell-Hyde cable car.* **(see p. 150)**

The Booksmith. A source for lots of books and a huge selection of domestic and foreign magazines and newspapers. Knowledgeable staff.... *Tel 415/863–8688. 1644 Haight St., 7 MUNI bus.* **(see p. 157)**

Brooks Brothers. In any word association game, definitely traditional, but not as stodgy as you might think. Men's, women's, and boys' clothing.... *Tel 415/397–4500. 201 Post St., Union Square, Powell St. BART station.* **(see p. 149)**

The Buddhist Bookstore. As the name suggests—a source for Pure Land, Zen, Tibetan literature. Altar supplies and gifts, too.... *Tel 415/776–7877. 1710 Octavia St. between Bush and Pine Sts., near Japantown, 38 MUNI bus. Closed Sun.* **(see p. 158)**

Buffalo Exchange. Come here for stylish used clothing in new condition—hip street fashions at very good prices.... *Tel 415/431–7733, 1555 Haight St., 7 MUNI bus, tel 415/ 346–5726, 1800 Polk St.* **(see p. 161)**

Burberry's. The famous Burberry plaid, inside raincoats and all over clothing, luggage, and other wearables....*Tel 415/ 392–2200. 225 Post St., Union Square, Powell St. BART station.* **(see p. 149)**

The California Gentleman by Astanboos. This custom clothier makes dress and casual shirts and suits for men and women.... *Tel 415/781–8989 or 800/697–4478. 490 Post St. Rm. 336, Union Square; Powell St. BART station. Closed weekends.* **(see p. 151)**

Carol Doda's Champagne and Lace Lingerie Boutique. San Francisco's No. 1 stripper sells some of the sexiest women's and men's underthings in town.... *Tel 415/776– 6900. 1850 Union St. #1, the Courtyard, 45 MUNI bus.* **(see p. 156)**

Cartier. Exclusive timepieces and fine jewelry.... *Tel 415/397–3180. 231 Post St., Union Square, Powell St. BART station. Closed Sun.* **(see p. 149)**

Citizen. The racks here are full of urban contemporary clothing for men—pricey, but worth it.... *Tel 415/558–9429. 536 Castro St., Castro St. MUNI Metro station.* **(see p. 151)**

City Lights Bookstore. The legendary beatnik hangout and bookstore.... *Tel 415/362–8193. 261 Columbus Ave., North Beach, 15, 30 MUNI buses. Open 10am–11:45pm daily.* **(see p. 157)**

Clothes Contact. Used clothing is sold here for $6 per pound. Lots of leather jackets.... *Tel 415/621–3212. 473 Valencia St., Mission District, 16th St. BART station.* **(see p. 152)**

Community Thrift Store. It's sort of junky, but there's a great book and record section here.... *Tel 415/861–4910. 625*

Valencia St., Mission District, 16th St. BART station.
(see p. 152)

Courtoué. Beautiful Italian designer clothing for men, classic to avant-garde.... *Tel 415/775–2900. 459 Geary Blvd., Union Square, Powell St. BART station. Closed Sun.*
(see p. 151)

Cronan Artefact. This showroom features men's attire by designer Michael Cronan.... *Tel 415/241–9111. 543 Eighth St., Powell St. BART station or 15, 30, 45 MUNI buses. Sat. by appointment only.* **(see p. 151)**

Crystal Way. Thousands of beautiful natural crystals and New Age books are sold here.... *Tel 415/861–6511. 2335 Market St. near Castro St., Castro St. MUNI Metro station.*
(see p. 153)

Curios and Candles. New Age emporium in the Upper Haight.... *Tel 415/863–5669. 289 Divisadero St., Upper Haight; 7 MUNI bus.* **(see p. 153)**

D & M Wine and Liquor Co. Simply the best selection of champagne in the country, and discount prices to boot.... *Tel 415/346–1325. 2200 Fillmore St. at Sacramento St., 6 blocks from 38 MUNI bus.* **(see p. 157)**

Daljeets. This store sells super-hip men's clothing at not-total-ly-expensive prices.... *Tel 415/752–5610, 1744 Haight St., 7 MUNI bus; tel 415/431–9100, 541 Valencia St., Mission District, 16th St. BART station. Closed Mon.*
(see p. 151)

Danilo Bakery. Wonderful breads and *panettone.... Tel 415/989–1806. 516 Green St., North Beach, 15, 30 MUNI buses.*
(see p. 157)

David Stephen. Featuring European clothing for men, this store has an experienced staff and offers same-day tailor-ing.... *Tel 415/982–1611. 50 Maiden Lane, Union Square, Powell St. and Montgomery St. BART stations. Open daily, Sun by appointment only.* **(see p. 151)**

Dianda's Italian American Pastry. Prize-winning Italian cakes have made this store's reputation.... *Tel 415/*

989–7745. *565 Green St., North Beach; 15, 30 MUNI buses.* **(see p. 157)**

Dinostore. Alternative clothing and clubwear for men.... *Tel 415/861–3933. 1553 Haight St., 7 MUNI bus.*
(see p. 151)

Discolandia. The selection of Latin music is enormous, so it helps to have an idea what you're looking for.... *Tel 415/826–9446. 2964 24th St., Mission District, 24th St. BART station.* **(see p. 158)**

Dog Eared Books. A fun place for browsing and buying.... *Tel 415/282–1901. 900 Valencia St., Mission District, 24th St. BART station.* **(see p. 158)**

Dottie Doolittle. Look here for designer clothes for infants, toddlers, girls 7–14 and boys 4–7.... *Tel 415/563–3244. 3680 Sacramento St. between Spruce and Locust Sts., 1, 3, 4 MUNI bus.* **(see p. 157)**

Dreamweaver. A huge selection of hand-knit sweaters makes this store a local favorite.... *Tel 415/981–2040. 171 Maiden Lane, Union Square, Powell St. BART station. Also at Pier 39.* **(see p. 150)**

East West Leather. The specialty here is cowboy boots plus jackets and clothing.... *Tel 415/397–2886. 1400 Upper Grant Ave., North Beach, 15, 30 MUNI buses.* **(see p. 150)**

Esprit Outlet Store. The place to buy Esprit outfits at discount prices.... *Tel 415/957–2550. 499 Illinois St., 15 MUNI bus.*
(see p. 152)

FAO Schwarz. Outpost of the world-class toy store.... *Tel 415/394–8700. 48 Stockton St., Union Square, Powell St. BART station.* **(see p. 157)**

First Step. Comfortable footwear: Nike, Reebok, Rockport, etc. Great shoes, great prices, great location.... *Tel 415/989–9989. 57 and 216 Powell St., Union Square, Powell St. BART station. Closed Sun in summer.* **(see p. 150)**

560 Hayes. Upscale vintage clothing and original works by local artists. Staff is helpful but not pushy.... *Tel 415/861–7993.*

560 Hayes St., Hayes Valley, Civic Center BART station.
(see p. 152)

Forever After Books. Here you'll find used books on many esoteric and mainstream subjects.... *Tel 415/431–8299. 1475 Haight St., 7 MUNI bus.* **(see p. 158)**

Gargoyle Beads. This store sells zillions of beads and offers ear piercing and jewelry-making classes.... *Tel 415/ 552–4274. 1324 Haight St., 7 MUNI bus.* **(see p. 153)**

General Bead. The biggest bead store ever.... *Tel 415/621–8187. 637 Minna St., Montgomery St. BART station, 15, 39, 45 MUNI bus. Closed Mon.* **(see p. 153)**

Gimme Shoes. An eclectic, chic mix of footwear merchandise.... *Tel 415/864–0691. 416 Hayes St., Hayes Valley, Civic Center BART station.* **(see p. 150)**

Global Exchange. Hand-crafted items from international artisans are sold at this Fair Trade Network store.... *Tel 415/648–8068. 3900 24th St. near Sanchez St., J Church MUNI Metro.* **(see p. 153)**

Globetrotter. The largest U.S. source for Tin Tin and Asterix fans.... *Tel 415/434–1120. 418 Sutter St., Union Square, Powell St. BART station.* **(see p. 155)**

Good Vibrations. This is a comfortable, clean, airy, healthy place to shop for sex toys, sex books, and videos.... *Tel 415/974–8980. 1210 Valencia St., Mission District, 24th St. BART station.* **(see p. 155)**

Goodwill Stores. Hit or miss secondhand shopping, but when you hit, the price is definitely right.... *Tel 415/575–2101. 820 Clement St.; 3801 Third St.; 1700 Fillmore St.; 241 Tenth St.; 2279 Mission St.; 822 Geary Blvd.; 1700 Haight St.; 61 West Portal.* **(see p. 152)**

Groove Yard. If you're into jazz, blues, and soul, you'll be thrilled with this store, where they buy, sell, and trade new, used, and rare records and CDs.... *Tel 510/655–8400. 4770 Telegraph Ave. (at 48th St.), Oakland; Ashby BART station. Closed Mon.* **(see p. 158)**

Gump's. What used to be a grand San Francisco department store; now scaled down, but still a local classic. Orientalia is a particular specialty.... *Tel 415/982–1616. 135 Post St., Union Square, Powell St. BART station. Closed Sun.* **(see p. 149)**

Gunne Sax Discount Outlet. You can get consistently good buys here on Gunne Saxe as well as Jessica and Scott McClintock fashions and fabric, including wedding dresses. It's a prom-dress paradise, with the clearance section of your dreams.... *Tel 415/495–3326. 35 Stanford St. off Townsend St., 15, 30, 42, 45 MUNI buses.* **(see p. 152)**

Guys and Dolls This vintage-clothing store for men and women specializes in tuxedos and formal accessories from the 1930s to the 1950s. Hats, ties, jewelry.... *Tel 415/285–7174. 3789 24th St., J Church MUNI Metro.* **(see p. 152)**

House of Cashmere. Cashmere, wool, and angora sweaters are the specialty of this men's and women's clothing store.... *Tel 415/441–6925. 2764 Octavia St., off Union St., 45 MUNI bus. Closed Sun.* **(see p. 150)**

Irish Castle Shop. Expect everything Irish, from claddagh rings to fishermen's sweaters.... *Tel 415/474–7432. 537 Geary St. Union Square, Powell St. BART station. Closed Sun.* **(see p. 150)**

Italian French Baking Co. Don't miss the delectable breads baked in brick ovens and the hand-rolled bread sticks.... *Tel 415/421–3796. 1501 Grant Ave., North Beach, 15, 30 MUNI buses.* **(see p. 157)**

Jacqueline Perfumery. The best selection of perfumes in the city.... *Tel 415/981–0858. 156 Geary Blvd., Union Square, Powell St. BART station. Closed Sun.* **(see p. 156)**

Jeffrey's Toys. Along with toys of all kinds, you can buy books and antique toys here.... *Tel 415/546–6551. 7 Third St., near Market St., Montgomery St. BART station.* **(see p. 157)**

Joseph Schmidt Confections. A local treasure, this shop sells the most beautiful edible sculptures you'll ever see or taste.... *Tel 415/861–8682. 3489 16th St., near Church St., J Church MUNI Metro line. Closed Sun.* **(see p. 156)**

Just Desserts. This mini-chain is famous for its decadent desserts.... *Tel 415/330–3600. 248 Church St.; 3 Embarcadero Center; 836 Irving St.; 3735 Buchanan; 1000 Cole St.; 1750 Fulton St.* **(see p. 156)**

Kenneth Cole. Footwear for the fashion-conscious.... *Tel 415/227–4536. 865 Market St., San Francisco Shopping Centre, Powell St. BART station. 2078 Union St., 45 MUNI bus.* **(see p. 150)**

Kinder Toys. Their motto is, "Come in and play"—and you will. The store sells classic, Old World toys, which can be personalized while you wait.... *Tel 415/673–1780. 1974 Union St., 45 MUNI bus.* **(see p. 157)**

La Rosa. On the upscale end of the vintage clothing spectrum, La Rosa focuses on formal clothing.... *Tel 415/668–3746. 1773 Haight St., 7 MUNI bus.* **(see p. 152)**

Lady Luck Candle Shop. Your basic Latino Catholic-voodoo-ritual botanica.... *Tel 415/621–0358. 311 Valencia St., Mission District, 16th St. BART station.* **(see p. 153)**

Let It Be. If there is a heaven for Beatlemaniacs, this may be where you buy your tickets to get there. Besides rare and out-of-print records, it has a variety of memorabilia.... *Tel 415/681–2113. 2434 Judah St., N. Judah MUNI Metro station. Closed Sun and Mon.* **(see p. 158)**

Louis Vuitton. This is the place to get that fancy luggage with the monogram that opens doors around the world.... *Tel 415/391–6200. 230 Post St., Union Square, Powell St. BART station.* **(see p. 149)**

Lucca Ravioli Co. Seemingly out-of-place in this Latino neighborhood, this wonderful Italian deli is always full of locals.... *Tel 415/647–5581. 1100 Valencia St., Mission District, 24th St. BART station. Closed Sun.* **(see p. 157)**

Macy's. This huge store occupies two full buildings and has always been a reliable favorite for locals and visitors alike.... *Tel 415/397–3333. 170 O'Farrell St. at Stockton St., Union Square, Powell St. BART station.* **(see p. 150)**

Magical Trinket. The gorgeous selection of beads here includes hand-blown pieces by Northern California artists. Friendly, helpful staff. Classes available in beadmaking; call far in advance.... *Tel 415/626–0764. 524 Hayes St., Hayes Valley, Civic Center BART station. Closed Mon.* **(see p. 153)**

The Mascara Club. Day of the Dead artwork and dashboard hula dolls share shelf space in this quintessential San Francisco gift store.... *Tel 415/863–2837. 1408 Haight St., 7 MUNI bus.* **(see p. 154)**

McB's Shoes. The specialty here is hard-to-find shoe sizes for women (or men who like to wear women's shoes).... *Tel 415/546–9444. 1701 Telegraph Ave., Oakland, 19th St. BART station. Closed Sun.* **(see p. 150)**

McDonald's Bookshop. More than a million used books in stock.... *Tel 415/673–2235. 48 Turk St., Powell St. BART station. Closed Sun.* **(see p. 158)**

Medium Rare Records. This is the place to find those old vinyl LPs you haven't heard for ages, as well as all the great jazz and Latin vocalists.... *Tel 415/255–7273. 2310 Market St., Castro St. MUNI Metro station. (K,L,M)* **(see p. 158)**

Minis By Profili. Local designer Christina Profili left the GAP to open her own business here. All the racks feature coordinating sportswear separates.... *Tel 415/567–9537. 2042 Union St., 45 MUNI bus.* **(see p. 157)**

Mod Lang. This English modern-rock music store caters to serious collectors, as well as curious onlookers. It's got a 24-hour fax line (510/486–1860).... *Tel 510/486–1850. 2136 University Ave. at Shattuck Ave., Berkeley, Berkeley BART station.* **(see p. 158)**

Molinari's. The traditional North Beach deli.... *Tel 415/421–2337. 373 Columbus Ave., North Beach, 15, 30 MUNI buses. Closed Sun.* **(see p. 157)**

Neiman Marcus. This branch of the Texas-based luxury store offers the city's best shopping experience. The cafe on the top floor is a real hoot.... *Tel 415/362–3900. 150 Stockton St., Union Square, Powell St. BART station.* **(see p. 150)**

Nordstrom. Get pampered with attentive, personal service on five floors. Don't forget the eateries and the spa.... *Tel 415/243–8500. San Francisco Shopping Centre, 865 Market St., Powell St. BART station.* **(see pp. 149, 150)**

North Beach Leather. This store sells the latest fashions— some custom-made—at prices to match.... *Tel 415/ 362–8300, 190 Geary Blvd., Union Square, Powell St. BART station.* **(see p. 155)**

North Face Factory Outlet. Quality outdoor gear at discount prices.... *Tel 415/626–6444. 1325 Howard St., south of Market St., 42 MUNI bus.* **(see p. 152)**

Open Mind Music. New and used records and CDs, in addition to assorted esoterica and an in-store vintage-clothing shop.... *Tel 415/621–2244. 342 Divisadero St. at Oak St., 7 MUNI bus.* **(see p. 158)**

Pacitas Bakery. One of dozens of bakeries in the Mission District, this is in the newly Bohemian part.... *Tel 415/452–8442. 10 Persia St. near Mission St., Mission District, 16th St. BART stop.* **(see p. 156)**

Patrick James. This store refers to itself as a "Purveyor to Gentlemen," if that gives you any idea.... *Tel 415/986– 1043. 216 Montgomery St., Financial District, Montgomery St. BART station. Closed Sun.* **(see p. 151)**

Paxton Gate. Truly a bizarre bazaar, this natural science/garden store is best known for its stuffed mice dressed in costumes.... *Tel 415/255–5955. 1204 Stevenson St. at Gough St., Upper Market, Van Ness Ave. MUNI station or 71 MUNI bus.* **(see p. 154)**

Piedmont Boutique. Absolutely outrageous women's garments and accessories—sold mostly to men. If you've ever coveted any of the gaudy get-ups you've seen on drag queens, this is the place to find them.... *Tel 415/ 864–8075. 1452 Haight St., 7 MUNI bus.* **(see p. 151)**

PlaNetweavers Treasures Store. The official UNICEF store is full of international trinkets and works of art.... *Tel 415/ 864–4415. 1573 Haight St., 7 MUNI bus.* **(see p. 153)**

The Polo Store/Ralph Lauren. For folks who affect the country-squire look. Tallyho.... Tel 415/788–7656. 90 Post St., Union Square, Powell St. BART station. Closed Sun. **(see p. 149)**

Quantity Postcards. Here's a place you can spend less than a dollar and come out with one of the best souvenirs of your trip. A true goofatorium.... Tel 415/986–8866. 1441 Grant Ave., North Beach, 15, 30 MUNI buses. Open 11–11.**(see p. 154)**

The Record Finder. More than 100,000 titles in stock. Good staff, too.... Tel 415/431–4443. 258 Noe St., Castro St. MUNI Metro station. **(see p. 158)**

Repeat Performance. Some of the stuff here—used clothing, records, books, knickknacks—is great, and some of it is definitely little-old-lady material. Check it out; the proceeds go to the San Francisco Symphony.... Tel 415/563–0366. 2436 Fillmore St., 22 MUNI bus. Closed Sun. **(see p. 152)**

Ria's. Birkenstocks, Timberland, Rockports, etc.... Tel 415/398–0895, 437 Sutter St.; tel 415/834–1420, 301 Grant Ave., tel 415/771–4393, 900 North Point St. **(see p. 150)**

Rolo SF. These 4 stores sell clothes for the modern urban guy, at modern urban prices (big). The one at 535 Castro—Undercover by Rolo—is a super-trendy designer store.... Tel 415/626–7171, 450 Castro St.; tel 415/861–1999, 1301 Howard St.; tel 415/431–4545, 2351 Market St.; tel 415/864–0505, 535 Castro St. **(see p. 151)**

Romantasy. Naughty stuff for upstanding citizens.... Tel 415/487–9909. 2191 Market St, at Sanchez St., Upper Market, J Church MUNI Metro line. Closed Mon. **(see p. 155)**

Saks Fifth Avenue. Not as glitzy as Nieman Marcus or as fun as Nordstrom's.... Tel 415/986–4300. 384 Post St., Union Square, Powell St. BART station. **(see pp. 149, 150)**

Sanrio at Union Square. Two floors of international toys.... Tel 415/981–5568. 39 Stockton St., Union Square, Powell St. BART station. **(see p. 157)**

Saturn Records. An eclectic collection of records, tapes, CDs, and 45s makes this music store a really fun place to stop....

Tel 510/654–0335. 5488 College Ave., Oakland, Rockridge BART station. **(see p. 158)**

The Scairy Hairy Toy Company. Voodoo games and handmade toys.... *Tel 415/864–6543. 3804 17th St. at Sanchez St., Mission District, J Church MUNI Metro line.* **(see p. 154)**

Shoe Loft. Come here for women's designer shoes at cheapo-cheapo prices.... *Tel 415/956–4648. 225 Front St., at California St., Montgomery St. BART station.* **(see p. 150)**

Sierra Club Bookstore. Heaven for walkers and hikers. If you plan to get outdoors, this is the place for maps and trail guides.... *Tel 415/977–5600. 85 Second St., Montgomery St. BART station. Closed Sun.* **(see p. 158)**

Stella Pastry & Caffe. The specialty here is Franco's *La Sacripantina*, a puffy slice of heaven.... *Tel 415/986–2914. 446 Columbus Ave., North Beach, 15, 30 MUNI buses.* **(see p. 156)**

Stephane Kelian. Très chic. One of the biggest French names in shoes.... *Tel 415/989–1412. Crocker Galleria, 50 Post St., Montgomery BART station. Closed Sun.* **(see p. 150)**

Stormy Leather. Kinky leather goods.... *Tel 415/626–1672. 1158 Howard St., South of Market, Civic Center BART station.* **(see p. 155)**

Streetlight Records. A major source for new and used vinyl, CDs, tapes, video, and laserdiscs.... *Tel 415/282–3550, 3979 24th St.; tel 415/282–8000, 2350 Market St., both near Castro St. MUNI Metro station.* **(see p. 158)**

Sulka. This exclusive store sells exquisite clothing for gentlemen.... *Tel 415/989–0600. 255 Post St., Union Square, Powell St. BART station.* **(see p. 151)**

Tassajara Cafe & Bakery. Once owned by the locally beloved Greens restaurant, this little Cole Valley bakery/cafe is now part of the Just Desserts mini-empire, but it hasn't suffered a bit.... *Tel 415/664–8947. 1000 Cole St. at Parnassus, 7 MUNI bus or N. Judah MUNI Metro station.* **(see p. 156)**

395 Sutter. This store's exclusive hand-loomed sweaters and knits for men and women come in classic designs and natural colors.... *Tel 415/989–1288. 395 Sutter St., Union Square, Powell St. BART station. Closed Sun.*
(see p. 150)

Thrift Town. The unique thing about this thrift store is its grab-bag section in the rear, with items stuffed into sealed plastic bags to be sold for a dollar or two..... *Tel 415/861–1132. 2101 Mission St. at 17th St., Mission District, 16th St. BART station.* **(see p. 152)**

Tiffany and Co. Jewelry and gifts, classic and very, very expensive.... *Tel 415/781–7000. 350 Post St., Union Square, Powell St. BART station. Closed Sun.* **(see p. 149)**

Tse Cashmere. This stuff is soft—really soft. Great colors, too.... *Tel 415/391–1112. 171 Post St., Union Square, Powell St. BART station. Closed Sun.* **(see p. 154)**

Uncle Mame. Toys for regressing grownups.... *Tel 415/626–1953. 2241 Market St., between Sanchez and Noe Sts., J Church MUNI Metro line.* **(see p. 152)**

Wasteland. Trendy secondhand clothing, for sure, but sometimes it's a little bit, you know, expensive. Especially, like, the denim, you know?... *Tel 415/863–3150. 1660 Haight St., 7 MUNI bus.* **(see p. 150)**

Wilkes-Bashford. The ultimate classic men's store. The local designers are literally top drawer.... *Tel 415/986–4380. 375 Sutter St., Union Square; Powell St. BART station. Closed Sun.* **(see p. 152)**

Worldware. Eco-elegant housewares and personal items.... *Tel 415/487–9030. 336 Hayes St., Hayes Valley, Civic Center BART station.* **(see p. 152)**

Yone of San Francisco. They call themselves a beehive of beads. Locals love 'em, but they're only open 12 hours a week.... *Tel 415/986–1424. 478 Union St., North Beach, 15, 30 MUNI buses. Closed Wed and Sun; call for hours.* **(see p. 153)**

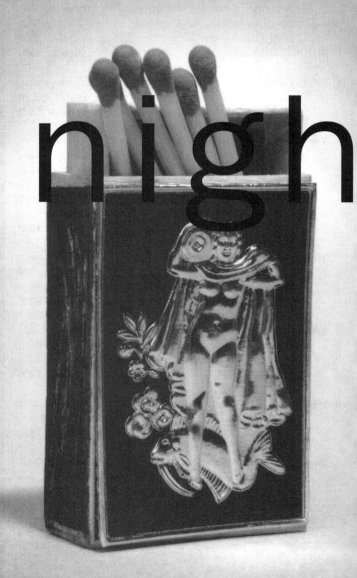

nigh

6

tlife

San Francisco is
an exotic cocktail
of world cultures,
stirred with a
liberal splash of
wild-West flavor
that dates to the

Gold Rush. State laws and politically correct teetotalers and anti-smoking fanatics have toned things down a bit since the notorious Barbary Coast days, but nothing can ever keep this city from being an exciting place to roam when its fabled sunsets are long extinguished.

The biggest problem a visiting roamer might encounter is actually finding the party. Movable clubs that host all-night raves are a huge part of the night scene in San Francisco, and both the addresses and the crowds can change. (See our section entitled "All-night techno-parties" for the latest information.) What doesn't change is that the club scene in San Francisco always has been dominated by three things: neighborhoods, music, and people in their 20s who have the stamina and cash to buy lots of drinks. Every neighborhood has its own bar scene, and some are so packed with worthy joints that you can usually bar-hop on foot. Go to 10th and Folsom streets, **South of Market**, for a pack of blues, rock, and contemporary music haunts as well as the "Miracle Mile" of gay sex clubs; stop off at 16th and Valencia streets in the **Mission District** for the city's hippest, funkiest bars full of lounge-crowd bohemians; head over to Castro and Market streets to enter the **Castro**, gay capital of the world; **Haight Street** (between Masonic and Stanyan streets) appeals to the new "Mod" set as well as hippies and thrashers; Broadway and Columbus streets form the axis from which **North Beach** jazz clubs, late-night cafes, and girlie strip joints flow. Acid jazz is still big, raves are huge, and rock music in all its variations will never go away, no matter how old or young the barflies are. Fancy cocktails, many of which

Fine music and fast women
*In New York, blues singer Billie Holiday had to fight to perform at uppity Carnegie Hall. That would never have happened in San Francisco, where the closest thing to Carnegie Hall is an ornate, turn-of-the-century concert hall that spent its first 30 years as a bordello and gambling hall. After the **Great American Music Hall** was taken over by a fan-dancer in the 1930s, it had many lives— a swank dance hall, a jazz club, a Moose Lodge. Saved from a wrecking ball in 1972, it was impeccably restored and has thrived as a concert hall/night club ever since, hosting jazz greats from Duke Ellington to Count Basie, rock legends from the Grateful Dead to Van Morrison, and comedians from Robin Williams to Rosanne Arnold. Visit the hall's web site at www.music hallsf.com for concert schedule, directions, and ordering information.*

are variations on the classic martini, are the rage, though some of us have never trusted drinks that are colored Tidy-Bowl blue. And despite California's controversial ban on smoking in bars, cigar rooms are still popular—even if they do make smokers of both sexes smell as though they just emerged from an off-track betting room in a bad part of town.

Liquor and Smoking Laws

The drinking age is 21 in California, and bartenders can ask for a valid photo ID, no matter how old you look. Some clubs demand identification cards at the door, so it's a good idea to carry one at all times. Once you get through the door, however, forget about cigarettes. On January 1, 1998, smoking was officially banned in all California bars. How that will affect the popular cigar bars and lounges is still a bit hazy, as enforcement of the controversial law has not been the top priority of San Francisco's police department, and cigar bars are allowed to open adjoining "tobacco shops" in which smoking is legal, anyway. But most bartenders will ask you to put out your cigarette or smoke it outside, so take a deep breath and accept it. Meanwhile, the dreaded last call for alcohol usually rings out at around 1:30 am, since state laws prohibit the sale of alcohol from 2 to 6 every morning. Don't be surprised to see crowded clubs empty just before the witching hour, as the revelers rush to buy enough six-packs to fuel them during the after-hours festivities, when some clubs stay open but stop serving alcohol. A very important word of warning: Driving under the influence of alcohol is a serious crime in California, with jail time for the first offense. You are likely to be legally intoxicated (0.08 percent blood alcohol) if you have had as little as one alcoholic drink an hour. Just don't do it. Take a taxi, as the locals do.

The Lowdown

It's only rock 'n' roll... Rock, in its various forms, dominates the music scene in San Francisco. Any night of the week you can hit a number of clubs and hear garage bands, ska, post-punk, rock-a-billy, thrash, metal—in other words, just about every rock style except that acidy Jefferson Airplane/Grateful Dead thing they once called the San Francisco sound. One of the most popular spots in town is **Bottom of the Hill** (South of Market), where most of the acts are locals who have landed recording contracts, but touring bands perform as well. Musicians like the cozy atmosphere and great acoustics; when U2 is in town, they hang out there. **Slim's** is the house that Boz built. In the 1980s, Boz Scaggs put South of Market on the map with his first-class music club, which originally leaned heavily toward blues but now features top names and new local faces in all popular genres, from Marianne Faithfull to Los Super Elegantes. Actor Danny Glover stops by here to see his favorites, but when the joint is jammed--as it often is--he has to stand in the crowd with everyone else. The **Trocadero** is a South of Market hot spot for record-release parties for up-and-coming acts. It's a great venue for a concert because the dance floor is huge and the entire second floor is a balcony. On Wednesdays, a leather-clad crowd steps in for "Bondage-a-Go-Go," when spanking and chains add a little variety to the old dance routines. The **Paradise Lounge** (South of Market) is less a club and more a rock saloon, where four separate performance rooms feature two or three acts playing simultaneously. Modern rock is the main attraction, but rock-a-billy, funk, acid jazz, gospel, and the spoken word are also on the bill. The **Fillmore Auditorium** has been synonymous with San Francisco's rock scene since Bill Graham put on his first psychedelic concert there in 1965. Shuttered up for years, the Fillmore reopened in the early 1990s, to immense popularity with both fans and musicians. Tom Petty wanted to play there so badly that he appeared every night for a couple of weeks in order to make enough money to pay his band (who usually play only in huge arenas for massive amounts of money). Across town in North Beach, the **Purple Onion** has become a hot spot for up-and-coming garage bands. This is truly a local party, down to the owner's keg of beer that invariable runs out before the night is over. When the keg is empty, it's empty. You can stay longer, but the beer is gone.

All-night techno parties... While modern rock dominates the city's live-music stages, techno is the music of choice for most clubs that host all-night dance parties. The clubs are often known simply by their addresses because the parties—which have distinct names—float from club to club. If a promoter comes to **177 Townsend**

with a party called "Colossus," for that night the location is known as "Colossus." Next week "Colossus" may be at **278 11th**. **650 Howard** and **715 Harrison** are also popular sites for floating fêtes. Each party has its own following, which can change over time. The *Bay Guardian* and *SF Weekly* are good sources for a start; parties at the legit clubs can lead you to the middle-of-the-night, deep underground scene, whose venues are even more unpredictable. For an up-to-the-minute party list, check out SF Rave's web site and map at www.hyperreal.org/raves/sf.

All that acid jazz... Acid jazz is the new fusion, a cross between modern jazz, hip-hop, rhythm and blues, funk, and even big band. It's vibrant and soulful, with big brass sections, lots of guitars, and rap-influenced vocals that all meet in an extremely danceable concoction. A leading venue for acid jazz is **330 Ritch**, a one-time warehouse where people who come for the music mix with a more trend-conscious set who come simply because it's the fashionable thing to do. There's also terrific Latin music that packs in a diverse crowd on Saturday dance nights. The **Elbo Room** has been a Mission District favorite for years, not only because of the music, but because it is truly a neighborhood bar, with pool tables and one of those photo booths that swallows your quarters and spits out a picture strip of you and your friends mugging for the camera. You can keep the pix or

Even Cowgirls Hit the Booze

You're in San Francisco and for some inexplicable reason you get a powerful hankering to do the Texas two-step. Trouble is, country music isn't exactly the hottest thing in the city, and the closest most people get to line dancing is late-night commercials for the Hank Williams Greatest Hits tapes "available only on TV." Not to worry—there's always the Rawhide (280 Seventh St., tel 415/621-1197). It's not exactly a traditional Western saloon—most of the regulars at the South of Market haunt are gay men—but it is a truly friendly, fun place for anyone who wants to get out there and kick up their heels, regardless of sexual orientation. Dance lessons are given Thursday through Sunday nights (7:30-9:30) for a $5.50 cover charge that includes two free cocktails. You'll learn how to do dances with names like "Ain't Goin' Down," and on a good night, you might catch a guy wearing chaps without a stitch underneath. Yee-haw!

NIGHTLIFE | THE LOWDOWN

leave them for the bar's collection. **Blondie's Bar and No Grill** used to be a laboratory where musicians flocked to jam and try out new (mostly acid jazz) riffs. Lately it has become a weekend haunt for the bridge-and-tunnel crowd, but there is still a free jukebox loaded with great jazz. Other clubs that feature jazz, including acid, are the **Up & Down Club** (South of Market), **Blues** (Cow Hollow), and **Cafe du Nord** (north Market Street).

All that other jazz... The best jazz club in the Bay Area, if not the entire West Coast, is across the bay. **Yoshi's** outgrew its former home in a small sushi restaurant near the Claremont Hotel and moved to Oakland's Jack London Square, but the setting is still so intimate that club owners insist you can be stuck in the back row and still see McCoy Tyner's fingers playing the piano. Some of the top jazz musicians in the world play at Yoshi's, which welcomes children and presents special shows and clinics for kids. In San Francisco, big-name artists tend to play at the hotels; check out the Fairmont's **New Orleans Room**. Otherwise, jazz gigs are spread around town, but there's always something going on in North Beach, for free. **Enrico's Sidewalk Cafe** has live jazz seven nights a week with no cover, and **Jazz at Pearl's** consistently presents such good music that players head over there to jam after their paying gigs are over. The indomitable Pearl opened her first jazz club in a Chinatown basement some 25 years ago, and usually gets the best of the local talent at her current address in North Beach. If you're near the Haight, cross the Panhandle to Fulton Street and check out **Storyville**, owned by jazz musician Don Pender. Storyville was the original Creole name of New Orleans' French Quarter, where jazz was born, but far from being a sort of Preservation Hall, Storyville welcomes contemporary as well as classic jazz sounds.

Blues joints... Until a few years ago, all of the real blues joints were in Oakland. Then clubs started to appear in San Francisco, and though some purists might argue that these are a bit too sanitized to qualify as "joints," they do book topnotch talent and you don't need a bodyguard to get to the door. One of the newest spots is the **Boom Boom Room** (Fillmore District), opened by blues legend John Lee Hooker. With his credentials, he could serve nothing but tap water and it would still be a bona fide blues joint. **Biscuits and Blues** is a highly regarded venue, despite its location in touristy Union Square. The down-home food is delicious and the headliners are the best in the business, from venerable stars like James Cotton to local hotshots like Paris Slim. North Beach has two dives—**The Saloon** and **Grant and Green**—that have survived more than two decades and have produced a signature house-band sound dubbed "North Beach blues," most often identified with the hard-rocking, rowdy, Southern-style blues played by Johnny Nitro and the Doorslammers. The Doorslammers and many other Bay Area blues bands also play frequently at a Cow Hollow haunt called **Blues**.

Disco infernal... If too much techno cools your dance fever, try some of these South of Market clubs, which offer a variety of sounds. **DV8** hosts up to three parties at a time, each with a different theme, a different promoter, and sometimes a different cover charge. On Saturday nights, though, you can usually dance all over the place for one admission. DV8 is a gathering place for hipsters and fashion slaves; socializing in the lines outside and gawking at the latest clubwear is all part of the fun. **Ten 15** (1015 Folsom St.) is another huge club (with a huge attitude) that usually has four different dance parties going at once, all for a $10 cover. House music booms in the multilevel main room; the gold room is a disco inferno, complete with a spinning, mirrored ball; in the basement are little alcoves and couches where you can take it easy and listen to acid jazz; and in the top room, anything goes. The crowd changes from night to night—Friday is a straight night, Saturday is a gay night, Tuesday is a deep underground party.

    Sound Factory is super-friendly and was built with people-watching in mind. The upstairs lobby looks out over the line outside and you can see everyone who enters. Then you can walk along a balcony and check out the different rooms, each with its own theme. This is a high-energy Generation-X crowd.

    DV8, **Ten 15**, and **Sound Factory** serve alcohol until 2am, but they all carry on after hours. There will definitely be lines outside their doors between 11:30pm and 1am.

Cool cocktail lounges... The lounge scene in the Mission District has made it the second-hippest neighborhood in America, according to the *Utne Reader*, a national magazine that ranked only New Orleans' Lower Garden District ahead on the hip-o-meter. The six-block stretch between 16th and 22nd streets is door-to-door cocktail world, on both Mission and Valencia streets; ditto every cross street that connects the two. At ground zero (16th and Valencia streets), step into the **Casanova Lounge** and try the signature cocktail, a butt-kicking blend of Mescal (a variation of tequila) and blue Curaçao. Then pop over to the **Skylark**, where you can sink into a gold vinyl booth and listen to Elvis (Presley, not Costello) on the juke box. Cross over to Mission Street and visit **Bruno's**, a cushy club where you can dance to live music, eat a real meal at an elegant restaurant, and check out the latest thrift-store cocktail dresses. Then go to the nearby **Elysium**, on the first floor of the Andora Inn. If the aqua cocktails and sea of goatees here gives you the whirlies, you can always check into a room.

Kiss me, I'm Irish... Aside from O'Greenberg's, a former Fisherman's Wharf watering hole where the logo was Moishe Daian with a shamrock for an eye-patch, San Francisco's Irish pubs for years have been clustered in the Clement Street neighborhood within a three-block radius of Third Avenue. The **Abbey Tavern** (Third Avenue and Geary Boulevard) is not as grungy or consistently lively as it was in the 1970s, when puddles of spilt beer and cigarette butts covered the floor and patrons stood three-deep around the huge bar, but it is still earthy enough to draw a flock of Irish regulars. Soccer posters are plastered on the walls alongside announcements of fundraising benefits for Irish political prisoners, and the bathroom stalls are covered with partisan graffiti. It's a bit too authentic to appeal to Americans who saw *Riverdance* and are now dying to share a pint with a "real" Irish person. (Not recommended for conservative Brits.) A Yankee-fied version of the Abbey is just up the block at **Pat O'Shea's Mad Hatter**. It is a mad house on weekends, when it's packed to the rafters with students from the University of San Francisco (a good Catholic college, mind you, and forget any nasty rumors you may have heard about scandals involving the erstwhile basketball team). With four satellites, 13 televisions, and a kitchen full of excellent pub food, Pat O'Shea's is also a magnet for local sports fans and out-of-towners who want to catch their team on the telly. The **The Plough and the Stars**, around the corner, is a good middle-of-the-road bet for Celtophiles who love traditional Irish music but would prefer to steer clear of football hooligans or political arguments. There's live music on weekends for a minimal cover charge (usually $3), but get there early to nab a good seat.

Just your basic, friendly neighborhood bar...
When you get sick of looking for a scene or a theme or a fancy cocktail, what you need is a good old neighborhood tavern, where the bartender will strike up a conversation and welcome you to the fold. **Gino & Carlo** has been serving cocktails to North Beach natives for as long as anyone can remember. Just pay your money, drink up, and get ready to hear some good stories from the local barflies. The **Edinburgh Castle** is a special treat, a Scottish dive in the no-man's land between Civic Center and the Tenderloin. Grab a pint of John Courage, then drop a few quarters in the jukebox and get blasted by bagpipes. The crowd ranges from sodden old lushes to luscious young bar-hoppers. Back over in the Mission District (we keep going there), the **Latin American Club** is a spot where locals meet for a quick one before they go out or end up for a nightcap when the party is over. If the company's lively and the beer is flowing, many a patron has been known to blow off other plans and hang around all night. Beware, though, the bathrooms are totally disgusting, so hold it in or sneak into the loo at another neighboring bars.

Three babes and a bus...
Get a taste of the different ingredients of San Francisco's nightlife with **Three Babes and a Bus**. About 80 percent of the bar-hoppers who take this tour are local residents, lured, perhaps, by the chauffeured ride, the pre-paid cover charges, the priority entry (no waiting in line), and, of course, the three fun-loving women who run the business. The bus will scoop you up at a downtown bar and chauffeur you to three or four more lively nightspots. Along the way, the babes introduce their passengers to one another and lay down a few house rules, the most important of which is "Never let the Three Babes buy their own drinks." Aside from that, the total cost of this party-on-wheels is about $30, which includes the clubs' cover charges.

NIGHTLIFE | THE LOWDOWN

Bustling brew pubs... Beware: The backlash against micro-breweries is in full force. More than one billboard in San Francisco has defiantly pitched its product as "macro" brew, and even **Gordon Biersch**, the king of the city's microbreweries, put up a sign that complained about wheat beers and apple beers, asking: "How about beer-flavored beer?" Gordon Biersch's loud, yuppie-infested brew pub is generally avoided by non-upwardly-mobile locals, but the beers are exquisite and it can be a lot of fun if you don't mind yelling to be heard by the person next to you. **Twenty Tank Brewery**, is more like an English pub—friendly but not deafening. Try the Red-Top Ale or Polly-Want-a-Porter. **Thirsty Bear Brewing Company** was named after an escaped circus bear who in 1991 bit the hand of a Ukrainian pub patron and ran off with his beer, or at least that's the story. This popular brew pub near the Museum of Modern Art is famous for its tapas and paella as well as the ales and beers brewed on the premises. Try the Lorca Ruby Ale, named after Spanish poet and playwright Garcia Lorca. All three brew pubs mentioned here are located South of Market.

Swingy supper clubs... There are supper clubs *per se*, where the meal is as important as the entertainment (see our Dining chapter), and there are supper clubs *perchance*, where the crowd often arrives long after dinner, and the only thing that makes it a supper club is that it looks like the ones in old movies. Among those are **Cafe du Nord** (Upper Market), a former speakeasy that features live swing, blues, and jazz, and still looks enough like a bordello to bring out the party spirit in its eclectic clientele; the **Hi-Ball Lounge** (North Beach), where bands like Lee Press-On and the Nails plus $2.50 well drinks pack in the stylish 20-something neo-swing crowd; **Club Deluxe** (Haight), a small neo-swing club that hosts a "Mod" night on Wednesdays; **Harry Denton's Starlight Room** (atop the Sir Francis Drake Hotel), where a slightly older crowd gets tanked on premium scotch and kicks up their heels on the dance floor; and **Bimbo's 365** (North Beach), a swanky, landmark nightclub opened in 1931, where Rita Hayworth got her start in the chorus line and headliners from Chris Isaak to Tito Puente still grace the elegant stage.

Lookin' for love... Aptly named, **Johnny Love's** in Polk Gulch is the best-known singles club in town, if you go in for that sort of thing. Its horseshoe bar is designed to allow eye contact from across the room, and the frisky crowd—all ages, some locals, and some visitors—come with the idea of meeting new friends, hopefully intimate ones. On the other side of town is **Harry Denton's Bar & Grill**, where Financial District singles gather; the suit quotient is exceptionally high, and the average age is thirty-something.

The **Cow Hollow District** along Union and Fillmore streets has for decades attracted large crowds of singles—now mostly college students. To find the liveliest spot on any given night, just walk down either street until you hear one you like.

Drag clubs... There are two kinds of drag shows in the city—the big, famous revues like North Beach's **Finocchio** (see Entertainment), and the small neighborhood clubs that are more oriented toward drag queens who come to see and be seen by their peers. One of the most interesting neighborhood drag bars is **Esta Noche**, a small, Latino-oriented club in the Mission District where the drag queens are more likely to be at the bar or on the dance floor than on stage. (Esta Noche does host drag shows, but not on a regular basis.) The disk jockeys play mostly salsa music—with some disco thrown in—and the dance floor is always jammed. The bartenders are friendly, as are most of the customers, but this is definitely a gay club and not recommended for curious heteros wondering what drag queens do in their spare time. It is also in a kind of seedy section of 16th Street, where there have been a few isolated gay-bashing incidents in the past, so take a cab to the door. A stone's throw away is **La India Bonita**, where drag shows on Friday and Saturday nights ($3 cover) are emceed in Spanish and the queens are definitely as *bonita* as they come. The audience is predominantly Latino, but both straight and gay customers are welcome as long as they are respectful during the shows. Again, the neighborhood is best reached at night by cab. The **Motherlode**, a Polk Gulch/Tenderloin institution, is an odd combination of both straight and gay men ogling the profusion of drag queens, transvestites, and transsexuals who hang out there. Friday and Saturday night shows

(11pm) include drag and strip, but the club itself is more aggressive than friendly, and the neighborhood is the pits (definitely take a cab).

Where the boys are... In practically any San Francisco neighborhood, there are too many gay bars to name, so we'll just mention a few "musts." If you are a gay man, you must go to **Twin Peaks** (Castro at Market St.), simply because it is the gateway to the **Castro** and is the first thing you see when you get out of the Castro Street MUNI/Metro station. The huge picture windows, the wonderful old burgundy-colored sign that beacons from a block away, and the antique wooden bar make it feel like a neighborhood cafe. Much of the crowd is over 40—it's not the top cruising spot in town—but it is a wonderful place to stop by for an afternoon pick-me-up, whether you are male or female. Around the corner is another historic Castro bar, the **Elephant Walk** (Castro at 18th St.), where in 1979 police stormed in, dragged out gay men, and beat them. The bar won a famous lawsuit against the police department, and has been a landmark in gay history ever since. It is cozy and candle-lit—a great place for a date for gay men and lesbians alike. A few doors down is the youngest cruise scene in the Castro, **The Phoenix**, where a racially mixed crowd—Asian, Latin, African-American, and white—squish into a packed room to dance and sweat and pick each other up, especially on weekends. We've been told to beware of pickpockets. The **The Pendulum** (around the corner on 18th St.) is frequented primarily by African-American men and those who can't resist them. Weekends are totally jammed—and jammin'. **The Mint** (upper Market St. near Guerrero) is one of the oldest gay bars in the city—open since World War II—and can be quite a hot spot during karaoke hours (9–2, Sun 4–2). If you think you may be Bette Midler trapped in a shy man's body, this is the place for you. The crowd applauds everyone who gives it a try, especially if they know it's your first time at the mike. For a full rundown on the gay scene in the city, stop by **A Different Light** (tel 415/431–0891, 4089 Castro St.), where you can pick up any number of free gay publications that include entertainment listings. Recommended: *Bay Times*, *Odyssey*, and *The Sentinel*.

Where the girls are... Until the late 1980s, the Bay Area's homosexual population was pretty much divided into two territories—gay men in San Francisco and lesbians in Oakland. Now there is a much more active lesbian community in San Francisco—particularly in the **Mission District** and nearby **Bernal Heights**—and there are a lot of fun lesbian hangouts, including a number of gay bars with special nights for women. The longest-running Saturday night lesbian dance party in the city is **The Girl Spot** (at the End Up, South of Market, Sixth and Harrison streets), commonly known as the G-Spot. It is extremely popular among a wide variety of women, and when the dance floor gets crowded and sweaty, there's a big outside patio where you and whoever you've got your eye on can go get a little fresh air. They've also got go-go dancers. The G-Spot is a must, but go before 10pm to get in for a reduced cover charge (usually less than $5). **Junk** (at the Stud, South of Market, Ninth and Harrison streets) is another rent-a-club dance party for women, on Thursday nights (10–2). It was originally a sort of leather and multiple-piercings scene for stylish, freaky urban Sapphites, but it has been infiltrated by suburban girls. It's still a safe and fun place for bad girls, though, and it still has a bit of an edge to it, so give it a try. Don't get there until at least 11:30—it's a late-night kind of place. Our favorite semi-lesbian bar is **El Rio** (Mission District, Mission and Army streets), with a mixed crowd and most definitely a mixed motif. It's predominantly Latin, but it also has a big backyard that would give it that Doris Day/Rock Hudson patio party kind of feel if it weren't for the bigger-than-life Carmen Miranda paper doll out there. The music schedule varies, but there is often good live salsa. Sunday afternoons are the best. Go kind of late and stay for the transition from a mellow afternoon to a wild night.

Poker palaces... Want a little Lowball to go with that highball? Poker rooms are legal and flourishing in the Bay Area, but you'll have to leave San Francisco's city limits to get to them. Most of the biggest clubs are in the South Bay (reachable by Cal Train), but you can hop on a local transit bus and get to **The Oaks** in Emeryville, a 15-table club where games range from seven-card stud to "California blackjack." **Pacific News** in San Mateo is smaller—four tables—for those who prefer a cozier atmosphere. Some of the South Bay "rooms" are huge casino-style clubs, with several gaming rooms, cocktail lounges, and live entertainment. Pai Gow, an Asian double-hand poker game, is very popular here. All of the clubs used to be so smoky it was almost impossible to breathe, but that changed with the law that banned smoking in all California bars and gaming rooms. The *Bay Area Poker Club Guide* lists all of the card rooms in the entire Bay Area, along with house rules, betting limits, and tournament information. Find them on the world wide web at www.aimnet.com/~jbs/BA-Poker_card_rooms.

The Index

Abbey Tavern. This low-profile corner tavern near Clement Street is San Francisco's most unadulterated Irish pub.... *Tel 415/221–7767. 4100 Geary Blvd. (at Third Ave.); 38 MUNI bus. Open nightly.* **(see p. 180)**

Bimbo's 365. Plush booths, a spacious dance floor, big-name headliners, and a diverse crowd dressed to the nines keep this classic night club a San Francisco favorite.... *Tel 415/ 474–0365. 1025 Columbus Ave., North Beach, 15 MUNI bus. Check listings.* **(see p. 182)**

Biscuits and Blues. A congenial atmosphere and delicious Southern-style food make this one of the city's most popular blues clubs.... *Tel 415/292–BLUE. 401 Mason St., Powell-Mason or Powell-Hyde cable car line, Powell St. BART/MUNI Metro station, 38 MUNI bus. Open nightly. Cover varies.* **(see p. 179)**

Blondie's Bar and No Grill. Go for the huge martinis (you get to keep the shaker) and stay for the free jazz jukebox at this Mission District bar.... *Tel 415/864–2419. 540 Valencia St., 16th St. BART station. Closed Sun.* **(see p. 178)**

Blues. A funky, dark saloon where blues and jazz are taken seriously. The crowd is mostly locals.... *Tel 415/771–2583. 2125 Lombard St. 28 MUNI bus. Closed Tue. Cover free–$5.* **(see p. 178)**

Boom Boom Room. John Lee Hooker's Fillmore blues joint features name acts and a Sunday jam session.... *Tel 415/ 673–8000. 1601 Fillmore St. (near Geary Blvd.), 38 MUNI bus.* **(see p. 178)**

Bottom of the Hill. Two or three bands play each night at this Potrero Hill club. It's way off the beaten path, but worth the effort to maybe catch a new rock sensation.... *Tel 415/626– 4455. 1233 17th St. take a cab. Open nightly. Cover $3–6.* **(see p. 175)**

Bruno's. You may get squished on the tiny dance floor at this ever-so-hip Mission District spot, but the music is great almost every night.... *Tel 415/550–7455. 2389 Mission St., 24th St. BART station. Live music Mon-Sat. Cover varies.* **(see p. 180)**

Cafe du Nord. One of the hippest clubs in town, located in a dark, ornate, former basement speakeasy. An artistic crowd comes here to hear acid jazz, jumpin' jive, salsa, and even some cabaret.... *Tel 415/861–5016. 2170 Market St. Church St. MUNI/Metro station. Open nightly. Cover $3–5.* **(see pp. 178, 182)**

Casanova Lounge. Be sure to check out the high-kitsch retro light fixtures in this cozy, crowded Mission District cocktail lounge.... *Tel 415/863–9328. 527 Valencia St., 16th St. BART station. Open nightly.* **(see p. 180)**

Club Deluxe. Big-band entertainment in a little bar. Most of the patrons are young hipsters who dress in 1940s garb and love to dance the boogie-woogie—which is not easy here, since there's not much room. Live music Thur–Sat; other nights, deejays keep the swing spirit alive.... *Tel 415/*

552–6949. 1511 Haight St., 7 MUNI bus. Open nightly. Cover free–$8. **(see p. 182)**

DV8. High-energy dance parties happen in this multi-room South of Market club. Special events include fashion shows and art exhibits.... Tel 415/957–1730. 540 Howard St.; Powell St. BART/MUNI Metro station, 30, 45 MUNI bus. Open Thur–Sun, after-hours each night. Cover $5–15.
(see p. 179)

Edinburgh Castle. Soak up the friendly atmosphere along with British Isles ale at this snug Civic Center/Tenderloin bar.... Tel 415/885–4074. 950 Geary at Polk. 38 MUNI bus.
(see p. 181)

El Rio. This eccentric Mission District dive is supposedly a Latina lesbian haunt, but it is also a friendly neighborhood bar, comfortable for men and women, gay and straight.... Tel 415/282–3325. 3158 Mission St., at Army St., 24th St. BART station. **(see p. 185)**

Elbo Room. Shoot some pool or mingle with local acid jazz freaks at this hip but friendly Mission District club.... Tel 415/552–7788. 647 Valencia St., 16th St. BART station. Open nightly. Cover for live music varies.
(see p. 177)

Elephant Walk. Made famous the night of the "White Night Riots" in 1979, this Castro bar is now a gay landmark. It is a quiet, romantic spot—perfect for a date.... Tel 415/252–8441. 500 Castro St., at 18th St.; Castro St. MUNI Metro station. **(see p. 184)**

Elysium. This bohemian-chic cafe cocktail lounge is on the ground floor of the Andora Inn, one of the only hotels in the Mission District.... Tel 415/282–2447. 2434 Mission St., 24th St. BART station. Open nightly. **(see p. 180)**

Enrico's Sidewalk Cafe. (See also Dining) A North Beach sidewalk cafe with great food and great jazz. The crowd is a good mixture of locals and tourists, who all like the European feel of the place.... Tel 415/982–6223. 504 Broadway; 15, 30 Muni bus. Open nightly. No cover. **(see p. 178)**

Esta Noche. This Mission District bar is a friendly neighborhood hangout for drag queens, with preplanned shows scheduled on an occasional basis (call for details).... *Tel 415/861–5757. 3079 16th St., at Valencia St.; 16th St. BART station. No cover.* **(see p. 183)**

Fillmore Auditorium. The infamous concert hall that made psychedelic music a household staple during the Sixties is going strong again.... *Tel 415/3456–6000 (show information). 1801 Geary Blvd., 38 MUNI bus.* **(see p. 176)**

Gino & Carlo. North Beach locals have been drinking in this friendly dive for longer than most of them can remember.... *Tel 415/421-0896. 548 Green St., 15 MUNI bus.*
(see p. 181)

The Girl Spot. Lesbian dance party held every Saturday night at a South of Market bar called the End Up.... *Tel 415/337–4962. 401 Sixth St., at Harrison, 42 MUNI bus (cab recommended).* **(see p. 185)**

Gordon Biersch. Probably the best micro-brew in the city, but the South of Market pub is unbearably loud.... *Tel 415/243–8246. 2 Harrison St. (at the Embarcadero), 42 MUNI bus.* **(see p. 182)**

Grant and Green. Crowded North Beach blues dive—after a few beers, it's a gas.... *Tel 415/693–9565. 1371 Grant St., 15 MUNI bus. Open nightly. Cover for live music varies.*
(see p. 179)

Harry Denton's Bar & Grill. A popular meeting ground for Financial District singles. Deejays spin Top-40 tunes for dancing in the back room. The San Francisco bistro fare isn't bad either.... *Tel 415/882–1333. 161 Steuart St.; Embarcadero BART/Muni Metro station, 7 MUNI bus. Open nightly; dancing Thur–Sat only.* **(see p. 183)**

Harry Denton's Starlight Room. The view of the city from this dance club on the top floor of the Sir Francis Drake Hotel is amazing. With the big-band sound and elegant surroundings, it's like dancing on top of the world.... *Tel 415/ 392–7755. 450 Powell St.; Powell St. BART/MUNI Metro* station, Powell-Hyde or Powell-Mason cable car. Open nightly. Cover $6–12. **(see pp.182, 183)**

Hi-Ball Lounge. The dressed-up neo-swing crowd at this North Beach night club is young but they can do the Lindy.... Tel 415/397–9464. 473 Broadway, 15, 30, Or 45 MUNI bus. Open nightly. Cover varies. **(see p. 182)**

Jazz at Pearl's. Straightforward jazz in an old-style jazz club in North Beach. Pearl, who greets most patrons herself and strictly enforces her two-drink minimum.... Tel 415/291–8255. 256 Columbus Ave.; 15, 30 Muni bus. Closed Sun. No cover; 2-drink minimum. **(see p. 178)**

Johnny Love's. A lively Polk Gulch singles bar popular with both locals and out-of-towners. The dance floor has an irresistible pull after a few drinks.... Tel 415/931–8021. 1500 Broadway, Powell-Hyde cable car. Closed Sun. Cover $5–8 after 9:30. **(see p. 183)**

Junk. Every Thursday night, the Stud, a South of Market gay bar, turns into a wild party for bad-girl lesbians with a high-style attitude.... Tel 415/863–6623. 399 Ninth St., at Harrison, 42 MUNI bus (cab recommended). **(see p. 185)**

La India Bonita. Friday and Saturday night drag shows are extremely popular at this Mission District bar ($3 cover). The audience considers female impersonation to be an art form, in its own way. The neighborhood is questionable at night, so take a cab.... Tel 415/621–9294. 3089 16th St., at Valencia St.; 16th St. BART station. **(see p. 183)**

Latin American Club. You don't have to be a lounge-crowd fashion model to feel comfortable at this Mission District neighborhood bar.... Tel 415/647-2732. 3286 22nd St., 24th St. BART station. Open nightly. **(see p. 181)**

The Mint. If you haven't been to a gay karaoke bar, you haven't lived. The key to having fun at this Upper Market spot is definitely participation.... Tel 415/626–4726. 1942 Market St., near Guerrero St., Church St. MUNI Metro station. **(see p. 184)**

The Motherlode. About half the customers at this crowded, smoky Polk Gulch bar are drag queens. The rest are transvestites, transsexuals, and assorted men (both gay and straight) who come to ogle the ostensibly 90 percent female clientele. Born-female women simply do not come here. Spooky neighborhood; take a cab.... *Tel 415/928–6006. 1002 Post St., at Larkin St., 38 MUNI bus. No cover.*
(see p. 183)

New Orleans Room. Some of the biggest jazz musicians in the world play at this intimate, plush room at the Fairmont Hotel. Music can range from the blues of Charles Brown to Pete Escavedo's Latin big-band sounds.... *Tel 415/772–5259. 950 Mason St., Powell-Mason cable car. Open Wed–Sun. Show times vary. Cover $5–30.* **(see p. 178)**

The Oaks. This legal gambling room in Emeryville (between Oakland and Berkeley) is a far cry from a Las Vegas casino, but you can win or lose a bundle just as quickly. Texas Hold 'Em and Pai Gow are two of the most popular games here.... *Tel 510/653–4456. 4097 San Pablo Ave., Emeryville, take an AC Transit bus from the TransBay Terminal at First and Mission Sts.* **(see p. 185)**

177 Townsend. An industrial-style South of Market space for floating dance parties, featuring huge columns around the dance floor, an extravagant lighting system, and a big, round bar that makes it easy to get drinks.... *Tel 415/974–6020. 177 Townsend St., 42 MUNI bus. Hours vary; usually includes after-hours. Cover $5–20.* **(see p. 176)**

Pacific News. With just four poker tables, this small San Mateo gaming room is a cozy place to ante up, depending on your definition of cozy. It used to be unbelievably smoke-filled, but the new anti-smoking laws have eliminated that problem... *Tel 415/348–9383. 204-B Second Ave., San Mateo, take a SamTrans bus from the TransBay Terminal at First and Mission Sts.* **(see p. 185)**

Paradise Lounge. Up to five bands play in this unusual South of Market club every night, where modern rock, blues, funk, poetry, and occasionally even a lounge-lizard act can be heard. Sometimes three bands will play simultaneously, each on a different floor. The crowd is unpretentious, enjoys playing a little pool on the side, and is as diverse as the entertainment.... *Tel 415/861–6906. 1501 Folsom St., 42 MUNI bus. Open nightly. Cover free–$10.*

(see p. 176)

Pat O'Shea's Mad Hatter. This large tavern kitty-korner from the more dive-ish Abbey Tavern is more of a college sports bar than an authentic Irish pub, but the satellite TVs do attract a lot of visiting Celts who want to see their home soccer teams in action.... *Tel 415/752–3128. 2848 Geary Blvd. (at Third Ave.), 38 MUNI bus. Open nightly.*

(see p. 180)

The Pendulum. This is the city's only predominantly African-American gay bar, and it is absolutely packed on weekends.... *Tel 415/863–4441. 4146 18th St., at Collingwood St., Castro St. MUNI Metro station.* **(see p. 184)**

The Phoenix. If you want loud, crowded, and sweaty—and you want it young—this is the gay bar to find it. It's a very popular Castro cruise spot, especially since the crowd is racially mixed.... *Tel 415/552–6827. 482 Castro St., at 18th St., Castro St. MUNI Metro station.* **(see p. 184)**

The Plough and the Stars. The traditonal Irish music can be heavenly, as long as you don't mind sitting quietly and listening to it with the earthy-earnest Birkenstock crowd.... *Tel 415/751–1122. 116 Clement St. (at Second Ave.), 38 MUNI bus. $3 cover Fri and Sat nights.* **(see p. 181)**

Purple Onion. Going to see the garage bands at this semi-secret North Beach club is like going to a private local party. The owner's beer keg sometimes runs out prematurely, but the party usually lingers on anyway.... *Tel 415/398–8415. 140 Columbus Ave., 15 MUNI bus. Open Fri and Sat nights only.* **(see p. 176)**

The Saloon. This rowdy North Beach blues dive has live music seven nights a week. It's usually loud, local, and not well known, but occasionally local legends like Charlie Musselwhite stop by to blow a few notes.... *Tel 415/986–7666. 1232 Grant Ave., (near Columbus), 15 MUNI bus. Cover varies.* **(see p. 179)**

715 Harrison. A high-tech dance club with an outrageous sound system. The floating parties at this South of Market space, are for a very young crowd; some nights, 18-year-olds are admitted.... *Tel 415/979–8686. 715 Harrison St., 42 MUNI bus. Hours vary. Cover $10–15.*
(see p. 177)

650 Howard. A three-level South of Market space for floating dance parties.... *No phone. 650 Howard St.; Powell St. BART/Muni Metro station, 30 or 45 MUNI bus. Hours vary. Cover varies.* **(see p. 177)**

Skylark. An Elvis-meets-Barbie cocktail lounge where stylishly dressed bar-hoppers from the Marina go slumming in the Mission District.... *Tel 415/621–9294. 3089 16th St., (near Valencia St.), 16th St. BART station. Open nightly.*
(see p. 180)

Slim's. Get tickets in advance for most shows at Boz Scaggs' premier South of Market music club. And go early or you'll be stuck in the suffocating crowd on the dance floor.... *Tel 415/522–0333. 333 11th St. (near Folsom), 42 MUNI bus (best to take a taxi). Cover varies.* **(see p. 176)**

Sound Factory. The biggest dance club in town, with six different rooms. The music is techno, with some funk, hip-hop, and disco thrown in. No athletic attire allowed.... *Tel 415/543–1300. 525 Harrison St., 42 MUNI bus. Open Fri & Sat until at least 4am. Cover $10.* **(see p. 179)**

Storyville. Don Pender's jazz club presents all kinds of jazz—straight ahead, outside, acid, alternative—and blues to a crowd that definitely appreciates the music.... *Tel 415/441–1751. 1751 Fulton St. (near Masonic Ave.), 5 MUNI bus. Cover varies.* **(see p. 178)**

Ten 15. A South of Market dance club with multiple rooms and multiple themes. Go early or you'll stand in a long line alongside plenty of attitude.... *Tel 415/431–1200. 1015 Folsom St., 42 MUNI bus. Open Fri & Sat and sometimes for special parties on other nights, always after-hours. Cover charge.* **(see p. 179)**

Thirsty Bear Brewing Company. Close to the Museum of Modern Art, this is the best of the South of Market brew pubs.... *Tel 415/974–0905. 661 Howard St., (near Third St.), 15, 30, or 45 MUNI bus.* **(see p. 182)**

Three Babes and a Bus. This is a tour of four different clubs guided by three women who have made fun their business. These traveling parties happen Fridays and Saturdays unless you can get enough people together for a special party on other days. Call 415/552–2582 for details and reservations. **(see p. 181)**

330 Ritch. A cool crowd gathers in this industrial building, located on a little South of Market alleyway, to enjoy the tapas and listen to the latest sounds.... *Tel 415/541–9574. 330 Ritch St.; 15, 30, or 45 MUNI bus. Food 5–11 or midnight, happy hour 5–8 Tue–Fri, music in two sets: 6:30–8 & 9–1:30. Closed Mon. Cover free–$10.* **(see p. 177)**

Trocadero. This South of Market club is often the site of record-release parties for up-and-coming rock bands. It also features Bondage-A-Go-Go Wednesday nights.... *Tel 415/995–4600. 520 Fourth St.; Powell St. BART/MUNI Metro station, 30 or 45 Muni bus. Hours vary. Cover free–$15.* **(see p. 176)**

Twenty Tank Brewery. This microbrewery is more like an English ale house than a San Francisco brew pub.... *Tel 415/255–9455. 316 11th St. (at Folsom St.), 42 MUNI bus.* **(see p. 182)**

Twin Peaks. This old-fashioned, picture-windowed bar sits on the corner of Castro and Market. The crowd is usually relatively quiet and 40-plus.... *Tel 415/864–9470. 410 Castro St., Castro St. MUNI Metro station.* **(see p. 184)**

278 11th. Another South of Market space for floating dance parties, this one used to be the Oasis Club, where pool parties were common. Now the pool has a plastic cover that serves as the dance floor.... *No phone. 278 11th St., 42 MUNI bus. Hours vary. Cover $5–20.* **(see p. 177)**

Up & Down Club. A fashionably quaint jazz dinner club downstairs, with a hip bar upstairs. Good food. The live music downstairs is usually acid jazz; upstairs, deejays spin a variety of dance tracks. Co-owner supermodel Christy Turlington stops in when she's in town.... *Tel 415/626–2388. 1151 Folsom St., 42 MUNI bus.* **Down** *is open Wed–Sat with dinner until 10pm.* **Up** *is open Wed–Mon. Cover $5, free if you have dinner.* **(see p. 178)**

Yoshi's. This is definitely the top jazz venue on the West Coast. If a world-class jazz concert is on your agenda, take the ferry or drive across the bridge to Jack London Square (Oakland). Call for a schedule or check out the web site at www.yoshis.com... *Tel 510/238–9200. 510 Embarcadero West, Oakland.* **(see p. 178)**

enterta

7

nment

San Francisco
sells more theater
tickets per capita
than any major
city in America.
Most people
would be shocked

to hear that little trivia gem, given the fact that so many of the high-profile productions in town are recycled Broadway musicals that appeal mostly to out-of-towners. Sure, you can spend your money on tickets to *The Phantom of the Opera* (yawn), but your hard-earned entertainment dollar would be more wisely spent on some of the most innovative, dynamic stage productions in the country—written, produced, directed, and performed by top local talent.

San Francisco leaves the monumental cost of producing mainstream shows to New York, concentrating its own money and effort on unconventional creations. The city's dozens of unusual options include the **Lorraine Hansberry Theater**, a small space in the downtown theater district that focuses on new and experimental works by established African American playwrights; **Theater Rhinoceros** in the Mission District, the oldest gay/lesbian theater group in the country; **The Marsh**, another Mission District venue for avant-garde theater and dance; and **Josie's Juice Joint and Cabaret**, a Castro District vegetarian cafe that stages informal productions in its back room. And by all means, don't leave town without going to North Beach to see San Francisco's trademark show, *Beach Blanket Babylon*, the longest-running musical revue in history.

Here's another surprising bit of trivia—the first ballet company in the United States was the **San Francisco Ballet**. And its glory is not at all in the past: the *New York Times* proclaimed the current troupe, led by artistic director Helgi Tomasson (formerly a principal dancer with the New York City Ballet), "one of the country's finest." If you're looking for more unorthodox dance performances, there are plenty of troupes to see, from the mid-size companies that perform at **Theater Artaud** (Potrero Hill) to the small, cutting-edge shows in the Mission District's **Footwork Dance Studio** and **Third Wave Dance House**.

The **San Francisco Opera** performs in the opulent 1932 War Memorial Opera House, which re-opened in September 1997 after extensive renovations. The refurbished auditorium has all the requisite high-tech improvements—state-of-the-art lighting and computerized scenery-rigging equipment—plus new gold leaf and bigger bathrooms for women. (We're not sure what amenities the men got.) The **San Francisco Symphony** has its own digs—Davies Symphony Hall—and a new maestro, Michael Tilson Thomas, who left the London Symphony to become the toast of the Bay Area. Most other music—jazz, blues, folk, and rock—is performed primarily at the clubs you'll find in the Nightlife chapter.

Getting a bit too highbrow here? Not to worry. There are enough spectator sports in the Bay Area to balance out the whole culture bit—two major-league baseball teams, two NFL football teams, an NBA basketball team, an NHL hockey team, and two major horse-racing tracks. There are even two professional roller-hockey teams. Oakland fans were deliriously happy when the **Raiders** became their home team again in 1995, but lately ticket sales have been weak, and so has the team. At least the owner hasn't been sent off to court on gambling charges, like the **49ers'** Ed De Bartolo. Not yet, anyway.

Sources

For theater and music listings, the best mainstream source is the "Datebook" tabloid in the Sunday *Chronicle*, known to locals as "the pink section" because it's printed on pink newsprint. The *Bay Guardian* and *SF Weekly*, free alternative weeklies that can be found almost anywhere you look, are recommended for listings of more offbeat or intimate happenings. Radio stations that offer diverse programming and information on local performances and concerts include KPOO 89.5 FM, KQED 88.5 FM, and KPFA 94.1 FM.

In Search of Tony Bennett's Heart

Did you ever wonder exactly where Tony Bennett left his heart? We knew his heart called to him from a spot "where little cable cars climb halfway to the stars," but we never guessed the spot was the Visitors Information Center at Hallidie Plaza, even though it's right next to the Powell Street cable-car turnaround. Take the escalator from the turnaround down toward the BART entrance and go into the center, where you'll find the "I Left My Heart in San Francisco" gold record, the original song manuscript, and an earlier rough draft (be sure to read it—some of the lyrics really stink). While you're there, pick up some free walking-tour leaflets and ask the multilingual staff for any information or advice you need (tel 415/ 391–2000). There's also a 24-hour telephone hotline—in five languages—that lists daily events and activities (English: tel 415/391–2001, Spanish: tel 415/391–2122, French: tel 415/391–2003, German: tel 415/391–2004, and Japanese: tel 415/391–2101).

ENTERTAINMENT | INTRODUCTION

Getting Tickets

San Franciscans are an odd lot when it comes to performing arts—they adore the opera and ballet, and snap up season tickets so fast you barely have time to read through the season's program if you hope to get a good seat, yet the major blockbuster shows that seem to be a priority to out-of-towners are not that big of a draw for locals. (They also dine before the theater, not afterward.) Here's the moral of that story: If you want to go to an opera, symphony, or ballet performance, make arrangements before you get to town. You can call BASS (tel 800/225–BASS outside California) for one-stop ticket shopping, but if you aren't familiar with the concert halls, you may prefer to deal directly with each company's box office, where ticket representatives tend to have much more information about the best seats. If you want to see a major Broadway-type show, mention it to your hotel concierge when you secure your room reservation, or call BASS. Tickets for smaller venues and more avant-garde productions are usually available on relatively short notice, but you should check out the *Bay Guardian* and *SF Weekly* as soon as you get to town to find out what's going on and to reserve your seats.

For half-price, day-of-performance tickets to major theater, dance, and music events at selected venues, go to the **TIX** booth on the Stockton Street side of Union Square (cash or traveler's checks only, Tue–Thur 11–6, Fri–Sat 11–7; tel 415/433–7827). Even fairly popular shows sometimes need to fill seats with the steep discount. TIX also sells full-price advance tickets (credit cards accepted). **BASS** is the primary advance-sales outlet for all major Bay Area events, including sports, and you can purchase tickets by telephone (tel 510/762–BASS, 800/225–BASS outside California). In every big city, there are scalpers on the street at sold-out events—even though the practice is against the law—but if you are not familiar with the seating chart, you can easily plunk down a bundle of cash for a "great seat" behind a pillar or up in nosebleed territory. Counterfeit tickets are also a common scam, and they are very difficult to detect—unless the nefarious scalper has neglected to wash the printer's ink off his hands. If you're willing to pay more than face value for a good seat or a sold-out event, it's probably better to go through a ticket broker. They will charge a steep price for a premium ticket, but they usually have choice seats and impossible-to-get tickets. The toughest ticket to get is one to a Golden State Warriors basketball game—all of their home games are sold out to season-ticket holders—but **Mr. Ticket** might be able to help. Mr. T is the biggest ticket broker in the Bay Area, specializing in premium seating—at premium prices (tel 415/775–3031; 2065 Van Ness Ave.). You can also check the Yellow Pages—there are more than two dozen agencies listed under "Ticket Sales."

The Lowdown

The play's the thing... San Francisco's "theater district" is just west of picture-pretty Union Square, but like its New York counterpart, it brushes up against a less cultivated neighborhood—in this case, the Tenderloin. There is no particular danger during performance times, but you might want to take a cab at night, especially if you're dressed up and look like you might have a purse or wallet worth snatching. All of the theaters that specialize in Broadway and Broadway-bound shows are within a few blocks of each other—if Andrew Lloyd Webber turned the O.J. Simpson trial into a musical, it would eventually end up at the **Curran**, the **Golden Gate**, or the **Orpheum** theaters. The Curran has been playing *The Phantom of the Opera* for what seems like eons; the run is open-ended, but call in advance to be sure it's still playing. The grand-old Golden Gate Theater is located a little deeper into the Tenderloin than some overdressed the-atergoers would prefer, but it stages lots of Broadway favorites and revivals—in 1995, Tommy Tune's new pro-duction of the fifties rock-and-roll musical, *Grease,* was a big favorite (the only thing missing was a young John Travolta). The Orpheum's meticulously restored Spanish baroque building is every bit as glamorous as the produc-tions it hosts; when Carol Channing came to town with the revival of *Hello Dolly!*, she came to the Orpheum. But the theater district is not limited to Broadway block-busters. One of the less-publicized casualties of the 1989 Loma Prieta earthquake, the Geary Theater—home of the **American Conservatory Theater (ACT)**, one of the most highly regarded repertory groups in the country—has reopened. ACT continues to be a company with great range, presenting modern classics such as *A Streetcar Named Desire* alongside weighty Shakespearean epics. The **Marine's Memorial Theater** presents both local and off-Broadway productions; it was the San Francisco home of Tony Kushner's *Angels in America*. The ornate **Alcazar Theater** often stages long runs of its plays; you won't see anything out of the ordinary, but classics like *The Lion in Winter* please drama lovers who can't stand the idea of another tap-dancing chorus line. The **Stage Door Theater** presents a mixed bag of top-quality local come-dy productions in an intimate space.

On the fringes... Predictably, San Francisco concentrates a great deal of its theatrical resources on gay and lesbian, multicultural, and avant-garde productions. Many of the most experimental companies are housed in or near San Francisco's "New Bohemia"—the Mission District—but non-mainstream theater can be found throughout the city. The current *ne plus ultra* avant-garde venue is **The Marsh**, a Mission District performance space where you pay your money (usually $18 to $22) and take your chances, and often see remarkably talented artists right before they become trendy and famous. Aspiring actors, dancers, playwrights, and performance artists, take note: The Marsh is also the best place in town to network. Its predecessor—still among the most respected progressive art centers in the city—is another Mission District space called **Intersection for the Arts**, where Sam Shepard and Whoopi Goldberg tried out their acts before they got their 15 light-years of fame. The not-yet-discovered performers here are generally cutting-edge. Downtown, amid all the Broadway musicals and other big-money productions, the cozy little **Exit Theater** serves beer and wine and stages avant-garde "classics," from one-act comedies set in cafes to absurdist murder mysteries. You don't have to be a sullen existentialist to be experimental—this is a place to be a tad eccentric and have fun at the same time. It's always a pleasure to see a dance, theater, or multimedia production at **Theater Artaud** (Mission District), because the space itself is so well-run; this medium-sized mainstay of the experimental-theater scene has been around long enough to know how to give impeccably professional stagings of the most avant-garde works. **Climate Theater** (South of Market) is so tiny that it makes the audience feel almost intimate with the performers. Expect all kinds of experimental works here, including individual readings and performance art. The **Lorraine Hansberry Theater** (downtown) provides a showcase for some of the top African American playwrights and artists in the country, presenting both experimental and well-known works. The **Mission Cultural Center for Latino Arts** (Mission District) emphasizes works written and produced by multinational Latino artists, much of it political in nature and aimed at the neighborhood's Mexican, Central American, and Chicano population (many of the productions are in Spanish). **Theater Rhinoceros** (Mission District) was the first theater group in the United States to focus strictly on contemporary gay and lesbian issues; their productions range from bizarre, avant-garde performance pieces to traditional plays that feature gay characters. There's often a line stretching down the block in front of **Josie's Juice Joint and Cabaret**, a Castro District vegetarian cafe/cabaret combo where local gay performers will have you in a belly-laugh frenzy. Both gays and straights love this place, which will be obvious to you the moment you see the line full of every possible combination of couples waiting to get in. New works by local playwrights and artists are staged at the **Magic Theater** (Fort Mason)—some are stars and some are starving, but all are very, very good. The progressive **Phoenix Theater** (South of Market) also features the work of local playwrights; the productions are often mounted on a shoestring budget, but they can be powerful.

The main drag... It was a very sad day for San Francisco when Steve Silver, the mastermind behind *Beach Blanket Babylon*, died in 1995, but he left a legacy that promises to keep people laughing for years to come—the longest-running, wackiest musical revue in history. Watch reasonable facsimiles of Tina Turner, Hillary Clinton, and James Brown—all wearing huge, ridiculous headdresses—give "Snow White" advice on how to find a good man. (It sounds reasonable to us.) And you won't believe the hats—one of the more famous ones is a huge model of the San Francisco skyline. Reserve a few weeks in advance for the cabaret-style performances in North Beach's cozy Club Fugazi (to be admitted you must be at least 21 years old, with photo identification, except for Sunday matinees). There are many small bars in town where drag queens congregate and strut their stuff (see Nightlife), but the most mainstream is **Finocchio**, a family-owned North Beach cabaret that has been presenting glitzy female-impersonator revues since 1936. It's one of the best-known drag clubs in the world, and by no means does it cater specifically to a gay clientele, as do some of the smaller neighborhood clubs around town. The cabaret atmosphere is completely comfortable for anyone who enjoys a good show, but you have to be 21—the minimum drinking age—to get in.

Mostly Mozart... Under the innovative direction of maestro Michael Tilson Thomas, who left the London

Symphony to become the toast of the Bay Area, the San Francisco Symphony grabbed national attention by winning both the 1997 Grammy award for Best Orchestral Performance and the American Society of Composers and Songwriters (ASCAP) award for Strongest Commitment to New American Music that same year. Davies Symphony Hall has had a slightly less direct route to public relations heaven. A huge, modern concert hall with what seems like acres of concrete and glass, it had a number of embarrassing acoustical glitches (echoes in the balcony among other problems) when it opened in 1980. Since then it has undergone a complete renovation and is now considered one of the finest modern concert venues in the world, with amenities that include the Ruffatti Organ, the largest concert hall organ in North America (eight divisions of 163 ranks and 9,235 pipes.

Men in tights... One of the city's cultural treasures, the world-class **San Francisco Ballet** normally shares its home with the opera, performing regularly at the War Memorial Opera House. Artistic director, Helgi Tomasson, is a darling of dance critics, especially in New York, where he was considered a premiere danseur, and worked closely with Balanchine. His production of *Romeo and Juliet* was hailed as one of the most inventive ever staged. The ballet's primary seasons are spring and fall, but there are special Christmas performances, including, of course, *The Nutcracker*. If you're inclined to take BART across the bay, you can see the **Oakland Ballet** perform at the gorgeous Paramount Theater, a perfectly restored landmark art-deco movie palace that alone is worth the trip. This exuberant, multiracial company is not as developed as its San Francisco counterpart, but some of the pieces are actually more interesting, in part because they feature a number of brilliant young dancers who are obviously delighted to be performing. Their enthusiasm is refreshing; the dancing isn't always perfect, but they are a lot of fun to watch. Artistic director, Ronn Guidi, loves to do historical reconstructions of old ballets and present new experimental ones. In 1997 he presented Nijinsky's *Chopin Concerto* along with a world premiere of *Dim Sum*, ancient Chinese folk tales set to Chinese music.

Dancing with the avant-garde... The city's unconventional dance companies gather where the rest of the avant-garde performing artists do—in the Mission District. Small, funky groups and extreme, cutting-edge choreographers showcase their work at **Dancers Group Studio Theater**, a small Mission District studio where local choreographers are having a creative field day and neighborhood audiences are eating it up. The best part is that the "attitude factor" is minor. Some very innovative productions have been staged at **Third Wave Dance House**, with local choreographers and ethnic traditions (a natural for the Mission District). The popular company closed its doors for awhile in 1997, but was scheduled to reopen in the spring of 1998. It's worth checking into. A few blocks away, experimental, mid-sized touring and local companies perform at **Theater Artaud**.

Grand opera... The **San Francisco Opera** is an experience, not just for the thrilling performances by top international stars, but also for the little risks the company takes just because, after all, this is San Francisco. There were, for example, the nuns (played by "supernumeraries," opera's version of extras) who stripped totally naked and physically climbed the walls to illustrate their possession by the devil, and an opera composed by jazz/pop vocalist Bobby McFerrin with progressive novelist Ishmael Reed as the librettist. Then there is the audience, half of whom are dressed to the nines while the other half arrives in jeans and sneakers. Boxes at the grand-old War Memorial Opera House are fabulous, with elegant brocade chairs and heavy velvet curtains. The opera season starts in September and runs through January, with a short summer season as well. Tickets are not easy to come by, so plan in advance. If you arrive without tickets, your only alternative may be standing-room tickets, available for every performance for $10 to $14. Line up at the box office at 10:00 that morning and hope they don't sell out before you get to the window.

Take me out to the ballgame... If you love sports, you came to the right place. From April to October, there is major-league baseball: The **San Francisco Giants** play at **3Com Park** (Candlestick Park). Candlestick which fans persist in calling by its former name, can get so cold at nights that the Giants used to give out a little orange pin—

a badge of courage called a *Croix de Candlestick*—to every fan who stayed until the end of an extra-inning night game. (The pin bore a motto that was Latin for "I came, I saw, I froze.") None of that will matter in a year or so. The Giants have already broken ground on a new downtown ballpark that promises to be cozy (42,000 seats), sunny, and open for business in April 2000. The **Oakland A's** play across the bay at the **Oakland Coliseum**, a sunny, warm, ballpark that used to have wide-open bleachers, until the Raiders came back to town and turned the Coliseum into a generic football bowl. Now there's a 10,000-seat, high-rise monstrosity where the bleachers used to be. Those seats aren't even used for baseball, which makes the already sparse attendance at A's games look utterly bleak. There are still a few good things about the Coliseum, though: an old-fashioned manual scoreboard, fantastic food, and imported beers. Tickets to see either baseball team have been plentiful since the strike that cancelled the 1994 World Series and made fans mad as hell. Come the end of summer, football teams start filling the stadiums—the **San Francisco 49ers**, which play on Sundays at Candlestick, and the **Oakland Raiders**. Bay Area football fans are often characterized as falling into two distinct molds: The wine-and-brie set at Candlestick and the Bud-and-burgers bunch at the Coliseum. Either way, tickets can be hard to come by, but if you're willing to spend enough money, you can usually snag one from a ticket broker.

Hockey and basketball start in October and November. The **San Jose Sharks**—whose logo of a shark devouring a hockey stick made their licensed hats and clothing into best-sellers before the team played its first game—skate at the **San Jose Arena**, about an hour south of San Francisco. The **Golden State Warriors** play at the Oakland Coliseum arena, which reopened in 1997 after renovations that added 4,000 seats (it now seats 19,200). The newest pro sport in the Bay Area is roller hockey, played June through August; the **San Jose Rhinos** play at the San Jose Arena. (Frankly, we preferred roller derby.) Finally, if you like to play the ponies (we love to), you have two choices for a sunny day at the races: **Bay Meadows** in San Mateo or **Golden Gate Fields** near Berkeley. Bay Meadows seems to be preferred by San Franciscans, who are loathe to cross the Bay Bridge for any reason, but Golden Gate Fields is a real salt-of-the-earth racetrack.

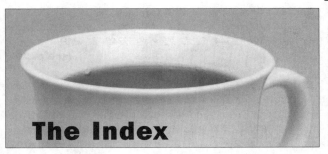

The Index

Alcazar Theater. A variety of top-quality, if not exactly new, plays are produced here, often for long runs…. *Tel 415/441–4042. 650 Geary St., 19 or 38 MUNI bus.* **(see p. 201)**

American Conservatory Theater (ACT). Earthquake damage to the Geary Theater has now been completely repaired and the renowned repertory company is back onstage at home.…*Tel 415/834–3200. Geary Theater, 415 Geary St., 5 MUNI bus.* **(see p. 201)**

Bay Meadows. This is a beautiful place for thoroughbred horse-racing, with picnic facilities and a playground for children…. *Tel 415/574–7223. 2600 S. Delaware St., San Mateo. Take CalTrain directly to Bay Meadows. To drive: Take Hwy. 101 South to the Hillsborough exit, head west, and follow signs to track. Seasons run Jan. 21–Mar. 29 and Sept. 4–Nov. 15. Post time 12:45, 6:45 on Fri.* **(see p. 206)**

Beach Blanket Babylon. It wouldn't be San Francisco without this totally wacky musical revue—and the gigantic, ridiculous headdresses that made it famous—at Club Fugazi, a cozy cabaret in North Beach. Reserve well in advance, or purchase your tickets by telephone before you get to town…. *Tel 415/421–4222. Club Fugazi, 678 Green St., 15, 30, or 45 MUNI bus. Shows Wed, Thur at 8, Fri, Sat at 7 & 10, Sun 3 & 7.* **(see p. 198)**

Climate Theater. This South of Market theater features monologues, plays, political satires, and performance art…. *Tel 415/978–2345. 285 Ninth St. (near Folsom), 10, 12, 20, 50, 60, 70, or 80 MUNI bus.* **(see p. 202)**

Curran Theater. The Curran presents both warmed-over Broadway hits and Broadway-bound musicals…. *Tel 415/551–2000. 445 Geary St., 19 or 38 MUNI bus.* **(see p. 201)**

Dancers Group Studio Theater. Most dance buffs are really excited about this small Mission District studio.... *Tel 415/824–5044. 3221 22nd St., 24th St. BART station.* **(see p. 205)**

Exit Theater. Closer to the mainstream than many neighborhood theaters, this small theater-district house is gaining a national reputation for avant-garde "classics".... *Tel 415/673–3847. 156 Eddy St., Civic Center BART/MUNI Metro station, 19 or 31 MUNI bus.* **(see p. 202)**

Finocchio. The Queen Mother of drag clubs, crossing over to an audience of straights as well as gays. There are three shows a night—for a cover charge of less than $15—and you can often get in without reservations.... *Tel 415/982–9388; after 7pm 415/362–9913. 506 Broadway, 15 or 30 MUNI bus. Open Thur–Sat 8:30, 10 & 11:30.* **(see p. 203)**

Golden Gate Fields. Across the bay in Albany (next to Berkeley), Golden Gate Fields offers thoroughbred horse racing and a view of the bay—but not at the same time: The track faces Interstate 80.... *Tel 510/526–3020. Seasons run Nov–Jan and Mar–June. Take shuttle or cab from N. Berkeley BART station. AC Transit (Tel 800/559–4636) runs buses direct from Transbay Terminal. To drive: cross Oakland–San Francisco Bay Bridge and take Interstate 80 east to Gilman St. exit; turn left to get to track.* **(see p. 206)**

Golden Gate Theater. This grand-old theater offers Broadway touring shows and revivals.... *Tel 415/551-2000. 1 Taylor St. (near Sixth and Market Sts.), Powell St. BART/MUNI Metro station, 6, 7, 8, 9, 21, or 66 MUNI bus.* **(see p. 201)**

Golden State Warriors. See Oakland Coliseum **(see p. 206)**

Intersection for the Arts. This Mission District institution, the oldest experimental arts center in the city, features plays, visual arts, dance performances, and readings.... *Tel 415/626–2787. 446 Valencia St., 16th St. BART/MUNI Metro station, 26 MUNI bus.* **(see p. 202)**

Josie's Juice Joint and Cabaret. Local gay performers wow an eclectic crowd at this Castro District cabaret. There's virtually no parking, so take public transportation. Reservations are recommended, but get there early, because there's always a line to fill in for last-minute no-shows.... *Tel 415/861–7933. 3583 16th St. near Market, Castro St. MUNI Metro station.* **(see pp. 198, 203)**

Lorraine Hansberry Theater. Some of the most prominent African American playwrights and performers are featured at this downtown theater. The emphasis is usually on new approaches or pieces with social significance.... *Tel 415/474–8800. 620 Sutter St., Powell-Mason cable car, 2, 3, 4, or 76 MUNI bus.* **(see pp. 198, 202)**

Magic Theater. New plays by American playwrights are the main attraction at this Fort Mason theater.... *Tel 415/441–8822. Building D, Fort Mason, Marina Blvd. at Buchanan St., 28 MUNI bus.* **(see p. 203)**

Marine's Memorial Theater. Theater district home to serious drama.... *Tel 415/771–6900. 609 Sutter St., 2, 3, 4, or 76 MUNI bus.* **(see p. 201)**

The Marsh. *The* place to see the latest avant-garde productions, it's hip, it's fun, it's good, and it's reasonably priced.... *Tel 415/641–0235. 1062 Valencia St., 24th St. BART/MUNI Metro station, 26 MUNI bus.* **(see pp. 198, 202)**

Mission Cultural Center for Latino Arts. Latino artists from many different cultures are featured at this Mission District showcase.... *Tel 415/821–1155. 2868 Mission St., 24th St. BART station.* **(see p. 202)**

Oakland A's. See Oakland Coliseum. **(see p. 206)**

Oakland Ballet. This lively young company is made up of brilliant young dancers from several countries. Their performance hall, the landmark art-deco Paramount Theater, is breathtaking.... *Tel 510/465–6400. 2025 Broadway, Oakland, 19th St. BART station, (3 stops from San Francisco's Embarcadero station).* **(see p. 204)**

Oakland Coliseum. The Oakland A's and, once again, the Oakland Raiders play across the bay here.... *For tickets to A's games, call BASS (tel 510/762–BASS, 800/225–BASS outside California); for Raiders tickets, call a ticket broker. Coliseum BART station.* **(see p. 206)**

Oakland Raiders. See Oakland Coliseum. **(see pp. 199, 206)**

Orpheum Theater. Fans of big Broadway musicals love this restored Spanish baroque theater in the theater district.... *Tel 415/551–2000. 1192 Market St., Civic Center BART/ MUNI Metro station.* **(see p. 201)**

Phoenix Theater. A progressive South of Market theater, the Phoenix presents works by local as well as world-famous playwrights.... *Tel 415/621–4423. 301 Eighth St., 19 or 26 MUNI bus.* **(see p. 203)**

San Francisco Ballet. The city's premier classical ballet troupe performs at the Opera House. Ordinarily, there are some balcony seats available for most performances, even without advance purchase.... *Tel 415/703–9400. 301 Van Ness Ave., Civic Center BART/MUNI Metro station.*
(see p. 204)

San Francisco 49ers. See 3 Com Park. **(see pp. 199, 206)**

San Francisco Giants. See 3 Com Park. **(see p. 205)**

San Francisco Opera. San Franciscans have had an uncondi-tional love affair with opera since the gold rush. You can go in a tuxedo or in blue jeans—nobody cares. The season runs from September through January, plus a short summer season. Get tickets far in advance.... *Tel 415/864–3330. 301 Van Ness Ave., Civic Center BART/MUNI Metro station.*
(see pp. 198, 205)

San Francisco Symphony. Try to get tickets before you get to town, or give your hotel concierge a generous tip to do it for you as soon as you arrive. If you can't get into a regular per-formance, though, try to get into a dress rehearsal (cheap, casual, and intimate) and definitely take advantage of the free tours of Davies Hall, Wednesdays and Saturdays by appointment ($3 general admission, $2 seniors and stu-dents).... *Tel 415/552–8338. 201 Van Ness Ave., Civic Center BART/MUNI Metro station.* **(see p. 198)**

San Jose Arena. Well, the Sharks haven't exactly brought home a Stanley Cup yet, but their fans don't care. The arena, is about an hour south of San Francisco.... *For tickets call*

BASS (tel 510/762–BASS, 800/225–BASS outside CA); for other information, call the arena (tel 408/287–4275). Take CalTrain from Fourth St. & Townsend St. depot to 65 Cahill station; free shuttle from station to arena. To drive: Take Hwy. 101 S. to Guadalupe Pkwy.; exit at Julian St.; take right. Follow Julian St. to Burns Ave. S., then turn left and follow signs to stadium. Free shuttle from parking lot. **(see p. 206)**

San Jose Rhinos. See San Jose Arena. **(see p. 206)**

San Jose Sharks. See San Jose Arena. **(see p. 206)**

Stage Door Theater. Downtown theater specializing in comedies, with local casts.... Tel 415/749–2228. 420 Mason St., Powell St. BART/MUNI Metro station. **(see p. 201)**

Theater Artaud. Dance, theater, or multimedia productions appear at this well-run Mission District experimental theater.... Tel 415/621–7797. 450 Florida St. (near 16th St.), 16th St. BART/MUNI Metro station, 12 or 33 MUNI bus.
(see pp. 198, 202, 205)

Theater Rhinoceros. This Mission District company, focuses in on gay and lesbian issues.... Tel 415/861–5079. 2926 16th St., 16th St. BART/MUNI Metro station.
(see pp. 198, 202)

Third Wave Dance House. This Mission District dance studio, which showcases local choreographers and ethnic traditions, was scheduled to reopen in Spring 1998.... Tel 415/831–1732. **(see pp. 198, 205)**

3Com Park. Home to the Giants for baseball and the 49ers for football, it's pretty cold on summer nights—you'll need a down parka—but it's fine during the day, and wonderfully balmy throughout the football season.... For tickets, call BASS (tel 510/762–BASS, 800/225–BASS outside CA) or a ticket broker. Express bus service available through MUNI (tel 415/673–MUNI). If you must drive (we don't recommend it), take Hwy. 101 S. to the stadium exit.
(see p. 205)

hotlines & other basics

Airports... Two major airports serve the city—**San Francisco International Airport (SFO)** (tel 415/761–0800; website www.ci.sf.ca.us/sfo) and **Oakland International Airport (OAK)** (tel 510/577–4000; website www.flyoakland.com). Most travelers will use SFO, which is served by 46 major airlines and is located 15 miles south of downtown San Francisco (Highway 101 or 280). Fares to either airport are usually identical, so if a flight to SFO is sold out, there may still be available seats on flights to the lesser-known stepsister, OAK, situated within a few minutes of the Coliseum BART stop (four stops from San Francisco's Financial District).

Airport transportation to the city... Super-cheap public transport is available from the airport to downtown via **SamTrans** (tel 800/660–4287; website www.samtrans. com); from the International terminal on the upper level or the United Airlines terminal, catch the 7F express bus for just $2.50 (you are allowed only one carry-on bag) or the 7B bus for $1 into the city, $2 outbound (bring as much baggage as you like). The 7F express takes about 30 minutes; the 7B takes about an hour. A taxi ride to the city center costs about $30 including tip and usually takes about 20–30 minutes, depending on traffic. Shuttle vans that carry up to six passengers offer door-to-door service for around $10 to most hotels and take 20–30 minutes; they're easy to catch at the airport, but reservations are recommended for your return trip from the city to the airport. Some of the most popular shuttles are **American Airporter Shuttle** (tel 415/876–0411); **Bay Shuttle** (tel 415/564–3400); **Door-to-Door Airport Express** (tel 415/775–5121); **Francisco's Adventures** (tel 415/821–0903); **Lorrie's Airport Shuttle** (tel 415/334–9000); **Pacific Airport Shuttle** (tel 415/252–8300); **Peter's Airport Shuttle** (tel 415/777–4899); **Quake City Shuttle** (tel 415/777–4899); **SF Advance Shuttle** (tel 415/495–2955); **SF City Shuttle** (tel 415/872–0440); **Super Shuttle** (tel 415/1558–8500); and **Yellow Airport Shuttle** (tel 415/282–7433). The **SFO Airporter** (tel 415/671–3100) is an express bus that offers door-to-door service to most major hotels for $10; no reservations are required.

All-night pharmacies... Got that itchy, sneezy, whatever-else-it-is, can't-sleep thing happening? Worse yet, did you just drop your last estrogen pill down the drain? Not to worry. **Walgreens 24-Hour Prescription Service** (tel 415/861–3136, 498 Castro St.; tel 415/931–6417, 3201 Divisadero St.) is there to help you.

Babysitters... First ask the concierge if your hotel offers child-care service. Otherwise, try these agencies (all members of the San Francisco Convention and Visitors Bureau): **American Childcare Service** (tel 415/285–2300), offers private in-room service at your hotel, excursions arranged for children 12 and older, and is fully licensed, bonded, and insured; **Starr Belly Child Care Services** (tel 415/541–8592) has on-call child care at your hotel, seven days a week, with all providers licensed, bonded, insured, and trained in CPR.

BART... **Bay Area Rapid Transit (BART)** is essentially a commuter railway that links neighboring communities with San Francisco. There are eight stations in the city itself. Fares depend on the distance of the ride, but for a special $2.60 excursion fare, you can ride the entire system as far as you want, any direction you want, as long as you exit the system at the same station you entered. All tickets are dispensed from machines at the stations. Contact their website at www.bart.org.

Buses... San Francisco Municipal Railway (MUNI) buses are marked on the front with the number of the line and the destination. Fare is $1 for adults, 35¢ for children and seniors. To find out which bus to take to get where you want to go, call 415/673–MUNI (website www. transitinfo.org). Official MUNI route maps are available throughout the city at newsstands and many other stores for $2.

Cable cars... There are three cable-car routes: the Powell-Hyde line begins at Powell and Market streets and ends at Victorian Park near the Maritime Museum and Aquatic Park; the Powell-Mason line also begins at Powell and Market streets, but it ends at Bay and Taylor streets near Fisherman's Wharf; the California Street line starts at California and Market streets and ends at Van Ness Avenue. Fare is $2.

Car rentals... Suit yourself—pick up a tiny little bread box on wheels from Enterprise Rent-A-Car at the airport for less than $20 a day, with unlimited free mileage; or cruise through your vacation in a Ferrari 348 Spyder convertible from Sunbelt Sports Cars for $850 a day and $2 a mile. Or settle for something in between—economy cars with unlimited mileage tend to rent for around $30–$40 a day, while a zippy convertible like a Mazda Miata will set you back about $80 a day. Here are several San Francisco rental companies (most have more than one location): **Alamo Rent-A-Car** (tel 415/882–9440, 687 Folsom St.); **Avis Rent-A-Car** (tel 800/331–1212 or 415/885–5011, 675 Post St.); **Bay Area Rentals, Cars, Trucks and Vans** (tel 415/621–8989, 229 Seventh St.); **Budget Rent-A-Car** (tel. 800/527–0700 or 415/875–6850, 321 Mason St.); **California Compacts Rent-A-Car** (tel 800/954–7368 or 415/871–4421, 245 S. Airport Blvd.); **Dollar Rent-A-Car** (tel 800/800–4000 or 415/244–4130, San Francisco International Airport); **Enterprise Rent-A-Car** (tel 800/325–8007 or 415/441–3369, 1133 Van Ness Ave.); **Hertz Rent-A-Car** (tel 800/654–3131 or 415/771–2200, ext. 518, 433 Mason St.); **Reliable Rent-A-Car** (tel 415/928–4414, 349 Mason St.); **Sunbelt Sports Cars** (tel 415/771–9191, 320 O'Farrell St.); **Thrifty Car Rental** (tel 800/367–2277 or 415/788–8111, 520 Mason St.).

Cash advances, check cashing, and ATM cards... If you aren't having any luck at automated teller machines and want to ask a human teller for a cash advance against your credit card, try calling **Bank of America** (tel 415/622–3546) or **First Interstate Bank** (tel 415/765–4511). **American Express** has four offices with full financial services, including personal-check cashing: Downtown (tel 415/398–8578, 124 Geary St.); Financial District (tel 415/536–2600, 560 California St. or 455 Market St.); and Fisherman's Wharf (tel 415/775–0240, 333 Jefferson St.). To find out the nearest ATM that will accept your **Cirrus Network** card, call 800/424–7787; for **Plus System**, call 800/843–7587.

Chauffeurs... Can't resist a man in uniform? Sometimes you've just got to lounge in the back of a long, black limousine with a chauffeur at the wheel. If the need arises while you're in San Francisco, call **Drivers Exclusive** (tel 800/395–3632) for 24-hour service, or **We Drive U, Inc.** (tel 800/773–7483). The company names may be a bit tacky, but what do you want for borrowed luxury?

Climate... Everybody knows that Mark Twain supposedly said the coldest winter he ever spent was summer in San Francisco. It's true that July can be downright chilly, but the truth is that the city is rarely—if ever—what a New England Yankee would call cold, or what a New Orleans belle would call hot. In fact, the weather is predictably unpredictable. A sunny morning can turn into a chilly afternoon, just as a thick morning fog often gives way to a gorgeous sun-drenched day. The standard pitch is that temperatures don't drop below 40°F (5°C) or rise above 70°F (21°C), but don't believe it. Every year there are many 80° days that are sworn to be the exception; there's just no predicting when they might occur. In general, September and October are the warmest months, and May through September are the driest. No matter when you visit, be sure to dress in layers. Whatever you expect the weather to be, it will almost certainly be otherwise—at least part of the time.

Concierges... If you're not staying at a hotel that offers the services of a resident concierge and you want personalized travel planning, shopping excursions, entertainment, ticket purchasing, or any other special arrangements, enlist your own private concierge—after you arrive or while you're still planning your vacation. Try **Ideas Unlimited/Unlimited Ideas** (tel 800/900–4884 or 415/668–7089), **Instead of You, Inc.** (tel 415/567–1985) or **Leisure Resources** (tel 800/758–5479 or 510/758–4868).

Convention center... The elegant—and extremely popular—**Moscone Center** (tel 415/974–4000, 747 Howard
St.) was named in memory of San Francisco's well-liked
mayor who was slain—along with the city's first openly
gay elected official, Harvey Milk—by a man who con-
vinced a jury he could not be held responsible because he
had eaten too many Twinkies and it made him insane. It
was a bitter tragedy for San Franciscans, but the Moscone
Center is a fitting tribute in its unparalleled success—it is
one of the most popular convention sites in the country,
despite all the bad press about the city's earthquakes and
frigid summer weather.

Dentists... The San Francisco Convention and Visitors
Bureau recommends **San Francisco Dental Office** for
24-hour emergency service (tel 415/777–5115, 131
Steuart St., Suite 323, between Mission and Howard Sts.;
Non-emergency hours: Mon and Fri 8–4:30; Tue–Thur
10:30–7; closed Sat and Sun).

Doctors... If you have a serious emergency, you should go
directly to a hospital emergency room, but for other medical needs, try **Traveler Medical Group** (tel 415/
981–1102), a 24-hour, multilingual medical staff of inter-
nal-medicine physicians who will make "house calls" to
your hotel. No appointments are necessary at **Physician
Access Medical Center** (tel 415/397–2881, 26 California
St.). Same-day appointments can be made at **Downtown
Medical** (tel 415/362–7177, 450 Sutter St.), whose doctors are familiar with all travel-related medical conditions.

Driving around... Lots of people drive in the city, and as a
rule they're much more courteous than in New York City
or Paris or Rome. The city is compact, but can be a bit
confusing, so if you're going to drive be sure to get a map.
Your driver's license from any other state (and most
Western nations) is valid in California for a year, but
there are a few things you should know about local safety
precautions and laws. Remember, San Francisco is a city
of hills (43, to be exact), and since you probably don't
want your car to roll down one while you're not in it,
there's only one sure bet: **Curb your wheels**. Turn the
front tires toward the street when you're parked facing
uphill and toward the curb when you're parked facing
downhill. This is not just a good idea, it's the law in San
Francisco. **Know what the curb colors mean: Red** means
no stopping or parking; **yellow** means all commercial
vehicles may stop for up to a half-hour; **yellow-and-**

black means only commercial trucks may stop for up to a half-hour; **green-yellow-and-black** is a taxi zone; **blue** is for cars with California disabled placards; **green** means all vehicles may stop for up to 10 minutes; **white** means all vehicles are limited to a 5-minute stop while the adjacent business is still open. **Towaway zones**: Nobody loves to tow cars more than San Francisco's Finest. It's big money for the city (almost 30% of all parking tickets issued in the state are issued in San Francisco), and the odds are always against you if you park illegally. You'll shell out a minimum of $20 for the most minor parking violation, plus another $100 for towing, plus storage fees. If you park in a disabled zone, the violation alone will cost $250 to $275, not to mention the towing fees and hassle of getting the car back.

Emergencies... Like anywhere else, **call 911**, but don't be surprised if you get put on hold. It's always best to try to stay out of dangerous areas and situations to begin with. Other emergency/information numbers: **Ambulance** (tel 415/931–3900); **Poison Control Center** (tel 415/476–6600); **Suicide Prevention** (tel 415/221–1424); and **Traveler's Aid** (tel 415/255–2252).

Events hotline... Call the **Visitor Information Center** 24 hours a day for a recorded message listing San Francisco's events and activities in five different languages: English (tel 415/391–2001); French (tel 415/391–2003); Spanish (tel 415/391–2122); Japanese (tel 415/391–2101); and German (tel 415/391–2004).

Ferries... Several ferries connect San Francisco with communities around the bay. Be sure to call for schedule information. The **Blue & Gold Fleet** (tel 415/705–5444) provides daily round-trip service from the Ferry Building and Pier 39 to Oakland, Alameda, and Vallejo. Fare to Oakland or Alameda is $3.75, $1.50 for children, $2.50 for seniors; to Vallejo, $7.50, $4 for children, $6 for seniors. Package fare to Marine World/Africa USA (Vallejo), including round-trip ferry, bus shuttle, and park admission is $36, $20.50 for children 5–12 (under 5 free), $30 for seniors. **Golden Gate Ferries** (tel 415/923–2000, TDD 415/257–4554) serve Sausalito and Larkspur from the Ferry Building. Fare is $4.25, $3.20 for children, $2.10 for seniors; weekdays to Larkspur, $2.50, $1.90 for children, $1.25 for seniors. **Harbor Bay Maritime Ferry** (tel 415/769–5500) goes to Harbor Bay Island in

Alameda from the Ferry Building. Fare is $4, $2 for children, $3 for seniors. The **Red & White Fleet** (tel 800/229–2784, 415/546–2700) serves Sausalito, Tiburon, Angel Island, and Alcatraz. Fare to Angel Island is $9, $4.50 for children, $8 for seniors; to Alcatraz (including audiocassette rental), $10, $4.75 for children, $8.25 for seniors; to Sausalito/Tiburon, $5.50, $2.75 for children, $5.50 for seniors.

Festivals and special events... From the crowning of Japantown's Cherry Blossom Queen and the Gay Pride Parade of self-styled queens to Chinese New Year and *Dia de los Muertos* (Day of the Dead), San Francisco's extraordinary diversity is celebrated year-round in one festival after another. A complete monthly listing is published in the *Bay City Guide*, free at information racks in the airports and at most hotels. Here is a brief sample of some of the major events:

January: **Sports and Boat Show** (tel 415/469–6065), Cow Palace; nine days. **Tet Festival** (tel 415/885–2743), Vietnamese New Year, held at Larkin and O'Farrell streets.

February: **Chinese New Year** (tel 415/982–3000) can be in late January or early February, depending on the lunar calendar; climaxes with giant parade down Chinatown's Grant Avenue. **Russian Festival** (tel 415/921–7631), three-day celebration around Sutter and Divisadero streets.

March: **St. Patrick's Day Parade** (tel 415/391–2000) starts at Market and 2nd streets and goes past City Hall.

April: **International Film Festival**, one of the most popular film festivals in America (schedule, tel 415/932–FILM; tickets, tel 415/931–FILM; Kabuki 8 Cinemas, Fillmore and Post Sts.). **Cherry Blossom Festival** (tel 415/563–2313), held in Japantown and Golden Gate Park's Japanese Tea Garden, offering traditional arts, music, theater, and food booths.

May: **Bay to Breakers** (tel 415/777–7771), a kooky-costume footrace across town from the Embarcadero (on the bay) to the ocean. **Black and White Ball** (tel 415/431–5400), a flashy fundraiser held in odd-numbered years to benefit the San Francisco Symphony; Civic Center is closed off for this all-night party-hop that attracts the city's biggest celebrities and those who are willing to pay $150 apiece to rub shoulders with them. **Carnaval** (tel 415/826–1401), a week-long fiesta in the Mission District, leading up to a parade that ends up on 14th Street (near Harrison Street)

SAN FRANCISCO | HOTLINES & OTHER BASICS

with a huge samba party. **Cinco de Mayo** (tel 415/826–1401), two-day fiesta; parade runs from 24th and Mission streets to Civic Center Plaza.

June: **Lesbian/Gay/Bisexual/Transgender Freedom Day Parade** (tel 415/864–3733), a celebration of gay pride with floats and groups from the Sisters of Perpetual Indulgence to Dykes on Bikes. **Stern Grove Midsummer Music Festival** (tel 415/252–6252), a series of free 2pm Sunday concerts held at 19th Avenue and Sloat Boulevard, featuring local performers, from the opera and symphony to jazz and ballet.

July: **San Francisco Marathon** (tel 415/296–7111), mid-month. **Jewish Film Festival** (tel 510/548–0556 held at Castro Theater and the U.C. Theater, Berkeley), the world's largest Jewish film festival; two weeks.

August: **San Francisco Shakespeare Festival** (tel 415/422–2222), free performances in Golden Gate Park run through October.

September: **Blues Festival** (schedule, tel 415/826–6837; tickets, tel 415/835–3849), outdoors at Fort Mason; two days. **San Francisco Fair** (tel 415/391–2000), sophisticated county fair (the city and county are one and the same) in Fort Mason, with vintage wines and California cuisine instead of corn dogs and carnival rides. **Opera in the Park** (tel 415/861–4008), a free opera in Golden Gate Park kicks off the San Francisco Opera's fall season.

November: *Dia de los Muertos* **(Day of the Dead)** (tel 415/826–8009), a Mexican fiesta and parade in the Mission District designed to honor the dead and to be so much fun it entices their spirits to return for the party. *The Nutcracker* (tel 415/776–1999, San Francisco Ballet box office) and **Sing-It-Yourself Messiah** (tel 415/431–5400, Louise M. Davies Symphony Hall box office) are extremely popular holiday traditions that are sold out far in advance.

Gay and lesbian resources... The lesbian and gay communities in the Bay Area are very well organized, and have countless resources at their disposal. The *Bay Area Reporter* is the best-known gay publication, with complete listings of organizations and events (website www.ebar.com). Some useful websites include the **Lavender Pages** (www.lavenderpages.com), **Amazon Online** (www.amazon.org), Q San Francisco (www.qsanfrancisco.com) and **Frontiers** (www.frontiersweb.

com/sfcurrent). All are distributed at bars, bookstores, cafes, and stores around the city. The **Gay/Lesbian/ Bisexual/Transgendered Switchboard** (tel 510/841– 6224) is in Berkeley. **Electric City Network** is a gay television show on cable channel 53, Fri 10:30pm. **Lavender Lounge** is a gay variety show, Tue 10pm, cable channel 47. **Fruit Punch** is a long-running gay radio show (since 1973), Wed 7pm, KPFA 94.1 FM and KPFB 89.3 FM; **Hibernia Beach** is a gay radio talk show, Sun 7am, KITS 105.3 FM. The **Gay and Lesbian Historical Society** (tel 415/626–0890, archive open weekends 2–5 by appointment) collects and preserves historically significant materials. The **Deaf Gay and Lesbian Center** (tel 415/ 266–9944 TDD or 800/735–2922 for Cal Relay voice callers) provides news and updates on community events. **Dial-A-Dyke** (tel 415/241–1564) is a free 24-hour bulletin board for lesbians. The **Names Project** (tel 415/ 882–5500) AIDS memorial quilt consists of more than 26,000 panels.

Liquor laws... Packaged alcoholic beverages are sold at liquor, grocery, and some drugstores 6am–2pm daily. Most bars and restaurants are licensed to sell all alcoholic beverages during those same hours, but some have only beer-and-wine licenses. No alcohol may be sold 2am–6am. Legal drinking age is 21; proof of age is required.

MUNI Metro streetcars... There are five streetcar lines that operate underground downtown and on the streets in the neighborhoods. Fares are the same as for buses—$1 adults, 35¢ for children and senior citizens.

Newspapers... There are more than 30 foreign-language publications in the Bay Area, not to mention the sex tabloids, business and professional journals, entertainment publications, and dozens of others. The two major English-language dailies are the *Chronicle* (website www.sfgate.com) and the *Examiner* (website www. examiner.com), which combine for a single paper on Sunday. Local weekly newspapers, such as the *Bay Guardian* (website www.sfbayguardian.com) and *SF Weekly* are free, and have better entertainment listings than the dailies.

Parking garages... You can spend a fortune to leave your car for a half-hour or a pittance to park it overnight, depending upon the garage. City-run garages tend to be cheaper than those privately owned, but you should call in advance to check rates and availability, if possible. The best deals in town are the **Sutter-Stockton and Ellis-O'Farrell garages**, where you can leave your car overnight for just $3. Other garages: **Chinatown** (tel 415/956–8106, 433 Kearny St.; tel 415/982–6353, 733 Kearny St.); **Civic Center** (tel 415/863–3187, 355 McAllister St.; tel 415/626–4484, 370 Grove St.); **Downtown** (tel 415/982–8522, 833 Mission St.; tel 415/771–1400 ask for garage, Mason and Ellis Sts.; tel 415/986–4800, Ellis-O'Farrell, 123 O'Farrell St.; tel 415/982–8370, Sutter-Stockton; tel 415/397–0631, 333 Post St.); **Embarcadero Center** (tel 415/433–4722, 250 Clay St.; tel 415/398–1878, Embarcadero Center Garage); **Fisherman's Wharf** (tel 415/673–5197, 665 Beach St., at Hyde St.); **Japan Center** (tel 415/567–4573, 1660 Geary Blvd.); **Mission District** (tel 415/567–7357, 90 Bartlett St., near 21st St.); **Moscone Center/Yerba Buena Gardens** (tel 415/777–2782, 255 3rd St.; tel 415/543–4533, Museum Center Park, 3rd and Folsom Sts.); **North Beach** (tel 415/558–9147, 766 Vallejo St.); **Union Street** (tel 415/563–9820, 1910 Laguna St.; tel 415/495–3772, 2055 Lombard St.); **Van Ness** (tel 415/567–9147, 1230 Polk St.).

Phone facts... The area code for San Francisco is 415. To call the East Bay (Berkeley, Oakland, or anywhere else in Alameda or Contra Costa County), dial 1, then area code 510, then the seven-digit telephone number. Local calls are free on private phones, 20¢ in a pay phone. For directory assistance, dial 411. **TDD users**: For operator assistance, TDD users call 800/855–1155. California Relay Service relays calls between a TDD caller and any other phone in the United States and allows people without TDD to call TDD users. It is a free, 24-hour service, 365 days a year. All calls placed through California Relay are billed at discounted Sprint rates. To use the service, call 800/735–2929 if you have a TDD, or 800/735–2922 if you don't have a TDD.

Taxis... It's fairly easy to hail a cab on major thoroughfares, especially in tourist areas, but if you're on a tight schedule, it's best to phone in advance for door-to-door service (the wait is usually 5–15 minutes during the day, occasionally up to a half-hour during rush hour or on busy weekend nights). There are more than 40 taxi companies listed in the Yellow Pages, but the most commonly used are: **Yellow Cab** (tel 415/626–2345); **City Cab** (tel 415/468–7200); **De Soto** (tel 415/673–1414); **Luxor** (tel 415/282–4141); and **Veteran's** (tel 415/552–1300). The fare is the same in every cab (regulated by the city): $1.70 when the meter is turned on plus $.30 for every 1/6 mile (about 2 blocks) thereafter. Since the city is no more than 7 miles in any given direction, most cab rides are around $5 to $7 plus tip (15% is customary).

Time... For the correct time, call 767–8900 from either the 415 or 510 area codes.

Tipping... Gratuities are not included in restaurant or bar checks. Most guides suggest 15% of the total amount as a decent tip, but 20% has become more commonly accepted at restaurants. Taxi drivers should be tipped around 15%; skycaps and bellpersons should get at least $1 per bag each time they carry it.

Visitor information center... The **San Francisco Visitor Information Center** (tel 415/391–2000; open 9–5:30, Sat until 3, Sun 10–2) is located at Benjamin Swig Pavilion on the lower level of Hallidie Plaza at Market and Powell streets. The center's neighborhood-walking-tour leaflets are really unbeatable. When you arrive, it's definitely worth a stop here to help plan your adventures.

A Clean Well-Lighted Place For Books, 157, 159
A Day on the Bay, 137
A Different Light, 158, 159, 184
A Taste of Leather, 155, 159
A.M. Walks, 116, 117
Aardvark's Odd Ark, 152, 159
Abbey Tavern, 180, 186
Abigail Hotel, 18, 27, 32
African Safari, 153, 159
Alain Rondelli, 65, 71, 76
Alamo Rent-A-Car, 215
Alamo Square, 113
Alcatraz Shark Fest, 134
Alcatraz, 138
Alcazar Theater, 201, 207
Alfred Dunhill of London, 149, 159
Ambulance, 218
American Bicycle Rental, 132
American Conservatory Theater (ACT), 201, 207
American Express, 216
American Property Exchange, 16
American Rag Compagnie, 152, 159
Amoeba Music, 158, 160
Andrews Hotel, 27, 32
Angel Island, 132, 136, 139
Angkor Borei, 63, 76
Angkor Wat, 63, 76
Anonymous Place, The, 158, 160
Ansel Adams Center for Photography, 108, 117
Aqua, 57, 76
Aquatic Park, 134
Archbishop's Mansion, 20, 27, 32, 113
Argonaut Book Shop, 158, 160
Asian Art Museum, 104, 107, 117
Asimakopoulos Cafe, 68, 77
Avalon Ballroom, 112
Avis Rent-A-Car, 215
AYH Hostel at Union Square, 22, 32
Babaloo, 60, 77
Backflip, 69, 77
Backseat Betty, 156, 160
Baker Beach, 134
Balmy Alley, 115
Bank of America, 216
Barbie Hall of Fame, 110, 117
Basic Brown Bear, 157, 160
BASS, 200
Bay Area Rapid Transit (BART), 214
Bay Area Rentals, Cars, Trucks and Vans, 215
Bay Area Reporter, 220
Bay City Guide, 219
Bay Guardian, 221
Bay Meadows, 206, 207
Beach Blanket Babylon, 198, 203, 207
Bead Store, The, 153, 160
Bed and Breakfast International, 16
Bernal Heights, 185
Best of Nob Hill-United Commercial Brokers, 16

Best Western Civic Center Motor Inn, 26, 33
Bimbo's 363, 182, 186
Birkenstock Natural Footwear, 150, 160
Biscuits and Blues, 66, 77, 179, 186
Black Stallion Inn, 23, 33
Blondie's Bar and No Grill, 178, 187
Blues, 178, 179, 187
Bock's Bed and Breakfast, 23, 33
Booksmith, The, 157, 160
Boom Boom Room, 178, 187
Bottom of the Hill, 175, 187
Boudin Sourdough Bakery, 103, 117
Brain Wash Cafe, 72, 74, 75, 77
Brooks Brothers, 149, 160
Brooks Island, 139
Brothers Restaurant, 63, 77
Bruno's, 66, 77, 180, 187
Buca Giovanni, 68, 77
Buddhist Bookstore, The, 158, 160
Buena Vista Cafe, 51
Buffalo Exchange, 152, 161
Burberry's, 149, 161
Burlingame Museum of Pez Memorabilia, 110, 118
Cable Car Barn and Museum, 106, 107, 118
Cafe Claude, 66, 78
Cafe de la Presse, 73, 78
Cafe du Nord, 178, 182, 187
Cafe Flore, 73, 78
Cafe Istanbul, 75, 78
Cafe La Bohème, 73, 74, 75, 78
Cafe Sausalito, 104, 118
Caffe Greco, 73, 78
Caffe Puccini, 75, 78
Caffe Trieste, 55, 73, 75, 79, 111
California Academy of Sciences, 105, 107, 118
California Canoe and Kayak, 139
California Compacts Rent-A-Car, 215
California Gentleman by Astanboos, The, 151, 161
California Reservations, 16
Campton Place Hotel, 27, 33
Carol Doda's Champagne and Lace Lingerie Boutique, 156, 161
Carta, 60, 79
Cartier, 149, 161
Cartoon Art Museum, 107, 118
Casanova Lounge, 180, 187
Castro, 18, 56, 174, 184
Cellar, 111
Center for the Arts at Yerba Buena Gardens, 106, 107, 118
Central YMCA, 15, 22, 33
Central Reservations, 16
Cha Cha Cha, 59, 60, 79
Chez Panisse, 58, 79
China Beach, 134
Chinatown, 17, 147, 222
Cho-Cho, 64, 79

Chronicle, 221
Church of John Coltrane, 101
Cirrus Network, 216
Citizen, 151, 161
City Cab, 223
City Guides, 114, 119
City Lights Bookstore, 111, 157, 161
Civic Center, 18, 222
Claremont Resort Hotel, Spa &
   Tennis Club, 28, 34, 142
Cliff House, 101, 134
Clift Hotel, The, 21, 26, 27, 34
Climate Theater, 202, 207
Clothes Contact, 152, 161
Club Deluxe, 182, 187
Coconut Grove, 66, 79
Co-existence Bagel Shop, 111
Coffeenet, 72, 80
Coit Liquors, 51
Coit Tower, 99, 114, 119
Commodore, 30, 34
Community Thrift Store, The, 152,
   161
Conservatory of Flowers, 105
Courtoué, 151, 162
Cow Hollow District, 183
Cronan Artefact, 151, 162
Cruisin' the Castro, 116, 119
Crystal Way, 153, 162
Curios and Candles, 153, 162
Curran Theater, 201, 207
Cyberworld, 72, 80
Cypress Club, 70, 71, 80
D & M Wine and Liquor, 147, 157,
   162
Daljeets, 151, 162
Dancers Group Studio Theater, 205,
   208
Danilo Bakery, 157, 162
David Stephen, 151, 162
Davies Hall, 10
Deaf Gay and Lesbian Center, 221
Devil's Slide, 135
Dial-A-Dyke, 221
Dianda's Italian American Pastry,
   157, 162
Dinostore, 151, 163
Discolandia, 158, 163
Dog Eared Books, 158, 163
Dollar Rent-A-Car, 215
Donatello Hotel, 20, 34
Dottie Doolittle, 157, 163
Dreamweaver, 150, 163
DV8, 179, 188
East Bay Regional Park District, 132
East Brother Island, 139
East West Leather, 150, 163
Edinburg Castle 181, 188
El Nuevo Frutilandia, 62, 70, 71, 80
El Rio, 185, 188
El Trebol, 62, 71, 80
Elbo Room, 177, 188
Electric City Network, 221
Elephant Walk, 184, 188

Elysium, 180, 188
Embarcadero YMCA, 133
Enrico's Sidewalk Cafe, 55, 58, 73,
   75, 80, 111, 178, 188
Enterprise Rent-A-Car, 215
Esperpento, 60, 80
Esprit Outlet Store, 152, 163
Esta Noche 183, 189
Examiner, 221
Executive Suites, 16
Exit Theater, 202, 208
Exploratorium, 106, 107, 115, 119
Fairmont Hotel, 14, 19, 25, 34
FAO Schwarz, 157, 163
Filbert Street Steps, 100
Fillmore Auditorium, 112, 176, 189
Fillmore Street, 56, 146
Financial District, 16, 56
Fina Estampa, 62, 81
Finocchio, 183, 203, 208
Firecracker, 59, 81
First Step, 150, 163
Fisherman's Wharf, 16, 103, 119
560 Hayes, 152, 163
Fleur de Lys, 65, 81
Flint's, 59, 81
Flower Power, 116, 119
Fly Trap Restaurant, 56, 71, 81
Flying Saucer, 57, 81
Footwork Dance Studio, 198
Forever After Books, 158, 164
Fort Funston Beach, 135
42 Belvedere Street, 112
Francisco Marathon, 131
French Laundry, 65, 82
Fringale, 65, 71, 82
Frisco Productions Crime Tour, 116,
   119
Galeria de la Raza, 108, 119
Ganges Vegetarian Restaurant, 63,
   67, 82
Gargoyle Beads, 153, 164
Gaylord of India, 63, 82
General Bead, 153, 164
Ghia Gallery/Discount Caskets and
   Urns, 109, 120
Gimme Shoes, 150, 164
Gino & Carlo, 181, 189
Gino and Carlo, 113, 120
Girl Spot, The, 185, 189
Glide Memorial Church, 102, 120
Global Exchange, 153, 164
Globetrotter, 155, 164
Golden Gate Bridge Beach, 135
Golden Gate Bridge, 99, 132
Golden Gate Ferry, 104, 120
Golden Gate Fields, 206, 208
Golden Gate Park Bowling Green,
   138
Golden Gate Park Course, 138
Golden Gate Park Fly Casting Pools,
   137
Golden Gate Park, 128, 131
Golden Gate Promenade, 130, 132

Golden Gate Theater 201, 208
Golden State Warriors, 206, 208
Golden Turtle, 64, 82
Good Vibrations, 109, 120, 155, 164
Goodwill Stores, 152, 164
Gordon Biersch, 182, 189
Grant and Green, 179, 189
Grant Plaza, 22, 35
Great American Music Hall, 174
Great Highway, 132
Green Tortoise Guest House, 22, 35
Greens, 67, 82
Grizzly Peak, 102, 120, 200
Groove Yard, 158, 164
Gumps, 149, 165
Gunne Sax Discount Outlet, 152, 165
Guys and Dolls 152, 165
Haight, 18, 55, 147, 174
Hama-Ko, 64, 82
Hamburger Mary's, 70, 71, 83
Harbor Village, 61, 83
Hard Rock Cafe, 115, 121
Harrington's, 113, 121
Harris', 57, 71, 83
Harry Denton's Bar & Grill, 183, 189
Harry Denton's Starlight Room, 182,
    183, 189
Hayes Street Grill, 57, 83
Hayes Valley, 56, 147
Hello Gorgeous!!, 110, 121
Helmand, 69, 83
Heritage House, 31, 35
Hertz Rent-A-Car, 215
Hi-Ball Lounge, 182, 190
Horseshoe Coffee House, 72, 74, 83
Hotel Astoria, 22, 35
Hotel Bijou, 25, 35
Hotel Bohème, 14, 24, 25, 36
Hotel Monaco, 14, 20, 36
Hotel Nikko, 23, 36
Hotel Reservations Network, 16
Hotel Rex, 23, 36
Hotel Richelieu, 17, 29, 36
Hotel Triton, 14, 30, 36
House O'Chicks, 23, 37
House of Cashmere, 150, 165
Huntington Hotel, 24, 37
I Can't Believe I Ate My Way
    Through Chinatown, 116, 121
Inn at the Opera, 14, 25, 28, 30, 37
Inn San Francisco, 23, 27, 37
Inter-Club/Globe Hostel, 22, 37
Internet Alfredo, 73, 84
Intersection for the Arts 202, 208
Irish Castle Shop, 150, 165
Italian French Baking Co, 157, 165
Italians of North Beach, The, 116, 121
Izzy's Steaks and Chops, 57, 84
Jackson Court, 27, 38
Jacqueline Perfumery, 156, 165
Jammin' Java Coffee House, 54, 72,
    73, 84
Japanese Tea Garden, 105
Japantown, 17

Javawalk, 116, 121
Jazz at Pearl's, 178, 190
Jeffrey's Toys, 157, 165
Jewish Community Center, 133
Jewish Community Museum, 108, 121
John's Grill, 56, 84
Johnny Love's, 183, 190
Joseph Schmidt Confections, 156, 165
Josie's Juice Joint and Cabaret, 198,
    203, 208
Jug Shop, 51
Juliana Hotel, 27, 38
Jungle, The, 115, 122
Junk, 185, 190
Just Desserts, 156, 166
Kabuki Hot Springs Spa and Shiatsu
    Center, 142
Keane Eyes Gallery, 109, 122
Kenneth Cole, 150, 166
Kinder Toys, 157, 166
Kirby Beach, 134
Kyung Bok Palace, 62, 70, 84
La India Bonita, 183, 190
La Rondalla, 62, 70, 84
La Rosa, 152, 166
La Taqueria, 62, 71, 85
Lady Luck Candle Shop, 153, 166
Lake Merced Boating and Fishing
    Company, 137
Lake Merced Park, 129,131
Lake Merced, 136, 137
Land's End Beach, 134,135
Latin American Club, 181, 190
Laurel Motor Inn, 26, 38
Lavender Lounge, 221
Lavender Pages, 220
Leisure Reservation Services, 16
Leland Hotel, 23, 38
Let It Be, 158, 166
Liberty Street, 114
Lincoln Cyclery, 132
Lincoln Park Golf Course, 137
Lombard Street, 18
Longshoreman's Hall, 112
Lorraine Hansberry Theater, 198,
    202, 209
Los Jarritos, 61, 85
Louis Vuitton, 149, 166
Lucca Ravioli Co, 157, 166
Lyle Tuttle's Tattoo Museum, 109, 122
M. H. de Young Memorial Museum,
    105, 107, 122
Macy's, 150, 166
Mad Magda's Russian Tea Room, 54,
    74, 75, 85
Magic Theater, 203, 209
Magical Trinket, 153, 167
Maiden Lane, 146
Manka's Inverness Lodge &
    Restaurant, 31, 38
Mansions Hotel, 26, 27, 39
Marina Green, 129
Marine World/Africa USA, 104, 122
Marine's Memorial Theater, 201, 209

Mario's Bohemian Cigar Store Cafe, 75, 85
Maritime Museum, 107, 122
Mark Hopkins International, 19, 39
Marsh, The, 198, 202, 209
Masa's, 64, 85
Mascara Club, The, 154, 167
Matrix, 112
Maxwell Hotel, 29, 39
McB's Shoes, 150, 167
McDonald's Bookshop, 158, 167
Mecca, 66, 85
Medium Rare Records, 158, 167
Mexican Museum, 108, 123
Mill Valley Inn, 31, 39
Millennium, 67, 86
Minis By Profili, 157, 167
Mint, The, 184, 190
Mission Cultural Center for Latino Arts, 202, 209
Mission District, 18, 50, 55, 148, 174, 185
Mr. Ticket, 200
Miyako Hotel, 23, 25, 39
Miyako, 142
Mod Lang, 158, 167
Molinari's, 157, 167
Moose's, 58, 86
Moscone Center, 217
Motherlode, The, 183, 191
Mount Diablo State Park, 140
Mountain Lake Park, 129,131
Muddy Waters Coffee House, 72, 73, 86
Muir Beach, 135
Muir Woods Nat. Monument, 141
Musée Mecanique, 107, 123
Museum of Modern Art, 106, 107, 123
New Orleans Room, 178, 191
Nick's, 103, 123
Neiman Marcus, 150, 167
No Name Bar, 104, 123
Nob Hill, 16
Nob Hill Lambourne, 14, 25, 40
Noe Valley, 18
Nordstrom, 149, 150, 168
North Beach Leather, 155, 168
North Beach Museum, 108, 123
North Beach, 54, 147, 174
North Face Factory Outlet, 152, 168
North Point Health Club, 133
Oakland A's, 206, 209
Oakland Ballet, 204, 209
Oakland Coliseum, 206, 209
Oakland Raiders, 199, 206, 210
Oaks, The, 185, 191
Ocean Beach, 134
Old Mint Museum, 109, 124
177 Townsend, 176, 191
112 Lyon Street, 112
1214 Polk Street, 111
1371 Haight Street, 112
Open Mind Music, 158, 168
Opera in the Park, 220

Orpheum Theater, 201, 210
Pacific Heights, 18
Pacific News, 185, 191
Pacitas Bakery, 156, 168
Palace of Fine Arts, 106, 124
Paradise Lounge, 176, 191
Park Cyclery, 132
Pat O'Shea's Mad Hatter, 180, 192
Patrick James, 151, 168
Paxton Gate, 154, 168
Pendulum, The, 184, 192
Pension San Francisco, 23, 27, 40
People's Temple, The, 102
Phoenix Theater, 203, 210
Phoenix, 14, 19, 29, 40
Phoenix, The, 136, 184, 192
Piedmont Boutique, 151, 168
Pier 23 Cafe, 103, 124
Pier 39, 103, 124
Pierce Street Annex, 112
Pinnacle Fitness Club, 132
Place, The, 111
PlaNetweavers Treasures Store, 153, 168
Plough and the Stars, The, 181, 192
Point Reyes Lodging, 142
Point Reyes National Seashore, 135, 141
Polo Field, 112
Polo Store/Ralph Lauren, The, 149, 169
Powell-Hyde cable car, 98
Precita Eyes Mural Center, 115, 124
Prescott Hotel, 14, 20, 29, 40
Presidio, 129,132
Psychedelic Shop, 113
Purple Onion, 176, 192
Quantity Postcards, 154, 169
R & G Lounge, 61, 86
Radio Valencia, 54, 74, 86
Record Finder, The, 158, 169
Red Dora's Bearded Lady, 54, 74, 75, 86
Red Victorian B & B Inn, 21, 40
Reliable Rent-A-Car, 215
Repeat Performance, 152, 169
Ria's, 150, 169
Ritz-Carlton San Francisco, The, 25, 41
Rodeo Beach, 134
Rodeway Inn, 26, 41
Rolling Stone, 112
Rolo SF, 151, 169
Romantasy, 155, 169
Rose Pistola, 67, 86
Rosicrucian Egyptian Museum, 110, 124
Sacred Grounds Cafe, 75, 87
Saigon Sandwich Cafe, 64, 71, 87
Saks Fifth Avenue, 149, 150, 169
Saloon, The, 179, 192
San Francisco Ballet, 198, 204, 210
San Francisco Brewing Company, 51
San Francisco 49ers, 199, 206, 210
San Francisco Giants, 205, 210

San Francisco International Hostel (AYH), 15, 22, 41
San Francisco Marriott, 26, 41
San Francisco Municipal Railway(MUNI)buses, 215
San Francisco Opera, 198, 205, 210
San Francisco Recreation and Park Dept., 132
San Francisco Reservations, 16
San Francisco School of Windsurfing, 136
San Francisco Symphony, 198, 210
San Francisco Zoological Gardens and Children's Zoo, 115, 124
San Gregorio Beach, 135
San Jose Arena, 206, 210
San Jose Rhinos, 206, 211
San Jose Sharks, 206, 211
San Quentin State Prison, 102
San Remo Hotel, 14, 18, 28, 41
Sanppo, 64, 87
Sanrio at Union Square, 157, 169
Santa Cruz Surfing Museum, 110, 125
Saturn Records, 158, 169
Scairy Hairy Toy Company, The, 154, 170
Sea Trek Ocean Kayaking Center, 136
Seal Rock Inn, 72, 87
Sear's Fine Foods, 72, 87
710 Ashbury Street, 112
715 Harrison, 177, 193
SF Net, 72
SF Weekly, 221
Sheraton Palace Hotel, 24, 42
Shoe Loft, 150, 170
Sierra Club Bookstore, 158, 170
Six Gallery, 111
650 Howard, 177, 193
Skylark, 180, 193
Slim's, 176, 193
Sol y Luna, 67, 87
Sound Factory 179, 193
South of Market, 56, 174
South Park Cafe, 74, 87
South Promenade, 130
Sparky's Diner, 72, 88
Specs, 111, 113, 125
Spinnaker Sailing, 137
Stage Door Theater, 201, 211
Stars, 58, 59, 88
Steinhart Aquarium, 115, 125
Stella Pastry & Caffe, 73, 88, 156, 170
Stephane Kelian, 150, 170
Stormy Leather, 155, 170
Storyville, 178, 193
Stouffer Renaissance Stanford Court Hotel, 21, 42
Stow Lake, 136
Stoyanof, 68, 88
Straits Cafe, 64, 88
Streetlight Records, 158, 170
Suicide Prevention, 218
Sulka, 151, 170

Sunset District, 18
Suppenküche, 69, 88
Tadich Grill, 56, 89
Tassajara Cafe & Bakery, 73, 75, 89, 156, 170
TDD, 222
Tea Garden Springs, 143
Ten 15, 179, 193
Tenderloin, 17
Tennessee Beach, 134
Theater Artaud, 198, 202, 205, 211
Theater Rhinoceros, 198, 202, 211
Thep Phanom, 59, 89
Third Wave Dance House, 198, 205, 211
Thirsty Bear Brewing Company, 182, 194
Three Babes and a Bus, 181, 194
3Com Park, 205, 211
330 Ritch, 177, 194
395 Sutter, 150, 171
Thrift Town, 152, 171
Thrifty Car Rental, 215
Tien Hon Temple, 101
Tiffany and Co, 149, 171
Timo's in the Zanzibar, 60, 89
TIX, 200
Tommy Toy's, 61, 89
Tosca, 113, 125
Trocadero, 176, 194
Tse Cashmere, 150, 171
24 Henry Guesthouse, 23, 42
24 Hour Fitness, 133
Twenty Tank Brewery, 182, 194
Twin Peaks, 184, 194
278 11th, 177, 194
2400 Fulton Steet, 112
Uncle Mame, 154, 171
Union Square, 16, 146
Union Street, 146, 222
Up & Down Club, 178, 195
Van Ness Avenue, 17
Vesuvio's, 111, 113, 125
Veteran's, 223
Victorian Inn on the Park, 21, 42
Visitor Information Center, 218
Wacky Jacky, 137
Walgreens 24-Hour Prescription Service, 214
Washington Square Bar & Grill, 113, 125
Wasteland, 150, 171
Waterfront Promenade, 130
Wave Organ, 129
Westin Saint Francis, 19, 26, 42
Wilkes-Bashford, 150, 171
Worldware, 152, 171
Yank Sing, 61, 89
Yaya Cuisine, 69, 89
Yerba Buena Square, 148
Yone of San Francisco, 153, 171
York Street, 115
York Hotel, 24, 25, 43
Yoshi's, 178, 195